MAINSTREAM MAVERICK

MAINSTREAM MAVERICK

John Hughes and New Hollywood Cinema

HOLLY CHARD

University of Texas Press Austin

Printed in the United States of America
First edition, 2020
First paperback printing, 2024

♾ The paper used in this book meets the minimum requirements of ANSI/NISO Z39.48-1992 (R1997) (Permanence of Paper).

Library of Congress Cataloging-in-Publication Data

Names: Chard, Holly, author.
Title: Mainstream maverick : John Hughes and New Hollywood cinema / Holly Chard.
Description: First edition. | Austin : University of Texas Press, 2020. | Includes bibliographical references and index.
Identifiers: LCCN 2020000758 |
ISBN 978-1-4773-2130-0 (paperback)
ISBN 978-1-4773-2132-4 (ebook) |
ISBN 978-1-4773-2131-7 (ebook other)
Subjects: LCSH: Hughes, John, 1950–2009. | Motion picture industry—History—20th century. | Motion picture authorship. | Motion picture producers and directors—Biography.
Classification: LCC PN1998.3.H84 C48 2020 | DDC 791.430/33092—dc23
LC record available at https://lccn.loc.gov/2020000758

doi:10.7560/321294

CONTENTS

ACKNOWLEDGMENTS

It has been more than a decade since I started researching John Hughes, and, consequently, I owe a debt of gratitude to a large number of people.

This work is based on research undertaken for my PhD at the University of Sussex. I am grateful to the following people for their support, feedback, and encouragement during my doctoral studies: my PhD supervisors, Frank Krutnik and Thomas Austin; my fellow PhD students; my colleagues in the School of Media, Film, and Music at Sussex; staff at the University of Sussex library, the British Library, and the British Film Institute; my coworkers and friends at Worthing Theatres; and Steve Neale and Niall Richardson, for examining my thesis and providing invaluable feedback. My doctoral research was partially funded by a UK Arts and Humanities Research Council studentship and a University of Sussex Doctoral Award. I sincerely hope that financial and institutional support for scholars in the humanities endures in this uncertain political climate.

The transformation of my doctoral research into a monograph has taken several years. Further expressions of gratitude are therefore due to another group of people: my colleagues in the School of Media at the University of Brighton; Brighton's library and support staff, particularly the amazing people who worked at the Hastings campus to create an inclusive, supportive environment for students and staff alike; my colleagues at City and Guilds Kineo; and the Certificate in English Language

Teaching to Adults crew. I am also grateful to Colin Cooper for assistance with proofreading of the manuscript.

Thank you to the team at the University of Texas Press, particularly Jim Burr and Sarah McGavick, for making this book a reality. Thanks also to Timothy Corrigan and Mark Gallagher for their detailed peer-review feedback, which has helped me improve this work significantly.

My family and friends helped me stick with this research project over the years. You are amazing, and I would never have gotten this far without your support. My brother, Dan, has displayed immense patience and dedication in helping me revise and edit my writing. My partner, Jack, deserves particular credit for keeping me sane during the last phase of my PhD and for putting up with me during the five years since, especially during the countless evenings and weekends devoted to writing this book.

The biggest thank-you of all has to go to my long-suffering parents, Mike and Elaine, who have supported me in countless ways.

MAINSTREAM MAVERICK

INTRODUCTION

The Making of "John Hughes"

John Hughes was never nominated for an Oscar, so when it emerged in 2010 that the 82nd Academy Awards would include a posthumous tribute to the filmmaker's career, it took many by surprise. Hughes, who had died unexpectedly of a heart attack the previous year, had also not had a major box-office hit for over ten years. The decision by the Academy of Motion Picture Arts and Sciences to dedicate six-plus minutes of the ceremony to a filmmaker who, during his lifetime, had won nothing more than a ShoWest Award for Best Producer was without precedent. The Academy had previously bestowed major posthumous memorials on only a few people—those who had been nominated for Oscars while alive or had had a strong affiliation with the ceremony. The press speculated why the Academy had decided Hughes was worthy of such unique treatment. Several media commentators argued it was an attempt to pander to a younger audience and an inappropriate celebration of the kind of commercial cinema antithetical to prestigious, Oscar-worthy fare.[1] In contrast, Roger Ebert, a longtime advocate for Hughes's work, declared it "one of the greatest moments in Academy Award history," suggesting that "Hughes was too great a legend to be simply included in the traditional 'In Memoriam' tribute."[2]

The Oscar tribute emphasized Hughes's talents as a screenwriter and centered primarily on his explorations of

American adolescence in a cycle of mid-1980s teen movies. Molly Ringwald and Matthew Broderick introduced a montage of clips from Hughes's films. The video positioned *Sixteen Candles* (John Hughes, 1984), *The Breakfast Club* (John Hughes, 1985), *Weird Science* (John Hughes, 1985), *Pretty in Pink* (Howard Deutch, 1986), *Ferris Bueller's Day Off* (John Hughes, 1986), and *Some Kind of Wonderful* (Howard Deutch, 1987) as Hughes's greatest achievements, alongside his highest-grossing box-office hit, *Home Alone* (Chris Columbus, 1990). Leading comedy performers of the 1980s and early 1990s such as Chevy Chase, Steve Martin, and John Candy also appeared in the montage. The memorial concluded with "Brat Pack" members Jon Cryer, Anthony Michael Hall, Judd Nelson, and Ally Sheedy joining Ringwald and Broderick on stage, along with the former child star Macaulay Culkin. The overall tone was one of nostalgia for the popular cinema of the 1980s and early 1990s, a period to which Hughes and his movies firmly belong.

The Academy Awards' appraisal of Hughes's career echoed the reports that proliferated after news of the filmmaker's sudden death on 6 August 2009 spread across the globe. While coverage was especially prominent in the United States and the United Kingdom, news outlets reported his demise in Canada, Australia, and a range of non-Anglophone countries, including Italy, Spain, Russia, and the Philippines. These reports and obituaries consistently highlighted Hughes's popular appeal and commercial credentials. Headlines described Hughes as the "Bard of Teen Angst," "leader of the Brat Pack," and "father of *Home Alone*."[3] ABC News online described him as "director of iconic films of the 1980s" and FoxNews.com dubbed him "Hollywood's youth impresario of the 1980s and 1990s," thereby emphasizing his connection with the period.[4] Many stories noted that Hughes was "one of the most prolific independent filmmakers in Hollywood history."[5] These assessments of Hughes's impact on Hollywood cinema and American culture marked the start of a process of memorialization and critical evaluation that continues to this day.

Filmmakers' creative reputations and the interpretations

of their films are, argues Barbara Klinger, "constructed" by factors that include their "publicized intentions, the practices of cultural institutions, the media, and social and political circumstances."[6] Therefore, their status can change over time. This is certainly the case with John Hughes. Following his death, his previous champions, including the popular critics Robert Ebert and Richard Corliss, remained constant in their appreciation of his work. But as the Oscars tribute demonstrated, other institutions began to lavish his work with far greater recognition and praise than they did during his lifetime. These shifts in Hughes's standing and critics' opinions of his work demonstrate that the construction of a posthumous legacy is an active process, fraught with tensions and contradictions. It is a phenomenon made even more complex by there being an actual person at the center of such claims. As Joli Jensen observes, "The struggle to 'own' a celebrity, especially after death, foregrounds the problematic differences between personal and familial claims, fan desires and critical commentary on what can constitute a star's legacy."[7] Thanks to these competing forces and shifting attitudes, Hughes's posthumous reputation is far from fixed and is instead a site of contestation and negotiation.

Hughes and Authorship in Hollywood Cinema

Even after Hughes's death, film critics and journalists conspicuously avoided describing him as an "auteur." Only one of the many obituaries and tributes published in the mainstream media used the term explicitly. In a *New York Times* article titled "The '80s Auteur of Teenage Angst," the film critic A. O. Scott contended, "Historians of cinema may be slow or begrudging in appreciating his achievement, but if auteur status is conferred by the possession of a recognizable style and set of themes, Mr. Hughes's place in the pantheon cannot be denied."[8] Scott's attempt to justify Hughes's significance in this way reflects the pervasive influence of auteurist discourse on American film culture. Auteurism, John Caughie suggests, has become "a critical position within discourses about cinema, a position which is supported institutionally and ideologically by the 'received' cultural aesthetic: a position, that is, which defines the space in which other discourses about cinema take place."[9] In this context, the debate over whether Hughes was an auteur was somewhat inevitable. But during his lifetime, Hughes consistently presented himself as a commercial filmmaker without artistic ambitions. When talking to reporters, he often made assertions to this effect, such as, "I don't think I'm making any great statements, and I certainly don't think I'm making art."[10] Nevertheless, Hughes could not escape the politics of taste that informs how films are variously celebrated and condemned by critics.

This book does not actively seek to make a case for Hughes's value on artistic grounds. He is worth researching and studying not because his films are "art" and deserve to be part of the canon, alongside the work of directors such as Alfred Hitchcock and Stanley Kubrick. Rather, his career and movies are of historical interest because they are industrially and culturally significant. This perspective contrasts with that underpinning most scholarship on specific filmmakers, which works within existing auteurist structures to argue for their admission to the pantheon and to promote expansion of the canon to include texts previously undervalued by scholars. Warren Buckland, for example, has argued that Steven Spielberg is an auteur in a traditional sense, contending that "Spielberg's blockbusters have their own complex structure, and their popularity does not preclude them from being considered worthy of serious study in themselves as *film*."[11] Moreover, debates continue to rage around other highly commercial New Hollywood filmmakers such as Ridley Scott and Michael Bay, who apparently fall short of auteur status because their work struggles to achieve certain aesthetic standards. Because of this preoccupation with artistic value, scholars often overlook mainstream filmmakers' involvement in the film industry and their engagement with commercial paradigms. This book contends that Hughes's work deserves greater scrutiny because his career offers intriguing insights into the operations and priorities of the American film industry in the New Hollywood era.

Even if considerations of artistic value are cast to one

side, authorship remains an inescapable part of how Hughes's body of work has been sold, consumed, and interpreted. Consequently, there are multiple, interconnected versions of "John Hughes": a man who worked in the film industry, a celebrity figure created through media coverage, a "brand" developed by several institutions, and a critical construct used to group and interpret films. This study engages with all these variants of "John Hughes" in an effort to show how they interact with one another and are, to no small extent, products of a particular set of historical circumstances. As Derek Johnson and Jonathan Gray state, "Authorship is . . . not just a question of art and individual expression, but also of social and institutional structures that govern cultural production, enabling, compelling, and authorizing some forms while constraining others."[12] Hughes is an excellent case study of how authorship has played a pivotal role in New Hollywood cinema as an industrial and cultural force.

Hughes occupied a variety of authorial roles, including screenwriter, director, and producer, on numerous productions. In certain cases, he played a dominant role during the production process; in others, he was more marginal, and creative power was dispersed. The studios may have sold them as "John Hughes films," but they were not exclusively *his* and, instead, were the products of collaboration. Numerous people, including actors, directors, editors, production designers, costume designers, sound editors, producers, and studio executives, had an impact on the development of movies that critics have dubbed Hughesian. As Berys Gaut argues, any film is "a product of many individuals, whose work is inflected in a complex manner by their interactions with their colleagues."[13] That said, although Hughes did not control every aspect of his films, he attempted to shape and regulate his body of work through his screenplays and production roles. Crucially, the overt thematic and stylistic continuities across his movies are the product of concerted, self-aware attempts to "author" his films for commercial purposes, rather than evidence of some unconscious authorial signature.

Hughes's approach to creating similarities among his films relied heavily on the use of genre frameworks and seriality. As this book explains, he adapted the conventions of both the teen movie and the family film to create a distinctive take on these established Hollywood genres. The similarities among his mid-1980s films allowed Hughes, Universal Studios, and Paramount Pictures to cultivate his reputation as a "teen-movie tycoon."[14] When Hughes decided to reorient his brand toward the cross-generational family film during the late 1980s and early 1990s, he did so by gradually altering the themes, narrative priorities, and style of his films. The nature of both genres meant that character types, settings, and overarching themes could remain remarkably consistent across his body of work. All of Hughes's movies center on the lives of white middle-class Americans, the majority of whom inhabit affluent suburban neighborhoods in the Midwest. His films explore familiar, mundane realities of suburban life, but they also probe Middle American fantasies, and thus include elements of escapism. Above all, Hughes aimed to make his films entertaining and appealing to a wide audience. In a 1985 interview, he disclosed, "My movies are not for people who want to think about the world's problems. . . . What I try to do is give moviegoers a couple of hours of entertainment so they can escape from the real world."[15]

The major Hollywood studios supported Hughes's attempts to create a recognizable product by branding numerous movies as John Hughes films. While the film industry had used directors' names to sell films for decades, from the late 1970s onward the auteur brand became an increasingly prevalent form of product differentiation in a competitive media marketplace.[16] In the New Hollywood, argues Timothy Corrigan, the auteur functioned "as a *commercial* strategy for organizing audience reception, as a critical concept bound to distribution and marketing aims that identify and address the potential cult status of the auteur."[17] Hughes played an active role in this process by participating in promotional activities that reinforced and developed his identity as a "commercial auteur." Over the course of his career, he became a brand in his own right and used his status to gain more control over productions. At the same time, the studios exerted significant influence over the production, promotion, and distribution of Hughes's movies. Despite claims that the collapse of the studio system created a "post-Studio era," major studio brands were incredibly resilient, and the US film industry continued to pursue strategies of "studio differentiation" through investment in particular kinds of movies.[18] Moreover, a studio's adoption of certain visual and thematic traits can constitute, argues Jerome Christensen, "studio authorship."[19] This book is structured to aid understanding of how studios' agendas and house styles shaped the production, marketing, and commercial exploitation of Hughes's movies.

In light of these contextual factors, this book considers Hughes's films both as industrial products and as cultural texts, synthesizing approaches from New Film History and New Cinema History. New Film Historians consider films themselves to be "the main primary sources" for their work.[20] Accordingly, they often use methods and theories for textual analysis that are specific to the discipline of film studies. New Cinema Historians, in contrast, are more preoccupied with "circulation and consumption" and "cinema as a site of social and cultural exchange."[21] These historians have investigated, notes Eric Smoodin, "the possibility for film scholarship without films; for using primary materials other than films themselves for examining the history of the cinema in the United States."[22] Consequently, New Cinema History has demonstrated how a range of primary materials can illuminate a historical understanding of cinema as well as highlight cinema's interactions with other media. As Charles Musser observes, "Cutting across media-specific histories rather than reinforcing them can facilitate rather than impede historical understanding."[23] Building on these developments in the field of cinema history, this research analyzes a variety of primary materials, including films, and situates them in a wider media landscape.

Hughes and New Hollywood Cinema

Despite Hughes's status within the US film industry, his career barely registers in academic studies of Hollywood cinema in the 1980s and 1990s. Stephen Prince includes a brief summary of Hughes's 1980s career in the corresponding volume of the History of the American Cinema series, describing him as "the decade's king of teen comedy" and "a filmmaker of the eighties."[24] Hughes is, however, noticeably absent from most studies of the American film industry. A major reason for this is that his body of work resists being situated in the main academic models used to write about New Hollywood. As Geoff King argues, scholarship has tended to center on two main versions of New Hollywood: the "Hollywood Renaissance" of the 1960s and 1970s and independent "auteur" cinema, and the blockbuster era.[25] Despite their prevalence, these perspectives, as Steve Neale maintains, "produce a partial and misleading picture of the American film industry, its output, and its audiences."[26] In particular, histories of New Hollywood have tended to obscure diversity within production strategies used since the 1970s, as well as the complexities of industrial organization. By charting Hughes's career, this book offers insights into the business agendas that shaped modestly budgeted mainstream cinema in the 1980s and early 1990s and therefore adds to historical knowledge of this period.

All of Hughes's movies were complexly determined industrial productions shaped both by a set of radically fluctuating commercial imperatives and by Hollywood's standardized formats and frameworks. The teen movie and the family film played a particularly key role in determining the commercial and textual logic of his movies. Both genres are defined in no small part by their relationship to the industry and their audiences. To develop an understanding of Hughes's career and the teen genre's industrial significance, this book locates his teen movies in their commercial contexts, placing particular emphasis on "high concept" marketing, home video, MTV, and recorded music. This approach is surprisingly uncommon in studies of 1980s teen movies: scholars often fail to give serious consideration to films' commercial origins and their cultural circulation, perhaps with the notable exception of Richard Nowell.[27] Through an examination of Hughes's family films in relation to changes to theatrical exhibition, home video, and merchandising, this book also develops the lines of inquiry outlined by scholars such as Robert C. Allen and Peter Krämer in their influential essays on the 1990s family film.[28] By arguing for Hughes's impact on the genre, this study also challenges Noel Brown's account of the family film during this period.[29] Interrogating the industrial underpinnings of Hughes's work and related aspects of New Hollywood cinema is, therefore, one of the major concerns of this study.

Building on approaches from New Cinema History, this account of Hughes's career is based on a wide range of sources. This book cites numerous trade publications, including *Variety*, the *Hollywood Reporter*, and *Screen International*, for their insights on the US entertainment industry and Hughes's business dealings. As well as providing relatively reliable evidence concerning production arrangements, contractual agreements, studio performance, and box-office data, these sources offer insights into industry-wide discourses during the 1980s and 1990s. Other specialized trade publications provide more detailed information on particular aspects of the entertainment industry. *Back Stage*'s "MidWest" section provided extensive coverage of Hughes's Chicago-based productions and wider trends within regional film production, and this reporting allows for greater reflection on his impact on the communities he depicted on screen. *Boxoffice*, which was aimed primarily at exhibitors, offers pertinent insights into how Hughes's films were marketed and targeted to the tastes of mainstream audiences. Newspapers, including the *New York Times* and the *Los Angeles Times*, are used as additional sources of information on, and analysis of, the US film industry. *Billboard*, which reported extensively on the music and home-video industries during the 1980s and 1990s, is one of the main sources of evidence for how Hughes's movies were promoted and distributed in these ancillary markets. Combining information drawn from these sources, each with its own strengths, allows a nuanced account of Hughes's career and films to emerge.

Although reviews are cited in this book, it should be noted that film critics, particularly those writing for prestigious publications such as the *New York Times*, the *New Yorker*, the *Washington Post*, and the *Los Angeles Times*, were often highly disparaging of Hughes's films and disapproving of his audiences. Hughes was clearly aware of this disconnection between critics' perspectives on his work and his target audience's tastes. In a 1985 discussion of the reception of *Sixteen Candles* and *The Breakfast Club*, he argued, "I think what critics don't look at is that these things are written for an audience and I took that audience's sensibilities into account."[30] The film industry was also conscious of this significant disparity in tastes. As *Variety*'s Richard Natale noted in November 1991, "Hughes's films have never been critics' movies."[31] The few critics who offered more favorable reviews of Hughes's work, such as Gene Siskel and Roget Ebert, tended to evaluate them as entertainment, reflecting on the pleasures that they offered audiences. Clearly, it is unwise, as Robert Allen and Douglas Gomery note, "to assert a correlation between critical judgment and 'public taste.'"[32] Reviews, instead, "display significant and value-laden suppositions about the social and (sub)cultural positions that [critics] and their assumed readerships occupy."[33] What they can do, therefore, is offer insights into the relationship between critical discourses, Hughes's reputation, and the positioning of his films as both authored texts and as examples of specific genres, as well as into matters of taste and cultural distinction.

Analyzing Hughes's Films

Despite the nostalgia that Hughes's films inspire, there has been a perceptible shift toward viewing his work more critically in the years since his death. In line with prevailing trends in American culture and society, the representations of gender, sexuality, and race in Hughes's movies have been subject to increased scrutiny. A personal history written in 2018 for the *New Yorker* by his former "muse," Molly Ringwald, remains the most public and widely circulated critique of the representational politics of his work. In the wake of the Harvey Weinstein scandal and the #MeToo movement, Ringwald felt compelled to revisit Hughes's films and to reflect anew on her experiences in making them. In a highly personal, well-informed essay, Ringwald explored Hughes's achievements and her feelings of affection for his teen films, but also contemplated how they "could also be considered racist, misogynistic, and, at times, homophobic."[34] She also noted how difficult it was to separate Hughes, the man she once knew, from his body of work. The vast majority of newspaper articles and online reactions were broadly supportive of Ringwald's attempts to wrestle with the question of how to appreciate much-loved movies that do not reflect contemporary attitudes to gender, sexuality, and race.

Rather than glossing over these problematic aspects of Hughes's work, it is important to acknowledge and interrogate them. As Ringwald pointed out in her *New Yorker* essay, "Erasing history is a dangerous road when it comes to art—change is essential, but so, too, is remembering the past, in all of its transgression and barbarism."[35] At the same time, critical analysis should remain mindful of the contexts in which films were made. As Andy Medhurst has observed in his work on comedy and identity, there is a danger that ideological analysis can become preoccupied with efforts to "construct a catalogue of chastisement" rather than engaging with the nuances of a text.[36] Accordingly, in several chapters of this book I reflect on the complex and sometimes contradictory politics of Hughes's films while acknowledging that his work is the product of a particular set of contexts. Through analysis of their representations of age, gender, sexuality, race, and class, I consider how Hughes's films engaged with social and cultural concerns. In their reflections on Hughes's teen movies of the 1980s, chapters 2 and 4 build on a growing body of work that engages with pertinent theories of identity and issues of film style and narrative in the teen films of the New Hollywood era, particularly the work of Timothy Shary, Christina Lee, Catherine Driscoll, Barbara Jane Brickman, and Frances Smith.[37] Using similar approaches, chapters 6 and 8 expand on recent scholarship on the family film, such as the work of Noel Brown and Bruce Babbington, which places particular emphasis on the cultural politics of childhood and the family.[38]

While Hughes's films are products of the 1980s and early 1990s, I resist dismissing them as "Reaganite entertainment," a term popularized by Andrew Britton and Robin Wood in their early-1980s writings. Britton claimed there was "a general movement of reaction and conservative reassurance in the contemporary Hollywood cinema."[39] Adopting a similar view, Wood argued that the 1980s was a period when Hollywood movies endorsed the ideology of the Right and audiences succumbed to "the easy satisfactions of reassurance and the restoration of the 'good old values' of patriarchal capitalism."[40] Wood declared the decade "the most impoverished, the most cynical, the most reactionary, the *emptiest*, in the entire history of Hollywood."[41] The residue of the concept of Reaganite entertainment can be found among more recent work on Hughes's films and 1980s Hollywood cinema, such as Chris Jordan's *Movies and the Reagan Presidency* and Leger Grindon's essay "1986: Movies and Fissures in Reagan's America."[42] In contrast, this book suggests that Hughes's movies negotiate ideologies in a number of ways rather than offering a simplistic reflection of conservative values.

Films do not offer direct insights into particular historical moments because, as Janet Staiger observes, "any relation of a text to its social context is complex, mediated and decentered."[43] This book uses both authorship and genre as frameworks that can help focus and contextualize an analysis of Hughes's movies. Although the analysis of films is always an act of interpretation, when it engages with established scholarly paradigms and is based on specific evidence, it can produce valuable insights and stimulate debate. As John Gibbs and Douglas Pye argue, "Interpretation developed through reasoned argument is . . . not simply 'subjective' or rooted in the tastes of an individual or group but, in establishing shared understanding, becomes a form of knowledge. It implies that a basis for dialogue and mutual understanding exists."[44] Of course, it is impossible to be entirely objective, and any interpretation, no matter how convincingly supported, is influenced by personal understanding, academic trends, and wider social and cultural concerns.

Therefore, the critical reflections on Hughes's films in this book are by no means definitive or comprehensive, but rather intended to spark further reflection on his body of work and New Hollywood cinema more generally.

The Focus and Structure of the Book

This study is, primarily for practical reasons, not a complete survey of Hughes's career and films. His prolific output means that it would be an immense undertaking to research in detail every film and television show he was involved in writing, producing, or directing. By focusing primarily on Hughes's teen movies and family-oriented films released between 1984 and 1994, this book offers a more focused and detailed reflection on certain aspects of his career, as well as engagement with relevant concepts such as authorship and genre. During this period, he exercised the greatest control over his work, and all the films that he wrote, directed, or produced were framed, to varying extents, as "John Hughes films." Focusing on a constrained time period facilitates contextualization of his career within wider shifts in the media industries during the late 1980s and early 1990s, as well as enabling an evaluation of the films in relation to relevant issues in American society.

Chapter 1, "Building a Brand," explores how, by focusing on teen movies while under contract at Universal, Hughes demonstrated both his exceptional understanding of a particular niche market of consumers and his awareness of marketing strategies suited to a changing media environment. By focusing on *Sixteen Candles*, *The Breakfast Club*, and *Weird Science*—all written and directed by Hughes— I show how he worked with Universal and its parent company, MCA, to establish himself as the dominant brand within the teen-film market. In particular, this chapter focuses on how he and MCA seized commercial opportunities offered by the burgeoning home-video and recorded-music markets in the United States, thereby laying the foundations for his success as a commercial filmmaker. This discussion of the industrial contexts of Hughes's first three teen films is followed by a chapter analyzing the movies themselves.

Chapter 2, "Realities and Fantasies of Suburban Adolescence," explores how, through his Universal teen movies, Hughes developed key textual features of his signature product, creating movies that shared themes, narrative tropes, and character types as well as aesthetic features. Besides reflecting on how the films use and rework the conventions of the teen genre, I consider how his coming-of-age movies engage with white middle-class suburban realities and fantasies.

Focusing on Hughes's career in the mid-1980s, chapter 3, "The Creative Producer," examines the slick, cross-promotional campaigns that Hughes and Paramount developed for *Pretty in Pink, Ferris Bueller's Day Off,* and *Some Kind of Wonderful.* Hughes's Paramount teen movies were particularly effective at engaging with the zeitgeist, bringing together numerous trends in American youth culture. Hughes and the studio not only adopted a consistent, cutting-edge approach to branding his movies and their paratexts, but also successfully harnessed the growing promotional power of music television and popular-music culture. It was through these movies that Hughes secured his reputation as an authority on the tastes of suburban American teenagers. Accordingly, chapter 4, "Gender, Generation, and Coming-of-Age in 1980s America," explores how the collaboration between Hughes, key creative personnel, and the studio helped differentiate Hughes's Paramount films from his Universal films and other teen movies of the period while replicating certain familiar elements from his Universal teen movies. I also examine how the politics of identity present in Hughes's earlier films, particularly in relation to gender and class, became more overt in his Paramount teen films. Alongside this analysis of representation, I explore how these films synthesize realistic themes and settings with fantasies of teen romance and, in the case of *Ferris Bueller's Day Off,* teen omnipotence, in a manner typical of Hughes's work.

Chapter 5, "Solid Family Fare," charts Hughes's move away from the teen film genre and his attempts to reorient the John Hughes brand toward the family audience while working with Universal and Warner Bros. in the late 1980s and early

1990s. I reflect on how he gradually shifted the emphasis of his movies onto the family and childhood by modifying specific elements of his previous box-office successes. This chapter also explores the studios' theatrical-release strategies, which were aimed at maximizing the films' appeal to cross-generational audiences, and their differing approaches to the exploitation of Hughes's movies in the home-video market. Hughes's family films are cultural artifacts as well as commercial products. Consequently, chapter 6, "Pressures of Parenthood and Fantasies of Childhood," examines how Hughes's Universal and Warner Bros. family films represent the American family through his characteristic mix of realism and fantasy. By doing so, I reflect on wider cultural myths and ideological debates concerning suburban family life in late-1980s and early-1990s America, a period when discourses of "family values" and moral panics about childhood were a staple feature of the period's culture wars. Through scrutiny of these movies, which were sold as escapist entertainment, I probe aspects of the complex relationship between films and society, reflecting on cinema's engagement with relevant political discourses.

Chapter 7, "Family Film Franchises," traces the commercial exploitation of the movies that emerged from the major multipicture deal that Hughes secured with 20th Century Fox following the unexpected global box-office success of *Home Alone*. Contextualizing the production and promotion of these movies within Hollywood's family-film production trend of the early 1990s, this chapter examines the production and marketing of the movies Hughes produced in close partnership with Fox. In particular, I focus on the studio's efforts to sell the *Home Alone* movies in ancillary markets, notably the rapidly expanding sell-through market for home video and the licensed-toy market. This chapter also examines the production and promotion of *Baby's Day Out* and *Miracle on 34th Street*, both of which were unable to replicate the box-office achievements of the *Home Alone* movies. Exploring the cultural resonances of these movies in more detail, chapter 8, "Slapstick, Sentimentality, and the American Family," focuses on how Hughes's 20th Century

Fox family comedies use a combination of physical comedy and appeals to emotion to work through issues relating to the contemporary American family. Significantly, all these films present white, upper-middle-class suburban life as the ideal and conclude with the (re)unification of the nuclear family. Consequently, I reflect on how slapstick sequences help work through apparent social problems and hint at anxieties concerning perceived threats to childhood and suburban life. The chapter also explores how *Miracle on 34th Street*, despite its lack of slapstick, nonetheless engages with themes and uses stylistic approaches characteristic of Hughes's other family films.

While this book is a history of Hughes's career, the commercial, textual, and cultural afterlives of his movies deserve attention, too. I therefore conclude the book by discussing the apparent decline of Hughes's career, beginning with a concise account of events in the late 1990s, including his deal with Disney and the founding of his new production company, Great Oaks. I not only consider how Hughes's seemingly abrupt departure from the film industry and public life fueled his elevation to almost mythic status but also explore how his reputation as a filmmaker continued to shift following his death. Finally, I close the book with a discussion of the textual afterlife of Hughes's films and some of the ways in which his movies continue to influence American popular culture.

CHAPTER 1

BUILDING A BRAND

Universal (1984–1985)

John Hughes, after directing one film, has been awarded virtual autonomy in a new three-year, $30 million production pact with Universal Pictures. He polishes off screenplays in one sitting, has assembled a talented cast of youngsters—headed by Molly Ringwald and Anthony Michael Hall—with whom he is making film after film, and works within jogging distance of his north suburban Chicago home.

Jack Barth, "John Hughes: On Geeks Bearing Gifts," *Film Comment*, June 1984.

In the summer of 1984, *Film Comment* announced John Hughes's entry into an elite group of directors who held multipicture production deals with major studios, an achievement made all the greater by the fact that he was not a well-known, big-budget filmmaker. As the article's author, Jack Barth, explained, Hughes specialized in modestly budgeted teen-oriented projects made without the participation of major stars. He also worked outside California, choosing instead to shoot his movies in his home state of Illinois. In fact, much about Hughes's profile—such as his lack of any formal training and limited experience of the Hollywood production process—did not fit with his newly acquired status as a major director. But his rapid ascent through the ranks of the US film industry was no coincidence; his success demonstrated how a changing media landscape was shaping the commercial priorities of the major studios in the mid-1980s and creating opportunities for mainstream filmmakers. Although *Sixteen Candles* (1984), *The Breakfast Club* (1985), and *Weird Science* (1985) were not major box-office hits, Hughes and Universal seized the opportunities created by the resurgent market for recorded music and the expanding home-video market in the United States. Hughes also drew on his background in the advertising field, developing projects that could be marketed and sold across multiple media platforms. While Universal initially underestimated the commercial potential of his films, Hughes showed a keen awareness of how American teenagers experienced and consumed popular culture, an insight that enabled his films to generate significant revenues in ancillary markets.

Although Hughes's elevation to the ranks of Hollywood's elite seemed sudden, he had laid the foundations for this move over a number of years. After dropping out of college, he began his career in advertising and worked his way up to become creative director at Leo Burnett. Immersed in the principles of the "Chicago school" of advertising, Hughes developed an acute understanding of what appealed to Middle American consumers. His tenure at the agency also helped him cultivate his midwestern sensibility as a writer. "A lot of my Chicago feeling comes out of Burnett: It's never pretended to be anywhere else but Chicago, to be proud to be a Chicago agency," he explained in a 1984 article.[1] When Hughes joined *National Lampoon* as a full-time writer in 1981, after writing freelance for the humor magazine for several years, he sought opportunities to gain experience as a screenwriter. The magazine wished to build on the success of *Animal House* (John Landis, 1978), and Hollywood studios were eager to invest in projects created by *National Lampoon*'s writers. His first two projects to make it past the development stage, a TV show based on *Animal House* called *Delta House* (ABC, 1979) and *Class Reunion* (Michael Miller, 1982), were not commercially successful. But the next film he wrote, *National Lampoon's Vacation* (Harold Ramis, 1983), starring Chevy Chase, was a major hit during the summer of 1983, grossing over $61 million at the domestic box office.[2] During the same period, another of Hughes's screenplays, *Mr. Mom* (Stan Dragoti, 1983), became a surprise hit movie. The family comedy starring Michael Keaton grossed over $64.5 million at the US box office.[3] As a consequence, when Hughes moved into film directing, he already had a wealth of creative skills and media industry experience.

Hughes's first three movies as a director, *Sixteen Candles, The Breakfast Club*, and *Weird Science*, were financed and distributed by Universal Pictures. Hughes originally conceived *The Breakfast Club*, which he wrote during July 1982, as a low-budget independent feature. After securing roughly $1 million in funding from A&M Records, he started planning the production in the winter of 1982.[4] According to Hughes, he decided to write another, more commercial script in order to improve his chances of having a career as a director.[5] The resultant screenplay, which became the movie *Sixteen Candles*, was a much more mainstream comedy than *The Breakfast Club* but deviated slightly from the established conventions of the teen movie. During the winter of 1982, Hughes's agent sent the script to Ned Tanen, the former president of Universal's film division.[6] Tanen, who favored inexpensive movies aimed at twelve- to twenty-four-year-olds, had championed several major youth-oriented hits, including *American Graffiti* (George Lucas, 1973), *Smokey and the Bandit* (Hal Needham, 1977), and *Animal House*.[7] Tanen acquired *Sixteen Candles* via his new production company, Channel Productions, and secured distribution through Universal. After he signed Hughes to direct *Sixteen Candles*, Tanen convinced Universal to purchase the rights to *The Breakfast Club* from A&M.[8] With Tanen's backing, Hughes found himself in the unusual position of directing two studio-funded motion pictures in short succession. In the summer of 1984, after shooting both movies, the filmmaker signed a deal, reportedly worth $30 million, tying him to Universal for three years.[9]

Hughes embarked on his directorial career when Universal and the other Hollywood studios were adjusting to the growing importance of nontheatrical release windows and ancillary markets. During the 1970s, the majority of the US film industry's domestic revenues came from the theatrical box office, and distributors received almost all their additional revenues from selling broadcast rights to television networks.[10] Between 1980 and 1984, the proportion of industry revenues generated by theatrical exhibition declined to below half; by 1989, it was just a third.[11] Box-office revenues did not drop significantly, however, because the major distributors increased ticket prices across the decade.[12] In addition, cable television, home video, and ancillary markets (such as soundtrack albums and merchandise) became increasingly important revenue streams, which helped offset rising production costs.[13] The concept of "synergy," as Jennifer Holt observes, became a guiding principle for media conglomerates in the 1980s as they sought to "exploit the rapidly imploding boundaries between film, television, and cable, and between various production, distribution, and exhibition outlets."[14] The expansion of ancillary markets also allowed media companies to spread financial risk because the profitability of a film no longer hinged solely on its performance at the box office.[15] This major shift in Hollywood's business model was a crucial factor in Hughes's success as a commercial filmmaker.

During the early to mid-1980s, Hughes successfully went from being a modestly successful screenwriter to an increasingly well-known and influential writer-director-producer. Focusing on teen movies at Universal allowed him to refine his approach to catering to a particular niche market of consumers—suburban teenagers. *Sixteen Candles, The Breakfast Club,* and *Weird Science* benefited from having strong, sellable commercial identities. Drawing on his knowledge and experience from the advertising world, he used genre, stardom, distinctive imagery, and memorable soundtracks to create strongly branded movies. This creative strategy suited the marketing and distribution strategies reshaping the American media industry at this time. As discussed in more detail in this chapter, MCA, Universal's parent company, harnessed the youth appeal of Hughes's teen movies to generate revenue in a range of markets. While the results varied, the success stories, besides boosting Hughes's reputation, fed into the entertainment industry's hyping of the benefits of cross-promotion and synergy. Thus, from the start of Hughes's career as a director and producer, his approach to the practice and business of filmmaking enabled him to build a distinct brand, founded on an increasingly recognizable, signature product: the John Hughes teen movie.

Battles for Control: Production and Marketing

During the early 1980s, MCA developed a reputation as "a conservative company with an unusual continuity of management for an industry that trades in its executives about as frequently as it trades in its automobiles."[16] Despite the success of *E.T.* (Steven Spielberg, 1982), Universal's executives viewed new projects cautiously, not least because they wished to avoid a repeat of the anxieties caused by the escalating budget on *The Blues Brothers* (John Landis, 1980).[17] In August 1982, the company's president, Sidney Sheinberg, stated, "MCA has a succinct philosophy about money. . . . By and large, we're not comfortable with bank debt."[18] Hughes's projects, which could be made quickly and relatively cheaply, therefore fit comfortably within MCA's guidelines. Ned Tanen's extensive knowledge of studio production and his contacts at Universal also helped Hughes navigate the business side of filmmaking. Before his departure from the studio in December 1982, Tanen had developed a reputation as a hit maker; his appointment as Universal's head of production in 1970, argues David A. Cook, was a major factor in the studio's turnaround during the following decade.[19] The executive producer guided Hughes through the production process and often acted as negotiator between the filmmaker and Universal. On the release of *The Breakfast Club*, Hughes stated that Tanen's "ramming it through the studio system" and protecting it from studio interference gave him the freedom to make the movie he had envisaged.[20]

Universal budgeted *Sixteen Candles* at $8 million, although later reports suggested the project came in under $6.5 million.[21] In a 1985 interview, Hughes stated that the final production budget for *The Breakfast Club* was in the region of $5 million, but the studio also had to cover the cost of purchasing the rights from A&M.[22] As part of their efforts to bring the film in on budget, Hughes and Tanen took advantage of changes in the Illinois film industry during the 1980s. From 1984 onward, the Illinois Film Office took a more "aggressive" approach to attracting major Hollywood productions, focusing in particular on the financial benefits of shooting in the state.[23] Members of the film labor unions in Chicago also agreed to substantial changes to their contracts, including more flexible working conditions and pay freezes.[24] The local workforce's flexibility, according to the director of the Illinois Film Office, ranked as "probably the biggest factor" in the growth of film and television production in Chicago.[25] These practical and financial incentives helped Tanen and Hughes convince Universal to allow the filmmaker to shoot his movies in Illinois. Consequently, Hughes filmed *Sixteen Candles, The Breakfast Club*, and parts of *Weird Science* on location in Chicago's North Shore suburbs, helping create the films' distinctive suburban aesthetic.

Hughes focused on securing control of as many aspects of his films as possible. In particular, he kept a tight grip on *The Breakfast Club*: "I took scale [payment] so I could have complete creative control. I made myself a producer. I had casting approvals. I didn't make any money on it, but I didn't care. This was my baby."[26] Hughes was not immune to studio interference, however, and points of conflict emerged during the shoot, most notably when production looked likely to run longer than the schedule set by the studio.[27] Toward the end of filming, Hughes had a major disagreement with newly appointed senior executives at Universal and threatened to leave the studio.[28] He then took legal action after the studio attempted to force him to edit the film in Hollywood.[29] Although Universal eventually released him from his contract, he was obliged to direct a third movie, *Weird Science*, which he shot in Illinois and Hollywood while editing *The Breakfast Club*.[30] Tanen had moved to Paramount in the meantime, and without his assistance Hughes was at a disadvantage when dealing with Universal. As well as facing studio pressure, Hughes had to join forces with Joel

Silver, a producer who owned the movie rights to EC Comics' *Weird Science* (1950–1953). A project that Hughes later tried to disown, *Weird Science* features much broader comedy than *Sixteen Candles* or *The Breakfast Club* and is laden with expensive special effects. While the movie represented Hughes's diminishing influence at the studio, it nonetheless bore several of the hallmarks of his work.

Another way in which Hughes exerted his influence over the commercial circulation of his work was by creating films that had obvious, built-in marketing hooks. The simple plots of his teen movies were easily conveyed in a wide variety of formats. Consequently, Hughes enabled Universal to use what John Ellis calls the "mechanism of the narrative image."[31] This method of product differentiation worked by building an impression of the film to appeal to a specific niche audience. Bold images alongside distinctive logos established a clear visual identity for each movie. Publicity materials relied particularly on the audience's awareness of the teen genre's tropes, harnessing intertextuality to pique viewers' interest. Thus, Universal sold each film through what Steve Neale terms its "generic image."[32] By foregrounding certain images and tropes—such as the suburban high school, wild parties, teenage cliques, sex, relationships, and coming-of-age—Universal's posters, trailers, and publicity stills shaped audience expectations. The studio also emphasized the recurrent presence of young stars, particularly Molly Ringwald and Anthony Michael Hall, across multiple films. In this way, the serial repetition of generic features and stars across the marketing campaigns for Hughes's three Universal teen films not only distinguished them from their competition, but also helped foster connections between the movies. By making a virtue of the films' similarities, Universal's publicity promised audiences that a John Hughes film would deliver a familiar set of pleasures.

Universal's promotional campaigns for *Sixteen Candles* and *Weird Science* created narrative images consistent with the style and tone of the films. The studio struggled to understand and capture the essence of *The Breakfast Club*, however.

Universal and Hughes had divergent perspectives on what would appeal to contemporary teenagers, and as one executive later put it, the studio and the director "were talking about very different movies."[33] When the final edit of *The Breakfast Club* was screened, studio executives expressed doubts about its commercial viability. "They thought it was unreleasable," Ned Tanen later claimed.[34] Neither Tanen nor Hughes was pleased with the marketing materials that Universal devised for *The Breakfast Club*. They were particularly unimpressed with the trailer, which included the teenagers smoking and a mixture of dancing, running, and comic moments, accompanied by a mixture of '80s synthesizer pop and guitar music in the style of Chuck Berry.[35] This selective presentation of *The Breakfast Club*'s content downplayed its serious dramatic intent. In a 1985 article describing the movie as a "commercial risk," Gene Siskel observed, "The film is being incorrectly referred to in publicity releases as a comedy, possibly in the hope of luring the unsuspecting."[36] Universal's attempts to broaden the film's audience in this way disregarded Hughes's perspective and emphasized the studio's ultimate control over the filmmaker's work.

Despite not fully understanding the appeal of Hughes's teen films, Universal was sufficiently confident to give all three of them a reasonably wide release, opening each film on over one thousand screens in the domestic market. In spite of somewhat confused promotional campaigns and mixed critical reviews, *Sixteen Candles*, *The Breakfast Club*, and *Weird Science* performed moderately well at the US box office. *Sixteen Candles* and *Weird Science* posted similar box-office receipts, grossing roughly $24.7 million and $23.8 million respectively. *The Breakfast Club* was by far the biggest success. The movie generated a box-office gross just shy of $45.9 million and ranked sixteenth in the 1985 annual box-office chart.[37] The films' theatrical releases proved that Hughes's economical approach to production and his ability to draw a niche audience could lead to a decent box-office return on the studio's investment. The key to Hughes's growing power within the US film industry, however, was his ability to create movies that could generate profits after their theatrical release. In the case of *Sixteen Candles, The Breakfast Club,* and *Weird Science,* recorded music and home video were the main sources of additional revenue, generating significant returns for MCA and A&M Records.

Recorded Music, Synergy, and MTV

Hughes's youth-oriented, mainstream entertainment provided myriad opportunities to exploit the economic potential of "mall culture." During the 1980s, multiplex cinemas were, as Jim Hillier notes, "often associated with shopping centers, exploiting the integration with other consumer and leisure activity."[33] An increasingly ubiquitous feature of American life, suburban malls became the focus of many adolescents' social activities, contributing to the development of mall culture.[39] Multiplex cinemas played an integral role in the expansion of this consumerist culture, as Josh Stenger argues: "Not coincidentally, multiplex theaters and youth markets were moving into the shopping mall at the same time: the mall and the multiplex became spaces for the mobilization of consumer desires, as well as dominant culture and political discourses which found voice and representation in the kind of mainstream films most likely to be exhibited in mall multiplexes."[40] The mall was, therefore, an architectural manifestation of the logic of synergy: a consumer could watch a movie and then purchase the soundtrack album or rent a video by the same filmmaker within the same shopping complex. Making such synergies a reality, though, was far from a foregone conclusion.

The evolution of MCA's business strategy facilitated the extension of Hughes's movies into ancillary markets. During this period, the corporation started to reorient its operations, developing links between Universal and MCA's record and music publishing operations and gradually shedding divisions unrelated to entertainment, such as its financial services and retail operations.[41] As early as 1979, in a move that signaled renewed efforts to develop "properties" that could be sold across a range of markets, MCA outlined a business strategy that included a focus on "the development of music related films and developing new artists for soundtracks."[42] The business incentives were obvious. As Jeff Smith observes, "Film and music cross-promotion can be seen more precisely as a strategy that not only creates multiple profit centers but also serves to spread risk and maximize resources."[43] MCA's business strategy proved particularly farsighted in the early 1980s, when, according to *Billboard*, Universal's box-office revenues helped offset a decline in MCA Music's record and cassette sales.[44]

The release of Hughes's teen movies coincided with the US record industry's emergence from a recession that had lasted several years. In the mid-1980s, young people were able to spend more money on recorded music because their disposable incomes increased and cassette tapes offered a cheaper, more portable alternative to vinyl.[45] The music industry also received an unexpected boost from a new cable TV channel, MTV, that by the mid-1980s was wielding considerable influence over the culture and commerce of popular music and youth culture more generally. Compared with the major networks, MTV did not have a huge audience—a potential viewership of 21.8 million—but it had become the most viewed basic cable channel by mid-1984.[46] Importantly, the average MTV viewer in the early 1980s was young and affluent.[47] Access to this particular demographic was a boon; in the 1970s, advertisers had struggled to target teenagers and young adults because they watched network television relatively infrequently.[48] Enticed by the access the channel gave to their main target audience, the major Hollywood studios were quick to jump on the bandwagon, and by mid-1983 they were among 140 companies jostling for advertising time on MTV.[49]

During the early 1980s, a music video cost roughly $50,000 to produce, and MTV's advertising rates were relatively low, especially when compared with those for network television.[50] Evidence that the promotion of movies via MTV could reap substantial financial rewards came in the form of Paramount's hit movie *Flashdance* (Adrian Lyne, 1983). The youth-oriented film offered a convincing demonstration of how MTV and Hollywood movies could cross-promote each other. The major

Hollywood studios, as Jeff Smith notes, "were quick to recognize certain promotional advantages afforded by the so-called 'music trailer.'"[51] Universal's executives soon integrated music videos and MTV into their business strategies. Following the success of Ray Parker Jr.'s "Ghostbusters," Frank Price, president of Universal Pictures, stated, "There's no question that music as a promotional tool for pictures is going to be around indefinitely."[52] The relatively conservative executives at MCA Records were, however, more hesitant to exploit cross-promotion. They remained skeptical about the commercial benefits of music television and resisted giving MTV clips for free.[53] Although the company soon fell in line with their competitors, MCA's continued conservatism meant Universal took the lead in creating cross-promotional opportunities.[54]

Universal and MCA initially underestimated the extent to which John Hughes's teen movies could help sell records and promote artists, nor did they fully exploit the potential crossover appeal between his soundtracks and MTV. The theatrical version of *Sixteen Candles* featured tracks from a diverse range of bands, including AC/DC, Paul Young, Altered Images, David Bowie, and the Specials. In contrast, the soundtrack album for *Sixteen Candles*, which MCA Records released on vinyl and cassette, contained just five tracks and omitted most of the film's standout songs. Despite being adorned with the *Sixteen Candles* logo and an image from the film, the "mini album" failed to capture the essence of the movie's use of music and included the bizarre juxtaposition of Patti Smith's "Gloria" with the Thompson Twins' "If You Were Here." Unsurprisingly, the album failed to make it into the Billboard 200 chart. Hughes had not considered whether MCA would be willing to pay for the rights to include songs from the film on its soundtrack. By prioritizing the music in the theatrical release, Hughes obstructed the creation of a proper tie-in album release. Shaped by this experience, Hughes conceived his future soundtracks with both aesthetic and commercial priorities in mind.

The Breakfast Club features a far less eclectic soundtrack than *Sixteen Candles*, comprising an original score by Keith

Forsey and a selection of new songs. The origins of *The Breakfast Club* meant that A&M records, which had originally funded the project, retained the right to produce and distribute the movie's soundtrack album. Crucially, A&M owned the rights for all the tracks featured in the movie, which kept costs down. The label was confident that it could target young consumers by selling the album primarily because of its association with *The Breakfast Club*. As well as excerpts from Forsey's score, the album featured all the songs from the movie's soundtrack: "Don't You (Forget About Me)" performed by Simple Minds, "Fire in the Twilight" performed by Wang Chung, "We Are Not Alone" by Karla DeVito, and "Didn't I Tell You," which featured Joyce Kennedy's vocals. Rather than emphasizing these artists, the LP cover featured the logo and main image from the movie's poster as well as Universal's official publicity stills of the cast.[55] In contrast, A&M issued two covers for Simple Minds' single "Don't You," with one highlighting the film and the other the band. For the second single release, "Fire in the Twilight" by Wang Chung, a more obscure band, the label opted for one cover that prominently featured images of the cast and the caption "From the Soundtrack of the Smash Film *The Breakfast Club*."

A&M Records invested considerably in the marketing of *The Breakfast Club: Original Motion Picture Soundtrack* and the single release of "Don't You" in the United States.[56] A&M, which was still independent of a major corporation, had ambitions to forge partnerships with film production companies in order to share in the cross-promotional benefits created by linking music with movies. Accordingly, A&M sunk more time and money into the album's promotion than MCA had done with *Sixteen Candles*, with advertisements for the album appearing in numerous national publications. To publicize the company's association with *The Breakfast Club*, A&M took out a full-page advertisement in *Billboard* on 23 February 1985, announcing that the movie's soundtrack album was "the first A&M Records soundtrack from an A&M Films / Channel Production."[57] The advertisement featured the movie's logo and an image of the album cover. Posters for the album

Figure 1.1. A&M Records advertisement for *The Breakfast Club: Original Motion Picture Soundtrack*, *Billboard*, 23 February 1985, 7.

prominently noted that "Simple Minds: 'Don't You (Forget About Me)'" was "the first single and MTV video."[58] The record company provided retailers with point-of-purchase materials, such as branded LP stands featuring images of the film's cast, to encourage them to display the album prominently. In this way, A&M actively targeted retailers and industry insiders as well as prospective customers.

A&M used two music videos to promote "Don't You" and "Fire in the Twilight." By 1985, music videos had become a standard part of record companies' promotional strategies.[59] The videos for "Don't You" and "Fire in the Twilight" are both relatively subtle in their inclusion of images from the movie, compared with other music videos of the period. Simple Minds' video for "Don't You" focuses primarily on the band's performance, and the first reference to *The Breakfast Club* comes almost halfway through the video. Brief excerpts from the movie's trailer appear on small television screens during the video. The video for Wang Chung's "Fire in the Twilight" also features movie footage and climaxes with the band's lead singer, Jack Hues, arriving at a cinema showing *The Breakfast Club*. Cast member Molly Ringwald makes a brief appearance in the video. Both music videos featured on MTV's playlists during 1985, providing promotional support for *The Breakfast Club*'s release.[60] MTV debuted the video for "Don't You" in its Breakout Rotation category a couple of weeks before the film's debut.[61] The video moved up the channel's rotation hierarchy, finally joining its Heavy Rotation list when the single rose into the Billboard Top 10 during May 1985.[62] It remained on the channel for eighteen weeks, an extremely rare occurrence, given MTV's prioritizing of new releases, and its longevity provided Hughes's film with considerable exposure on the youth-oriented channel.

A&M's investment in marketing and its faith in cross-promotion paid off. Both *The Breakfast Club* and its soundtrack proved popular with American consumers. Released on 19 February 1985, shortly after the film debuted in theaters, *The Breakfast Club: Original Motion Picture Soundtrack* sold well and remained in the Billboard Top 200 album chart for twenty-six weeks, peaking at number 17; it ended up ranked seventh in *Billboard*'s Top Pop Album: Soundtracks chart for 1985.[63] "Don't You," released the same week, became even more successful, reaching number 1 on the Billboard Hot 100 singles chart and remaining on the chart for twenty-two weeks.[64] The single was also an international hit, reaching the top 10 in Britain, Canada, West Germany, the Netherlands, Italy, and Australia.[65] The single's achievements seemingly validated Hughes's musical instincts. Association with *The Breakfast Club* did not guarantee chart success, however; Wang Chung's "Fire in the Twilight" failed to break into the Billboard Hot 100 and appeared on MTV for just a month.[66] The single releases from *The Breakfast Club* soundtrack therefore demonstrated the capricious nature of the "synergies" between film and recorded music.

Nonetheless, the trade press celebrated the commercial success of "Don't You" as a triumph of the synergistic relationship between film and music, downplaying the other factors involved. A photograph of A&M Records and Films president Gil Friesen and Simple Minds' Jim Kerr, printed in *Billboard*'s "Newsmakers" section, applauded the single's cross-promotional achievements.[67] Similarly, in June 1985, *Billboard* printed an image depicting MCA executives and Steve Schiff, the song's cowriter, posing with boxes of breakfast cereal to celebrate the single's chart success.[68] While the entertainment industry may have been keen to promote the song's commercial achievements, Simple Minds were more restrained. According to *Billboard*, the band's lead singer, Jim Kerr, denied that the band had significantly benefited from its relationship with *The Breakfast Club*, even though "Don't You" was their first US number 1. When Simple Minds embarked on its 1986 tour, Kerr asserted that the band's increased popularity should be attributed to its "socially conscious" music rather than the success of "Don't You."[69] Simple Minds' decision to perform the single at the Philadelphia concert for Live Aid demonstrated, however, that the band's politics could not be easily disentangled from its commercial success.

Hughes obviously understood popular music culture, and after the cross-promotional success of *The Breakfast Club* and "Don't You," his insider knowledge about music trends became a cornerstone of his reputation as a filmmaker. His ability to compile soundtracks that were either fashionable or sometimes ahead of mainstream trends quickly became a major selling point for his movies. Via interviews in media outlets aimed at a youth demographic, Hughes tried to assert his credibility as a music fan. Interviews are, as Timothy Corrigan suggests, "one of the few, documentable extratextual spaces where the auteur, in addressing cultures of fans and critical viewers, can engage and disperse his or her own agency as auteur."[70] In a 1986 interview with MTV, for example, Hughes maintained that he was more interested in the music than in the potential synergies created by his movie soundtracks. When referring to the relationship between "Don't You" and *The Breakfast Club*, he asserted, "We didn't put the song in there to sell records. We put the song in there because it was part of the movie. You couldn't take that song out of the movie and you couldn't take the movie out of the song. That's what I try to do, not sell records."[71] By directly addressing his youth audience through the music channel, Hughes demonstrated an awareness of who made up his target market and of how retaining a "cool," anticommercial image would strengthen his brand.

Music critics largely ignored the soundtrack for *The Breakfast Club*, despite its popularity. In his "Consumer Guide" on 25 June 1985, the *Village Voice*'s Robert Christgau awarded the album a D- and gave it his "Must to Avoid" label, describing it as a "consumer fraud" filled with "utterly negligible songs."[72] Christgau's hostility toward this form of commercial pop music was shared by many "serious" rock musicians and journalists who felt that the music video and cross-promotion between pop songs and other media contributed to an increased emphasis on marketability.[73] But as Andrew Goodwin points out, "Pop has always stressed the visual as a necessary part of its apparatus—in performance, on record covers, in magazine and press photographs, and in advertising."[74] Hughes's movie soundtracks are arguably a continuation of this long-standing practice of using popular music to promote other commodities.[75] Rock critics' antipathy seemed to stem particularly from the genre of music on the album. As Simon Frith suggests, critics and rock fans condemned "New Pop," with its appeal to white, suburban youth, as "mall music, shiny and confined," lacking the rebellious legitimacy of rock n roll's "fantasy of the streets."[76] *The Breakfast Club* soundtrack's reception was, therefore, tightly bound to wider cultural battles concerning taste and popular music.

After the success of *The Breakfast Club*, the soundtrack for *Weird Science* garnered significant publicity. From July 1985 onward, *Billboard* printed several updates on its progress.[77] The publication linked the project with MCA's efforts to develop Oingo Boingo's commercial prospects, following the band's five mediocre years at A&M.[78] Danny Elfman, the band's front man, expressed ambitions to have a mainstream hit, and MCA seemed confident that for all the band's quirkiness, it was "right smack in the middle of center."[79] *Weird Science* was not Oingo Boingo's first foray into film music; the band's music had appeared on several movie soundtracks in the early 1980s, including those for teen movies such as *Fast Times at Ridgemont High* (Amy Heckerling, 1982) and *The Last American Virgin* (Boaz Davidson, 1982), as part of its management company's plan to increase the group's exposure.[80] The *Weird Science* soundtrack, however, placed the band center stage. Oingo Boingo aside, the track listing for *Weird Science: Music from the Motion Picture* was eclectic. The album includes artists signed to MCA and performers affiliated with other record labels, demonstrating MCA's increased confidence in the commercial viability of tie-ins for Hughes's movies.

The music video for Oingo Boingo's "Weird Science" first appeared on MTV's playlist in early July 1985, providing the single, the album, and the film with additional publicity.[81] In late August 1985, MTV executives moved the single into the Heavy Rotation category to coincide with the single's release.[82] Whereas A&M released both the *Breakfast Club* soundtrack album and "Don't You" within a week of the movie's release, MCA did not release Oingo Boingo's single and the soundtrack album for *Weird Science* until a couple of weeks after the movie debuted in US theaters. "Weird Science" peaked at No. 45 in the *Billboard* Hot 100 and dropped out of the chart after just twelve weeks.[83] *Weird Science: Music from the Motion Picture*, which reached number 105, dropped out of the Billboard 200 the same week. By then, Oingo Boingo had a new album on sale, *Dead Man's Party*, which offered fans the opportunity to buy a version of "Weird Science" alongside the band's other new tracks.[84] In a *Billboard* article debating the benefits and drawbacks of the "current soundtrack craze," Larry Solters, an executive at MCA Records, argued that the inclusion of Oingo Boingo's music on the *Weird Science* soundtrack helped bring the band to a "national audience," beyond its established fan base in Los Angeles.[85] Indeed, the staying power demonstrated by the music video for "Weird Science," which remained on

MTV's playlist until late October 1985 despite the single's lack of commercial success, suggested the band's and the video's appeal exceeded that of the movie and the song itself.[86]

While rock music critics remained suspicious of Hughes's commercial motives, a November 1985 interview in *Rolling Stone* was acknowledgment of the filmmaker's growing influence on American popular music. The interviewer, Rob Tannenbaum, described Hughes as "a frustrated guitarist" who was "among Hollywood's hippest directors," and positioned him alongside the film producers Don Simpson and Jerry Bruckheimer, as well as Gary LeMel, the head of music at Columbia who supervised the soundtracks for *The Big Chill* (Lawrence Kasdan, 1983) and *St. Elmo's Fire* (Joel Schumacher, 1985).[87] In keeping with his earlier interviews, Hughes explained how his creative process was designed to realize a "complete symbiosis" between the narrative and the soundtrack. He stated that his screenplays were "written to the style of a couple of bands," noting that *The Breakfast Club* was from his "Clash–Elvis Costello period."[88] The emphasis that Hughes placed on listening to records and on his knowledge of older rock groups suggested an attempt to gain legitimacy among rock fans by appealing to the discourses of authenticity associated with rock music, and to disavow the commercialism associated with New Pop and MTV. Further validation came in an August 1985 interview with Oingo Boingo's Danny Elfman; he stated that Hughes was "one of the only guys out there who really takes chances musically," in contrast with the majority of "film people," who "know nothing about music, and their tastes are three or four years behind wherever the music scene is."[89] Hughes's interactions with the popular-music press and with music industry personnel suggest a conscious effort to assert his musical knowledge and to position his soundtracks as genuine attempts to convey the subjectivity of youth experience through music.

MCA, Home Video, and Youth Audiences

Home video became a significant source of ancillary income from Hughes's Universal teen films. His movies were an excellent match for the clientele of the video stores that spread across the United States during the 1980s. One survey suggested that viewers under the age of twenty "tripled their video viewing to 58 million films in August–September 1985 while reducing their theatrical viewing by a fifth."[90] The developing culture of video stores as spaces where teenagers could socialize, along with the central role that home entertainment played in slumber parties, further added to video's status within 1980s youth culture.[91] Hughes later claimed that home-video releases also performed a promotional function: "There was a strategy. I'm a growing market: *Sixteen Candles* will come out on videocassette as *The Breakfast Club* is opening. *Breakfast Club* will be on cassette as *Pretty in Pink* is coming. It created this wave. It took three years to get through it. And it worked."[92] Given MCA Home Video's struggles to capitalize on video's commercial potential during the early 1980s, this outcome seems as much a happy coincidence as the product of coherent business strategy.

The rapid change in MCA Home Video's strategy, between the releases of *Sixteen Candles* and *The Breakfast Club*, reflected broader transformations in the home-video market, most notably increased spending on the advertising of individual releases as well as promotion of the companies themselves. MCA did not heavily publicize the home-video release of *Sixteen Candles*. In contrast, the release of *The Breakfast Club* on video in July 1985 was accompanied by several full-page advertisements in *Billboard* aimed at video distributors and retailers. The eight months between the movie's theatrical release and the video's launch gave the studio time to prepare a high-profile marketing campaign. The video also benefited from MCA's increased promotion of its home-video division. Under the slogan "Everyone's Watching MCA," a series of advertisements appeared in *Billboard* and other trade publications. The claim that "variety gives us the edge" formed the main selling point of these materials, which boasted, "Look to us for the brightest stars, the most popular titles, and incredible musical performances."[93] The ads featured several current video releases, including *The Breakfast Club*, which was described as "one of the year's biggest box

Figure 1.2. "Everyone's Watching MCA": advertising *The Breakfast Club* on VHS, *Billboard*, 31 August 1985, VSDA-51.

office hits."[94] To promote the video's chart success, MCA Home Video also took out a full-page advertisement in *Billboard* on 16 November 1985 that proclaimed, "Thanks to our sales staff and yours for making us the Number 1 for the 4th week in a row."[95] The successful promotion of *The Breakfast Club* on videocassette helped advance MCA's more strategic approach to video marketing during the mid-1980s.

Hughes's teen movies were well suited to the "exploitation" marketing that was prevalent in the home-video market of this period. As video producers adjusted to the rapidly expanding market for VHS and Betamax, distributors and retailers often devised their own marketing strategies to supplement the major studios' publicity materials. Since hundreds of video titles competed for consumers' attention, wholesalers and stores had to develop creative ways to make new releases stand out. *Billboard* reported how one video wholesaler, Sight

& Sound Distributors, developed a major sweepstake promotion to boost sales of *Sixteen Candles*. The contest, which attracted 6,000 entries, required the coordination of several hundred dealers and the in-house production of publicity and entry materials.[96] An image included with the article depicted a sixteenth-birthday cake that was presented to the contest winner.[97] The hand-decorated cake attempted to replicate the MCA Video logo, the film's logo, and the image of the movie's young stars used on the movie's poster. Similarly, in August 1985, *Billboard* described how the owner of a small chain of video stores in Michigan devised his own promotional campaign for the release of *The Breakfast Club* as part of a larger series of "aggressive promotions that include private screenings, free meals, and giveaways."[98] To celebrate the movie's video release, the retailer opened his store at seven in the morning and gave away free coffee mugs and breakfast vouchers for a local restaurant.[99]

By promoting such local marketing strategies, *Billboard* helped share the expertise of successful home-video businesses with a wider community of small and midsize companies. Video distribution companies also took responsibility for transferring knowledge between retailers during the early 1980s. "The video distributors," argues Joshua M. Greenberg, "acted as knowledge brokers and helped shape a shared consensus on how to market and sell movies on video cassette."[100] For example, VTR Distributing, a midsize video distributor based in Pittsburgh, held a brunch and seminar for *The Breakfast Club*. The event was part of larger series of seminars set up to explain to retailers how to market tapes and set up promotions, as well as to supply them with additional advertising and point-of-purchase display materials.[101] In the buildup to the video release of *Weird Science*, MCA Home Video mimicked these kinds of independent promotions. As Greenberg observes, "Corporations were continually playing catch-up with the small business owners and enthusiasts who were creating the [video] industry."[102] In January 1986, MCA announced a sweepstakes for the video release of *Weird Science*. Distributors, retailers, and consumers were eligible for cash prizes, and consumers could win a European vacation.[103] MCA still did not take full responsibility for the video's promotion at the store level, but instead encouraged retailers to create their own displays for the video release and invited them to send in photographs as part of a contest to win an Apple computer.[104] It was not until later in the decade, as the shift to retail video sales (as opposed to video rentals) gained momentum, that MCA and other video producers started to habitually provide and control display materials for new releases.

Consistent with wider industry practices, MCA released Hughes's teen films on VHS and Betamax from five to eight months after each movie's theatrical debut, with a LaserDisc release one to two months later. It released *Sixteen Candles* on tape in October 1984, *The Breakfast Club* in October 1985, and *Weird Science* in February 1986. MCA positioned the VHS and Betamax versions for the rental—rather than purchase—market, pricing all three at $79.95.[105] Consistent with the corporation's promotion of the format, LaserDisc versions of the movies were much cheaper, with suggested retail prices of $30 to $35.[106] Although the major studios were experimenting with sell-through pricing for blockbusters during the mid-1980s, most home videos were priced for rental. And the rental market was where *Sixteen Candles, The Breakfast Club*, and *Weird Science* thrived.[107] Average fees of $3 or less meant that renting a video was affordable for Hughes's primary audience, suburban adolescents.[108] *Sixteen Candles* remained in the top 40 of Billboard's Top Videocassette Rentals chart for twenty-seven weeks.[109] *The Breakfast Club* seized the top spot on 26 October 1985, just two weeks after first appearing on the chart, and remained at number 1 for four weeks.[110] Altogether, the video stayed on the chart for thirty-one weeks.[111] *Weird Science* entered the Top Videocassette Rentals chart at number 7 and remained in the top 40 for twenty-one weeks.[112] All three videos generated significant revenues for MCA, thanks to demand from private buyers as well as from rental stores; both *The Breakfast Club* and *Weird Science* gained platinum certification for over $6 million worth of sales income.[113] The videos' success therefore affirmed that Hughes's teen movies were, as *Billboard*'s Tony Seidman suggested in relation to *The Breakfast Club,* "a superb match for the demographics of the VCR-owning audience."[114]

John Hughes successfully launched a career as a mainstream Hollywood filmmaker by capitalizing on his strong commercial instincts and creating films that could be commoditized. Each of his Universal teen films had a clearly defined identity, which increased opportunities for cross-promotion with record labels and the home-video industry. *The Breakfast Club* and *Weird Science,* in particular, gave A&M and MCA opportunities to take advantage of growth in the recorded-music market during the early to mid 1980s. Hughes's focus on New Pop and British New Wave bands meant that his films were suited to promotion via MTV. Translating his ambitions into reality was not a straightforward process, however; his commercial credentials were untested, and the differing agendas of Universal and the soundtracks' record labels sometimes hindered cross-promotion. The success of the movies' soundtrack albums and singles hinged on MCA Music's and A&M's investment in rights, marketing, and music videos. Following the success of A&M's aggressive promotion of the *Breakfast Club* soundtrack and Simple Minds' "Don't You," MCA increased its spending on the soundtracks to Hughes's films. As the mixed chart results for other singles and albums showed, being linked with a Hughes teen movie did not guarantee success. Hughes's reputation nonetheless benefited from the music industry's push for successful cross-promotions. Moreover, his teen movies—alongside the so-called MTV movies of the same period—helped reinvigorate the long-standing relationship between youth-oriented movies and popular music.

Hughes's teen movies were also well positioned to capitalize on the growing home-video market in the United States. Affluent suburban teenagers, who embraced the entertainment technology with particular enthusiasm, were instrumental to the success of the video releases of *Sixteen Candles, The Breakfast Club,* and *Weird Science.* While the major studios were often slow to react to changes in audiences' consumption habits during the early 1980s, MCA soon recognized that to maximize profits, home video had to be treated as an important part of a film's commercial life cycle, rather than as an afterthought. The increasingly elaborate campaigns for the video releases of Hughes's movies reflected the corporation's attempts to keep pace with the rapid changes in the home entertainment industry, as well as MCA's growing confidence in his output.

Through *Sixteen Candles, The Breakfast Club, Weird Science,* and the films' paratexts, Hughes became associated with a signature product—the John Hughes teen film. Universal and Hughes's commercial strategy relied on similarities between the films and on a degree of regulated difference. That said, Universal's efforts to diversify the appeal of his teen films were consistent with Barbara Klinger's observation that studios are "not primarily concerned with producing coherent interpretations of a film," but instead "produce multiple avenues of access to the text that will make the film resonate as extensively as possible in the social sphere in order to maximize its audience."[115] Alongside attempts to exploit genre and stardom, Universal worked to position Hughes as the teen films' creative origin. Looking toward the next phase in his Hollywood career, Hughes used interviews to assert his central role in the development of these commercial successes, and as his reputation in the industry developed, he embraced opportunities to assert greater creative control over his projects. Thus, his career trajectory serves as a reminder that, as Jon Lewis argues, in the New Hollywood, "Auteurs gain notoriety less for a signature style, than for a signature product."[116] As shown in more detail in the next chapter, *Sixteen Candles, The Breakfast Club,* and *Weird Science* share narrative and stylistic attributes that aided their packaging as a cohesive group of films. They also demonstrate a thematic engagement with social and cultural issues shaping suburban adolescent life, which was key to their appeal to Hughes's target audience.

CHAPTER 2

REALITIES AND FANTASIES OF SUBURBAN ADOLESCENCE

Sixteen Candles (1984), *The Breakfast Club* (1985), and *Weird Science* (1985) respond to and develop the conventions of the teen film. They are now widely considered, in both popular and academic discourse, to be paradigmatic examples of the genre. The movies' marketing, exploitation in ancillary markets, and wider cultural impact played key roles in this genre designation. Genre is an inherently intertextual phenomenon, and Janet Staiger argues, "The text is inevitably impure because it cannot but be known by the context in which it exists."[1] Nevertheless, as mainstream Hollywood movies that address a teenage audience and focus on teenagers' lives at home and high school, Hughes's teen movies are uncontentious examples of the teen film on a textual level.[2] To use Rick Altman's framework for genre analysis, *Sixteen Candles, The Breakfast Club,* and *Weird Science* showcase the "semantic" features associated with many examples of the American teen film, including the high school, suburbia, the teenage "hangout," cars, and the general paraphernalia of youth culture—such as posters, magazines, and "hip" clothes—the exact nature of which is determined by a range of factors, including time period, geographic location, and the character's social class. The movies also engage with the "syntax" of the teen film through their explorations of the closely interrelated themes of coming-of-age, identity, sex, romance, social acceptance, and generational conflict. It is Hughes's articulation of the syntax of the teen film, the way in which his movies inflect the "genre's meaning-bearing structures," that distinguishes them from many of their precursors.[3] Through their emphasis on female characters and "geeky" male characters, Hughes's movies deploy the genre's conventions in distinctive ways and for different purposes than do many earlier teen movies.

All three of Hughes's Universal teen films explore suburban teenage experiences and emotions by condensing a variety of events into a short time frame. Explaining the ethos of his directorial debut, *Sixteen Candles*, Hughes recounted, "I wanted to make a very realistic movie about what it's like to be sixteen, what it's truly like to be sixteen. And to compress a lot of those things that you feel and experience when you're sixteen into one day."[4] *Sixteen Candles* depicts the incidents that unfold on Samantha Baker's (Molly Ringwald's) sixteenth birthday as her family prepares for her older sister's wedding. Taking this distillation of teenage experience one step further, *The Breakfast Club* relies on an extremely simple premise: five teenagers (played by Molly Ringwald, Anthony Michael Hall, Judd Nelson, Emilio Estevez, and Ally Sheedy) spend a Saturday in detention in their high school's library. They argue, joke, and engage in lengthy discussions of their problems, discovering that they share similar insecurities. In fact, *The Breakfast Club* is more like a stage play than a typical Hollywood movie. With a more concept-led approach, *Weird Science* fuses elements of the Frankenstein story with a fairly conventional coming-of-age narrative. Two geeky teenage boys, Gary (Anthony Michael Hall) and Wyatt (Ilan Mitchell-Smith), use a computer to create their perfect woman, Lisa (Kelly LeBrock). Over the course of a weekend, Lisa uses her superior intellect, magic powers, and sexuality to teach the boys self-confidence and to elevate their social status.

In their narrative structures, engagement with generic frameworks, and use of film style, *Sixteen Candles*, *The Breakfast*

Club, and *Weird Science* embody what Richard Maltby has dubbed Hollywood's "commercial aesthetic," since they are constructed to satisfy the audience's emotional desires and "turn pleasure into a product."[5] Hughes combines different elements to maximize the films' appeal, and he shows a keen understanding of how "Hollywood plot structure engages the spectator in a carefully articulated mental and emotional experience."[6] His teen films have just one or two major plotlines, which aids audience comprehension and identification. Cuts between lines of action and shifts in focalization between characters permit shifts in tone and style as well as the deployment of a variety of genre conventions. By using tropes from melodrama, comedy, fantasy, and science fiction, Hughes is able to release his characters from the reality of their suburban experiences. All three films mix comedy and sentiment, using one mode to offset the other. In a 1984 interview about *Sixteen Candles*, Hughes pointed out that this strategy was intentional: "It's part of my style. I like to take things to a comic extreme, once in a while. Just to say: 'No, I'm not afraid to go this far. This picture is not afraid to go this far.' Just as it's not afraid to be touching."[7] Thus, Hughes's teen films rely heavily on the interplay between the reality of everyday suburban teenage life and moments of fantasy in order to appeal to audiences.

Hughes, as critics noted at the time, visibly attempted to distinguish his movies from "the standard teen romp."[8] In interviews, he criticized Hollywood's failure to engage meaningfully with the real-life concerns and experiences of American teenagers: "I just don't think 16-year-olds are being served well by my generation," he told *Film Comment*'s Jack Barth in 1984.[9] Hughes framed his movies as being about, as Roger Ebert put it, "fairly typical American teenagers . . . kids who are vulnerable and serious and spend infinitely more time speculating about sex than actually experiencing it."[10] Accordingly, this chapter explores how Hughes's emphasis on less stereotypical teenage characters in *Sixteen Candles* and *The Breakfast Club*, including complex female characters, had a significant impact on the films' articulation of genre tropes. Even *Weird Science*, which at first glance appears to be a fairly run-of-the-mill sex comedy, offers a layered perspective on masculinity and the pressures of social conformity. *Sixteen Candles, The Breakfast Club,* and *Weird Science* engage with the rites of passage typically associated with coming-of-age narratives, such as the loss of virginity, embarking on relationships, consuming alcohol, and taking drugs. By doing so, they not only touch on the anxieties of many American teenagers, but also expose how social identities and social structures shape adolescent experiences.

Shermer: One of America's Towns

The creation of a strong sense of place figured centrally in Hughes and his collaborators' efforts to create a "realistic" portrayal of Middle American teenage life. The characters in *Sixteen Candles, The Breakfast Club,* and *Weird Science* live in Shermer, Illinois, a fictional suburb on Chicago's North Shore. While not a full-fledged hyperdiegesis, the Shermer "universe" forms part of a system of intertextuality that Hughes developed through his 1980s films. "Everybody, in all of my movies, is from Shermer, Illinois," Hughes once explained. "Del Griffith from *Planes, Trains & Automobiles* lives two doors down from John Bender. Ferris Bueller knew Samantha Baker from *Sixteen Candles*."[11] This serial recurrence of certain locations within Hughes's films acts as a form of shorthand, supporting his efficient approach to storytelling. John Ellis observes that the repetition of locations aids narrative economy because the viewer's familiarity allows the filmmaker to focus on introducing novelty through other aspects of the film.[12] Moreover, familiar locations "carry memories of events that have already been staged there, and so intensify the accumulation of meaning within the film."[13] The repeated use of locations such as high schools and tree-lined suburban streets also encourages audiences to make associations between Hughes's films.

Marilyn Vance's costume design and John W. Corso's production design play a crucial role in creating the world of Shermer. Vance's costume design adds to the realism of *Sixteen Candles, The Breakfast Club,* and *Weird Science*. After her work on *Fast Times at Ridgemont High* (Amy Heckerling, 1982), Vance became highly aware of the richness of detail required to portray teenage subcultures realistically.[14] For Hughes's films, she carefully researched teenagers in the Midwest. Her costume designs were not, however, constrained by the demands of authenticity. In step with Hughes's production philosophy, she prioritized character and storytelling. For instance, when the characters are introduced in *The Breakfast Club,* Vance noted, "every little thing determines who these characters are, what their families are like."[15] Similarly, the films' sets do not simply provide a realistic backdrop; Corso's designs shape the audience's understanding of the action, since the "décor becomes the narrative's organizing image, a figure that stands for the narrative itself."[16] The characters' confinement to the windowless library in *The Breakfast Club,* for example, reinforces the oppressive nature of high school, and the demarcation of space reinforces the characters' shifting relationships with one another. Through their synthesis of realistic and symbolic elements of design, both Vance and Corso helped create a seemingly authentic representation of mid-1980s suburban teenage life, which was key to the films' appeal to teenagers and to the development of a Hughesian aesthetic.

The soundtracks of *Sixteen Candles, The Breakfast Club,* and *Weird Science* work closely with the films' visuals to build an enticing portrayal of mid-1980s suburbia. The predominance of New Pop bands across Hughes's teen films links them with an aspirational form of white suburban culture that prizes style and consumption as markers of identity.[17] While the films' soundtracks had a strong commercial aspect, Hughes's use of popular music was also a significant feature of his filmmaking style. Working in conjunction with his editors and music supervisors, he used music to score scenes of teenage life, accentuating their affective impact. In *Sixteen Candles* and *Weird Science,* music often sets the general mood for a scene, as it works in conjunction with editing to create a particular tempo. Music can also signal characters' feelings. For example, at the high school dance in *Sixteen Candles,* Spandau Ballet's "True" scores both Samantha's longing gazes at Jake Ryan and the moment when he returns her look. Similarly, the Thompson Twins' "If You Were Here" scores the couple's unification in the film's final scene. Both these moments emphasize female desire and fantasy as the soulful lyrics and vocals of the New Romantic tracks suggest the strength of Samantha's feelings. This blending of commercial, narrative, and cultural motivations was typical of Hughes and his collaborators' use of music. Through this approach, they created a distinctive aural identity for mid-1980s suburban Chicago.

Hughes maintained that despite the persistent recurrence of the same readily recognizable locales, his teen films were not simply about a particular corner of Illinois. In a 1986 interview, he asserted, "No, they weren't about Chicago. Chicago's a setting."[18] Hughes's comment points to why the settings of *Sixteen Candles, The Breakfast Club,* and *Weird Science* have a wider cultural resonance. Shermer's function as a microcosm of American life is clearly underscored by its slogan: "One of America's Towns." This suggestion of universality reflects a discourse that positions the Midwest as quintessentially Middle American. Shermer's portrayal on-screen is also closely connected with a vision of suburbia that came to the fore in the postwar era, when, observes Amy Maria Kenyon, suburbia was inextricably bound up with the American Dream and when "white, middle-class suburban life was commodified and equated with 'America' and with 'American national identity.'"[19] Hughes's depiction of Middle American life in *Sixteen Candles, The Breakfast Club,* and *Weird Science* as suburban, white, and affluent is consistent with suburbia's portrayal in much American cinema and culture. Even the "reality" of suburban life that Hughes sought to create in these teen films is inseparable from what Bennett M. Berger has dubbed "the myth of suburbia."[20]

The suburban imaginary that Hughes and his collaborators refer to and develop through his teen films relies heavily on a set of images and tropes that hark back to the early to mid-twentieth century. The image of suburbia created in *Sixteen Candles,* in particular, is imbued with nostalgia. The film's

Figure 2.1. The streets of suburban Shermer, Illinois, in the opening shot of *Sixteen Candles*.

opening shot, of a truck delivering newspapers in a leafy neighborhood with large, colonial-style houses and manicured lawns, immediately establishes a wistful, storybook vision of suburban life. *Variety*'s reviewer pointed to the "flavorful backdrop" created by "the tree-lined Midwest aura," and commented that the "tone of the film . . . actually suggests the Middle America of a Norman Rockwell Saturday Evening Post Cover."[21] In contrast, *The Breakfast Club* focuses on the institutional setting of a 1970s-built high school, its brutalist concrete façade suggesting a less nostalgic vision of suburbia. Nonetheless, the opening and closing sequences of the film show that trees, grass, and neat suburban housing surround the school. Returning to a more idealized perspective, *Weird Science* centers on the highly aspirational setting of an extremely affluent prewar neighborhood. In all three movies, Hughes and his collaborators not only use suburbia as a backdrop, but also draw on its status as a "potent cultural signifier" capable of connoting numerous meanings.[22]

The recognizable backdrop of Shermer accentuates Hughes's emphasis on the more mundane aspects of teenage experience. Much of the humor and drama in *Sixteen Candles, The Breakfast Club,* and *Weird Science* concerns the awkwardness of being a middle-class suburban teenager. The angst felt by many of the teenage protagonists in his teen films comes from being "normal" and forgettable rather than exceptional. Accordingly, Hughes's teen films place particular emphasis on familial relationships, a thematic concern that is rare in the teen sex comedies and slasher movies of the 1980s. *Sixteen Candles* and *Weird Science* ground the concerns of their teenagers in interactions taking place within a domestic setting. In *Sixteen Candles,* in scenes recognizable to many teenagers, Samantha spends the majority of her time on-screen bickering with her siblings and engaging in awkward interactions with her parents and grandparents. In *Weird Science,* the boys' families are also a source of conflict and embarrassment. In their rich parents' absence, Wyatt's brother Chet is an emasculating bully, and Gary's parents are painfully out of touch. Although the parents in *The Breakfast Club* are almost entirely absent from the screen, the teenagers' relationships with them loom large in their conversations. As Hughes explained in a 1985 interview, "If their parents weren't important to them, they wouldn't have said anything about them. It wouldn't even have come up."[23]

Dialogue plays a significant role in grounding *Sixteen Candles, The Breakfast Club,* and *Weird Science* in the everyday world of white middle-class American teenagers. The three films are relatively dialogue heavy, and the characters frequently engage in rapid-fire conversations filled with teenage slang. In Pauline Kael's *New Yorker* review of *Sixteen Candles,* she reflected on this strength of the filmmaker's work: "John Hughes has a feeling for verbal rhythms, and he knows how kids toss words around, especially the words that set them apart from their elders. What gives *Sixteen Candles* its peppiness is his affection for teenagers' wacko slang phrases."[24] Phrases such as "By night's end, I predict me and her will interface," "You're a neo maxi zoom dweebie," and "You're stewed, butt-wad" celebrate the inventiveness of adolescent speech. In "Is There Life after Teenpix?," Richard Corliss of *Time* magazine said of Hughes in 1985, "He knows how ordinary teenagers, the ones who don't get movies made about them, think and feel. . . . He has learned their dialect and decoded it for sympathetic adults."[25] The filmmaker was aided in his interpretation of teenage experience by the shrewd use of his casts' firsthand experiences as middle-class youths. The producer of *Sixteen Candles*, Hilton Green, commented, "John is extremely talented at making scenes blossom because he gets very close to the cast, and if they have a new idea, that's the way he will do it. That's a knack you don't find very often in directors."[26] This actor-focused approach to directing helped Hughes further develop the authenticity of his scenes of teenage life.

In a 1984 television interview, John Hughes explained his creative strategy as a director: "My main intent in directing is to get the performances from the actors, to execute the story correctly and clearly, [and] fill it up with wonderful little performance pieces. I'm not a technical director. I'm not interested in lenses or all the other technical aspects of it. I establish a look for the picture and a visual style. . . . I spend most of the time working with the actors."[27] Consistent with Hughes's deference to proven approaches to commercial filmmaking, his direction relies heavily on the same "invisible style" that sustained studio-era "Hollywood cinema's illusion of reality" by using mise-en-scène and film style to reinforce narrative priorities and to maintain a sense of spatial and temporal continuity.[28] By working with increasingly skilled cinematographers, he gradually built up his repertoire of shots and adopted a more precise approach to framing, staging, and editing. This enabled him to reinforce characters' emotions and relationships as well as to emphasize key aspects of the mise-en-scène.

Even as Hughes's understanding of cinematography developed, he still shot a considerable amount of footage for his films, because of his performer-centered approach. His editors, therefore, played a crucial role in creating logical and engaging narratives that placed characters at their center, as well as in determining the pace and rhythm of the films. Hughes frequently claimed that *The Breakfast Club*'s editor, Dede Allen, known for her pioneering work on movies such as *Bonnie and Clyde* (Arthur Penn, 1967), transformed his approach to filmmaking by making him more conscious of framing, characterization, and the coordination of sound and image.[29] Through the progression of *Sixteen Candles, The Breakfast Club,* and *Weird Science,* Hughes began to develop a directorial style that prized narrative efficiency and supported his character-led approach.

Hughes was particularly focused on finding actors who could deliver convincing performances that would support his directorial style. In fact, critics frequently commented on Hughes's "talent for casting."[30] During the casting process, over which he had considerable influence, Hughes was careful to choose young performers who were, or could plausibly be, in their teens. Both Molly Ringwald and Anthony Michael Hall were just fifteen during the filming of *Sixteen Candles.* Ringwald's attractive, slightly awkward, postpubescent appearance is consistent with Hughes's notes in the final draft of the screenplay: "She's young and pretty. No seething, precocious sexuality. Just a pretty, young girl."[31] Similarly, Hall's gangly frame, unruly hair, and orthodontics captured the transitional nature of teenage physicality. Even as the two actors matured, Hughes showcased their distinctive physical traits as well as their talents as performers, aiding their development as stars. The other cast members of *The Breakfast Club,* Emilio Estevez, Ally Sheedy, and Judd Nelson, were more established performers, associated with the Brat Pack, and their largely conventional good looks and maturity made them aspirational figures. Conversely, Hall's costar in *Weird Science,* Ilan Mitchell-Smith, who was only fifteen during the movie's production, embodied a "cute" version of male adolescence, more likely to appeal to younger teens and preteens. By embodying realistic or slightly idealized versions of suburban teenagers, these young stars increased the authenticity of the movies' worlds and their engagement with contemporary concerns.

Teenage Gender and Sexuality in 1980s Suburbia

Hughes's teen films demonstrate how gender and sexuality, in conjunction with race and social class, shape both the realities and fantasies of suburban teenagers. Heteronormative romance, a cornerstone of suburban existence, figures centrally in *Sixteen Candles, The Breakfast Club,* and *Weird Science.* Hughes's teen films only hint, however, at the reality of teenage sexual activity in the mid-1980s. Rather than engaging directly with issues such as teenage pregnancy, which affected one in ten American teenage girls during the early 1980s, the movies promote the virtues of a more restrained female sexuality, one based on romance.[32] "Most of my characters are romantic rather than sexual," Hughes claimed in a 1986 interview. "I think that's an essential difference in my pictures."[33] *Sixteen Candles* markedly avoids representing Samantha as a sexual object and sets limits on young female sexuality. Romance rather than lust drives the narrative and frames her interactions with Jake. Although the sex survey that she completes in homeroom indicates that she would like to lose her virginity to Jake Ryan, she seems more focused on having a boyfriend than on realizing any sexual desires. This is in stark contrast to the female characters in films such as *Little Darlings* (Ronald F. Maxwell, 1980) and *Private School* (Noel Black, 1983), who are focused on engaging in sexual acts. Sex and its attendant cultural politics nonetheless feature in Hughes's teen films. As Catherine Driscoll explains, "Because puberty, gender and sex are crucial to adolescence[,] there is no such thing as a teen film that does not include sex, even if there is no sex on screen."[34]

A tension between the teenage girl as subject and the teenage girl as object pervades Hughes's teen films. While central female characters are represented as complex individuals, their subjectivity is often constrained by their romantic ambitions and by the limits placed on teenage girls by society. Although Samantha is ostensibly the protagonist in *Sixteen Candles*, she is passive for the majority of the film. Consequently, part of what makes *Sixteen Candles* enjoyable for female audiences is Hughes's use of structuring devices associated with the "melodramatic narrative."[35] Steve Neale suggests the melodramatic narrative creates suspense and, ultimately, pleasure through "the production of discrepancies between the knowledge and point of view of the spectator and the knowledge and points of view of the characters."[36] The audience possesses knowledge of Samantha's and Jake's feelings from an early point in

Sixteen Candles, through scenes in which the characters express their interest in each other. For much of the film, however, the couple are unaware of their mutual affection, and suspense is built through a series of failed communications and delays. Samantha's desires are finally realized in the final sequence of the film, when Jake appears outside the church after her sister's wedding. Although the movie's romantic resolution is perhaps undermotivated from a realist perspective, *Sixteen Candles* is, as John Hughes noted, "to a certain extent, a fantasy."[37] But the fantasy it creates is based on the teenage girl as passive and not directly in control of her romantic destiny.

Allison's character arc in *The Breakfast Club* similarly illustrates how romance and the pursuit of social acceptance constrain the subjectivity of more active suburban teenage girls. Initially, through her silence and eccentric behavior, she distances herself from the group, seemingly uninterested in their approval. While Curran Nault argues that her "destabilizing influence" declines once she starts to speak, in fact Allison's words reinforce her lack of conformity, her self-awareness, and her outward-looking perspective.[38] In particular, Allison demonstrates an astute understanding of gendered attitudes toward adolescent sexuality. She points out to Claire that a girl's virginity is "kind of a double-edged sword": "If you say you haven't, you're a prude. If you say you have, you're a slut. It's a trap." She also dreams of existing in a less regulated world beyond the confines of the Chicago suburbs, arguing that she could "run away" and go to "the ocean," "the country," "the mountains," "Israel, Africa, Afghanistan." Close to the end of the film, however, Allison undergoes a transformation, shedding her fantasies of escape, her cynicism toward her peers, and her alternative clothes and makeup. Succumbing to her desire to belong, Allison allows Claire to give her a makeover that transforms the edgy, grungy outsider into a smiling, perky girl dressed in pink.

Allison and Claire's ability to transform their appearances, and by extension their social status, is linked with wider debates about teenage girls' agency. As Maryn Wilkinson observes, at the core of the makeover-sequence trope is the contradiction

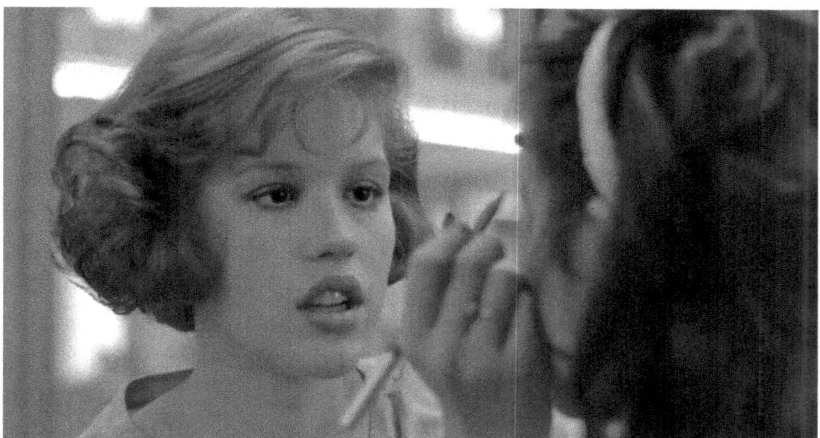

Figure 2.2. A feminist move? Claire's makeover of Allison in *The Breakfast Club*.

between, on the one hand, its emphasis on the female body as active and capable of self-transformation and, on the other hand, its promotion of traditional gender norms.[39] Anthony C. Bleach, for example, interprets Allison and Claire's "bonding over eyeliner" as an empowering "feminist move."[40] In contrast, Curran Nault asserts that Allison's makeover "provides access to her previously hidden body, salvaging her for male desire."[41] To some extent, the makeover in *The Breakfast Club* signals a progression in the girls' relationship and centers on Claire helping her new friend transform herself. But Brian and Andy's admiration of Allison's new look in the following scene reinforces the message that her makeover has primarily been for the satisfaction of male desire. Furthermore, by showing that Allison was correct to abandon her alternative look, as Maryn Wilkinson observes, "the sequence validates Claire's upper middle-class, virginal expertise on appearance and the 'appropriate' performance of femininity."[42]

The ways in which teenage boys in Hughes's teen films engage with their female counterparts help shore up the boundaries of suburban masculinity. As R. W. Connel and James W. Messerschmidt argue, "Gender is always relational, and patterns of masculinity are socially defined in contradistinction from some model (whether real or imaginary) of femininity."[43]

Jake Ryan in *Sixteen Candles* serves primarily as a fantasy figure onto whom Samantha and the heterosexual female audience can project their romantic desires. The high school senior is popular, good-looking, physically mature, and rich, but fairly subdued. Compared with most leading male characters in earlier teen movies, Jake is seemingly unthreatening and uncomplicated. His development is largely sidelined, and instead, focalization shifts to the Geek and his quest to increase his social status and "bag a babe." Hughes uses film style to accentuate the fantasy aspect of the freshman's evening of partying and cruising around town in a Rolls-Royce with the prom queen. After a collision between the car and some trashcans, Caroline (Haviland Morris) throws herself at the Geek, who looks directly into the camera and says knowingly to the audience, "This is getting good." While his friends, Cliff and Bryce, witness his triumph and describe him as "a legend," they point out that no one at their high school will believe what happened. The Polaroid photos his friends take as proof appear on-screen, and they are simply blurred close-ups of the Geek's face. Consequently, the evening's wild events are dreamlike and fleeting, nodding to the fact that a geek could never seduce a prom queen in real life.

The boys in *The Breakfast Club* represent three established stereotypes of the teen film: the jock (Andy), the juvenile delinquent (Bender), and the nerd (Brian). The dynamics between these characters and their female peers not only point to forms of masculinity valorized in the mid-1980s high school but also align with the wider promotion of strong and assertive masculinity in mid-1980s Hollywood cinema.[44] Bender competes, both verbally and physically, with Andy for status because the jock's physical strength and popularity threaten Bender's standing within the group. The interactions between Bender and the teacher, Mr. Vernon, are highly confrontational, almost spilling over into physical violence. Frustrated with the student's disrespect, the jaded teacher tries to provoke a fight by pushing the teenager against a filing cabinet. The scene serves as a reminder that scuffles for masculine authority extend beyond teenage life and that adult males will use violence to assert their power. As a sensitive, nerdy "cherry," Brian poses no immediate threat to Bender's or Andy's status. Bender mocks the younger boy's awkwardness, his academic interests, and his solidly middle-class lunch, but is never physically aggressive toward him. Similarly, Mr. Vernon belittles Brian verbally when he contradicts him, saying, "Shut up, Peewee!" Andy, in contrast, adopts a more protective attitude to Brian, which nonetheless reinforces his superior status. *The Breakfast Club* thus demonstrates how displays of masculine aggression and virility were central to the high school social hierarchy in the 1980s.

The teenage boys in *The Breakfast Club* also perform their masculinity through their exchanges with the girls in the group. This is particularly noticeable in the case of Bender, who "proves" his apparent masculine prowess by his hostility to Claire and, to a lesser extent, Alison. His verbal and physical harassment of Claire forms part of his wider strategy to assert his dominance and superior masculinity. He jokes about impregnating her, asks loaded questions about her sexual experience, and feigns disgust at her lipstick application trick. Bender's actions conform to a social script followed by many white American teenage boys who, observes C. J. Pascoe, "assert masculine selves by engaging in heterosexist discussions of girls' bodies and their own sexual experiences."[45] In an early moment in the film, Bender puts his head between Claire's legs and then gropes her, presumably in an effort to reinforce his "bad boy" credentials. Despite his unpleasant attitude and sexual aggression, Claire expresses desire for him near the end of the film, and the two kiss twice, although her interest in the working-class boy seems to be at least partly motivated by her desire to upset her rich parents. Consequently, Bender and Claire's interactions suggest the complexity of teenage relationships and sexual politics, albeit filtered through a mid-1980s lens.

The liaison between the Geek and Caroline in *Sixteen Candles* points to a similarly troubling link between hegemonic teenage masculinity and the mistreatment of teenage girls. Caroline's primary role is to aid the fulfillment of the Geek's

Figure 2.3. The prom queen (Haviland Morris) and the Geek (Anthony Michael Hall): male desire in *Sixteen Candles*.

desires. As is often the case in the teen sex comedy, the sexually experienced girl becomes a prop for the adolescent male's coming-of-age through sexual activity. Caroline provides a vision of teenage girlhood designed to appeal to heterosexual male fantasies. Although just a year older than Samantha, she is physically mature, as is clearly demonstrated in a locker room scene in which Samantha and Randy jealously discuss why Caroline is perfect while she showers in front of them. Evidently, the scene is primarily for the gratification of heterosexual males, a point underscored by the opening close-up of Caroline's pert wet breasts accompanied by a "boing" sound effect. Anthony C. Bleach argues that middle-class Samantha must both compete with and emulate Caroline.[46] But what happens to Caroline suggests that Samantha's more "sensible" and "innocent" behavior is preferable to the older girl's excess. After binge drinking at a party, Caroline is unable to stand or recognize her boyfriend, Jake, who bundles her into a Rolls-Royce with the Geek. During the ensuing events, Caroline loses almost all agency and is reduced to an object, which becomes all the more problematic when it transpires that she and the Geek had sex. The male fantasy of coming-of-age through sexual experience, which this conquest represents, conflicts with the female fantasy of romance and reveals a contradiction at the core of Hughes's films: teenage girls are, on the one hand, expected to be chaste and focused on relationships, whereas teenage boys can achieve manliness only through sexual encounters and displays of control.

Weird Science, in contrast with Hughes's first two teen films, focuses solely on adolescent male subjectivity. The movie commences with a tilt shot tracing the figures of two awkward teenage boys—Wyatt and Gary—from their worn sneakers and dirty gym socks, past their pale skinny torsos clad in ill-fitting tank tops, to their gawky faces. The camera captures their enthralled expressions as they watch a girls' gym glass. Gary outlines his dream scenario for a party, and despite Wyatt pointing out the impossibility of such a party ever happening—"Nobody likes us. Nobody"—Gary continues to describe his elaborate fantasy until two older boys pull down their gym shorts and humiliate them. This opening scene sets up two main characteristics of the film: a willingness to objectify young women, and what Timothy Shary describes as its "nerd transformation narrative."[47] Gary and Wyatt's repeated humiliation in the first half of the film aptly illustrates that young white men still face personal challenges and experience pressure to conform, a viewpoint that Hughes hoped would resonate with the everyday experiences of his target audience. But Lesley Speed somewhat overstates the matter by asserting that "in vulgar teen comedies, the repeated humiliation of protagonists exposes to scrutiny the presumed social freedoms of white, middle-class males."[48] While their status as straight white males may not fully insulate them from failure, particularly when it comes to their interactions with females, as Shirley Steinberg and Joe Kincheloe observe, the two boys benefit significantly from both class and racial privilege throughout the movie.[49]

Weird Science's narrative suggests not only that being a male geek who fails to meet hegemonic standards of masculinity is undesirable but also that geekdom is a phase that boys can outgrow. A common plotline in 1980s teen films showed the transformation of the male nerd into a more experienced and popular but still intelligent young man.[50] This narrative trope also aligns with wider representations of teenage male protagonists, who frequently secure their transition to manhood by facing specific, conventionally "masculine" challenges.[51] In the case of *Weird Science*, the boys are guided by Lisa, who becomes, as Steinberg and Kincheloe note, "a vehicle for Gary's and Wyatt's transition to manhood, to the assumption of dominant masculine power."[52] Lisa, suggests Catherine Driscoll, uses her magical powers and knowledge of stereotypical male culture to teach the boys how to perform masculinity.[53] To help them attract female partners, she creates tests that focus on their ability to withstand aggression from more physically mature men. A scene in which members of a mutant biker gang start groping teenage girls clearly signals that men should protect "their" women from other men and from sexual assault. *Weird Science* therefore reinforces the idea that masculinity is tied to dominance, control, and heterosexuality.

The fantasies of hegemonic masculinity in Hughes's teen movies are underpinned by assertions of heteronormativity and what C. J. Pascoe describes as the "repeated repudiation of the specter of failed masculinity."[54] The characters' casual use of insults such as "fag," "faggot," and "queer" is the starkest illustration of this impulse. When *Weird Science*'s Gary takes a stand against the chief biker, who publicly humiliates the boys for their social and sexual inadequacy, the teenager calls the biker a "bitch" and refers to his "faggot friends." The character's homophobic language reflects, of course, how many teenagers talked in the mid-1980s. Nonetheless, as Steinberg and Kincheloe argue, homophobia in youth films "serves to reinforce a need to acknowledge a dominant masculinity and manliness."[55] Accordingly, the term "faggot" is used in all three of Hughes's Universal movies when young men are competing to assert their masculinity. When the freshmen are nervous about crashing the party at Jake's house in *Sixteen Candles*, the Geek exclaims, "Don't be such faggots!" in an attempt to show bravado. In *The Breakfast Club*, Andy calls Bender a "faggot" when he suggests his peer lacks the discipline and focus to understand the appeal of competitive wrestling. Bender responds by retorting, "I have such a deep admiration for guys that roll around on the floor with other guys!" and points out that Andy has to wear "tights." This prompts aggression from Andy, who is upset at the implication that there is something "queer" about the sport, having expressed similar outrage at Bender's earlier declaration, "You're pretty sexy when you get angry." Thus, while Hughes's teen films sympathetically portray a variety of white heterosexual teenage boys, masculinity remains closely aligned with sexual desire for girls, and homosexuality remains the Other, an identity that is deviant and seemingly absent from the idealized midwestern suburb of Shermer.

Masculinity in Hughes's teen films is also an implicitly racialized identity. Perhaps Hughes's most controversial character, *Sixteen Candles'* Long Duk Dong, serves to reinforce, argues Helen L. Key, "normative expectations around American masculinity" because of his failure, as an "unassimilable foreigner," to meet these standards.[56] Dong is a haphazard composite of broadly "Oriental" stereotypes. Samantha's family refers to him "the weird Chinese guy," and at various points a nondiegetic gong sounds when characters speak his name. He utters American colloquial phrases in heavily accented English and lacks understanding of the "American" way of life, making him an object of ridicule. Dong is also socially inept, sexually repressed, and, at times, feminized. Whereas the white geeks of Hughes's films can prove their masculinity through heterosexual encounters, Dong's attempts to do so only reinforce his Otherness. Although he succeeds in engaging in consensual sexual activity, it is with a large athletic girl who exhibits "masculine" traits. A later scene between Jake Ryan and Dong also hints at the latter's queer proclivities. Jake tells him, "You grabbed my nuts." Dong explains, "I thought you were my new-style American girlfriend." As Kent A. Onon and Vincent Pham observe, "While this representation aims to provide comic relief, it both feminizes Asian American men and simultaneously constructs alternative gender and sexuality as aberrant."[57] Through Dong, *Sixteen Candles* thus reinforces the apparent normality of white heterosexual masculinity.

Weird Science, too, positions white masculinity as the norm while simultaneously tapping into white suburban males' fantasies of authenticity. In a scene at a blues club, The Kandy Bar, Wyatt and Gary interact with heavily stereotyped black and Latino men and learn to express their feelings with confidence, albeit through cultural appropriation and mimicry. A drunken Gary, who is wearing a Latino man's hat and tie and smoking a cigar, lapses into an impression of a black man as he recounts his rejection by a girl. This encounter ultimately reasserts the whiteness and class status of the boys. As well as using misogynistic language while mimicking the speech of the black men, the white boys are the focus of the scene, with the club's patrons hanging on their every word. Although many Hollywood films of the mid-1980s featured similarly dubious representations of race, even critics of the time were unimpressed by this scene. One reviewer lamented the "racism" in *Weird Science*, pointing to how the boys "take over a black nightclub and mock its clientele."[58] Another critic described the scene as "insulting and loathsome" and queried whether "the racially offensive character or sequence" had become a standard component of Hughes's movies.[59] Although it is crude and offensive, this scene in *Weird Science* nonetheless points to anxieties that surround the nature of whiteness as both normative and a seemingly "empty" identity, and the desire of white middle-class males to find more authentic ways to express their feelings.

The party scenes in *Sixteen Candles* and *Weird Science* display the contradictions underpinning the seemingly rebellious actions of the white middle-class teenagers in Hughes's films. In teen films, a wild party typically functions as a rite of passage. Steve Bailey and James Hay suggest that the "out-of-control party" represents a "tentative reclamation of the family space for youth," in which the home "is freed from parental control and becomes the site of a social and sexual freedom."[60] This scenario is taken to comic extremes in *Weird Science* when hundreds of teenagers descend on Wyatt's house and the boys' attempt to create a second fantasy woman prompts a series of bizarre and destructive events. The family home is transformed into a scene of teenage hedonism as well as the stage on which the boys must prove their manliness. Whether the wild party constitutes rebellion against the dominant social order remains less certain. Antony C. Bleach interprets the damage to Jake Ryan's house during the party in *Sixteen Candles* as a "gleeful celebration of the destruction of upper-class privilege."[61] The Ryans' large mansion, complete with wine cellar, certainly represents yuppie excess. And yet the teenagers' attitude to material possessions as easily replaceable means that the destruction of property emphasizes the teenagers' affluence rather than their disaffection. The teenage party is, moreover, a space enabled by the social status quo.[62] Teenagers are allowed to enjoy the temporary absence of parental control, but meaningful resistance to authority is a distant prospect.

All of Hughes's teen films for Universal thus take a constrained and personal attitude toward rebellion that is fairly typical of that seen in mainstream youth-oriented cinema of the 1980s. The misconduct of the teenagers in *The Breakfast Club*, for example, is fairly minor and typical of much suburban high school acting out. During the course of the day, the group causes only minor damage to school property. For the most part, this destruction is led by Bender, who flaunts his rebellious credentials by dismantling a door, ripping pages from a library book, and falling through a ceiling during his escape from the utility closet. The most wayward activities that the teenagers indulge in are smoking cannabis and then dancing around the library to Karla DeVito's "We Are Not Alone." Drinking, smoking cigarettes, and consuming drugs, notes Robert C. Bulman, are some of the ways in which films about suburban youth "express fantasies of self-expression and individual rebellion" against middle-class values.[63] These activities also feature in *Sixteen Candles* and *Weird Science*, but instead of indicating disaffection and introspection, they imply middle-class teenagers' relative freedom to experiment during their high school years. Thus, Hughes's characters never do more than probe the limits of acceptable behavior, and their transgressions do not pose a significant challenge to the high school as an institution or to the class, gender, and racial boundaries present in suburbia. In fact, as John Taylor contends, Hughes's protagonists ensure the continuity of suburbia by using "the suburban milieu to negotiate their differences and eventually join a normative adult social order."[64]

The implication, made by critics and journalists, that John Hughes entirely rewrote the rules of the teen film is not accurate. The teen films of the late 1970s and early 1980s were not quite as monolithic as the mainstream press or Hughes or his cast members suggested. The "New American teenagers" of 1970s cinema, argues Barbara Jane Brickman, lay the foundations for a shift in representations of adolescence on-screen. Films such as *Badlands* (Terrence Malick, 1973), *Freaky Friday* (Gary Nelson, 1976), and *Halloween* (John Carpenter, 1978) demonstrated that the teen film was a highly flexible genre capable of responding to shifts in American culture and society.[65] Even the producers of teen sex comedies and slasher movies of the early 1980s made concessions to female audiences, argues Richard Nowell, by including female characters and elements of romance.[66] Moreover, movies such as *Fast Times at Ridgemont High* had opened the door for teen films that combined comedy with drama while telling stories about both boys and girls. Nonetheless, although Hughes's work was not revolutionary, the development of a consistent set of textual features and commercial visibility made him something of an icon; as Catherine Driscoll observes, "Hughes came to represent the 1980s teen film."[67] Significantly, Hughes played a central role in reorienting the teen film toward more feminine concerns, and since the late 1980s, the genre has been gendered as female, with the label typically applied to commercial "girl films."[68]

Hughes's decision to start directing his own screenplays allowed him to pursue more nuanced portrayals of suburban teenage life in *Sixteen Candles*, *The Breakfast Club*, and, to some extent, *Weird Science*. Rather than being overly ambitious, Hughes devised the screenplays for those films with his limitations as a novice director in mind. As he explained in interviews, he deliberately wrote screenplays that would be straightforward and cheap to shoot and that focused on younger casts, who would be less likely to challenge his expertise.[69] Hughes was, by his own reckoning, not a particularly innovative director, and his lack of technical prowess did not go unnoticed by critics. For example, in his review of *Sixteen Candles, Boxoffice*'s Jimmy Summers asserted, "The rather artless directing style he displays here suggests his main talent is in the area of writing. He does, however, show a talent for getting the best from his perfectly chosen cast and in creating nice moments of throw-away business."[70] Nonetheless, Hughes's films show an astute understanding of how to use film style to tell character-centered stories, and he worked to improve his filmmaking techniques on *The Breakfast Club* and *Weird Science*.

There were clear incentives for Hughes to develop his directorial style and develop a particular aesthetic for his films. It was and remains possible, as Henry Jenkins suggests, for directors to increase their "market value" through the "development of an idiosyncratic style."[71] There are strong similarities and intertextual links between Hughes's Universal teen movies, which aided the studio's efforts to sell them as "John Hughes" films. The filmmaker exerted a certain degree of "authorial" control over these films through his roles as screenwriter, director, and producer. But the overall visual style of his Universal teen films was the product of collaboration. John W. Corso's production design and Marilyn Vance's costume design played indispensable roles in the realization of Hughes's creative vision for the world of Shermer, Illinois, and its inhabitants, as well as in supporting his approach to visual storytelling. By maintaining a consistent approach to portraying Shermer, Hughes and his collaborators developed a familiar but distinctive vision of mid-1980s suburban adolescent life.

Realistic dialogue and familiar scenes of suburban life ground *Sixteen Candles, The Breakfast Club*, and *Weird Science* in the everyday and commonplace. Moreover, by using dependable narrative formulas, he could balance the elements of realism and fantasy in his teen films. As his proclivity for happy endings shows, Hughes was extremely aware of the pleasures created by narrative scenarios that would be implausible in real life. In 1985 he explained, "I get hit a lot of the time for having sentimental endings. And I do it deliberately. . . . When you're that age you want things to come out right. And they never do."[72] These endings are underpinned by a utopian impulse that, as Richard Dyer puts it, implies "something other than what is can be imagined and maybe realized."[73] The utopia that *Sixteen Candles, The Breakfast Club,* and *Weird Science* promotes is, in fact, a conservative one, designed to appeal primarily to white suburban youths. In these films, seemingly universal experiences are shaped by wider attitudes toward gender and sexuality, class, and race, offering insights into identity politics during the mid-1980s. Heterosexuality is at the core of both the feminine and the masculine ideals promoted by the movies. Alternative femininities and masculinities are marginalized through ridicule or transformation. The Universal teen films were not Hughes's last word on the topic of teenage identity, however. In his next batch of teen films, released through Paramount, he continued to explore, with increasing sophistication, the realities and dreams of suburban adolescents.

CHAPTER 3

THE CREATIVE PRODUCER

Paramount (1985–1987)

John Hughes quickly capitalized on his early success at Universal, signing a contract with Paramount in March 1985, shortly after the release of *The Breakfast Club*.[1] Ned Tanen, who had become president of Paramount Pictures during early October 1984, was instrumental in attracting Hughes to the studio.[2] In an upbeat press release, Frank Mancuso, the chairman and CEO of Paramount, stated: "John Hughes is a boundless talent, and we are exceptionally pleased to welcome him to the Paramount family of filmmakers. I am particularly delighted that we can provide a home-base for John to further his collaboration with Ned Tanen, with whom he has so successfully worked in the past."[3] Hughes was poised to become one of the most powerful producers in Hollywood. In a move that signaled an expansion of his commercial interests and the formation of a distinct John Hughes brand, the pact allowed him to produce movies through his own unit, the John Hughes Company. Hughes soon adjusted his business operations to accommodate the scope of his ambitions, and in the fall of 1985, he restructured and expanded his production company to create Hughes Entertainment. In a move that signaled industry insiders' confidence in Hughes, the vice president of Universal Studios, Michael Chinich, became head of the new company in October 1985, alongside John Hughes as chairman.[4] The filmmaker's commercial shrewdness and ability to prioritize marketability seemed a good match for Paramount's business strategies during the mid-1980s.

Paramount had a relatively diverse output when Hughes formed his alliance with the studio. During the late 1970s and early 1980s, the studio developed a variety of modestly budgeted mainstream comedies and dramas as well as critically acclaimed films such as *Ordinary People* (Robert Redford, 1980) and *Terms of Endearment* (James L. Brooks, 1983), and lucrative blockbusters including the *Star Trek* (1979–) and *Indiana Jones* (1981–) franchises. This variety of releases appears to confirm Janet Staiger's and Richard Maltby's arguments that following the shift to the package-unit system, the brand identities of individual Hollywood studios became less clearly defined.[5] But as Paul Grainge notes, "The majors have the industrial muscle to be more varied in their project investments, but this does not preclude the accretion of brand style in specific moments, and around particular film cycles."[6] A cycle of youth-oriented movies with popular-music soundtracks, including *Saturday Night Fever* (John Badham, 1977), *Grease* (Randal Kleiser, 1978), *Flashdance* (Adrian Lyne, 1983), and *Footloose* (Herbert Ross, 1984), provided the clearest distillation of Paramount's approach to mainstream filmmaking during the period. The cycle also demonstrated how the concentration of power within a small elite of executives ensured consistency among Paramount's projects and aided the development of a studio brand.

Under the direction of Chairman Barry Diller, a former television executive, Paramount overhauled its approach to the business of filmmaking. Diller represented a new breed of studio head. As a 1977 feature in the *New York Times* described it, "The day of the almighty mogul is over. Now moviemaking is in the hands of packagers and budget-watchers who are the hired hands of the conglomerates who own the studios."[7] With Diller at the helm, Paramount refined its strategies in several areas of the movie business. The ability to "identify and exploit a particular market segment," as Justin Wyatt notes, underpinned many of the studio's projects.[8] Paramount executives devised more cost-effective ways to sell movies to specific groups, for instance, by buying TV spots on local television stations rather than the national networks and by using MTV to attract youth audiences.[9] At the box office, the studio performed consistently well, topping the annual rentals chart in 1978 and placing second during the following four years.[10] The studio was also at the forefront of experimenting with sell-through pricing for home-video releases of major blockbusters.[11] In 1983, the *New York Times*' Sandra Salmans proclaimed, "Mr. Diller has built what is widely regarded as perhaps the best-run, most stable, and most consistently successful movie company in Hollywood."[12]

Diller and his team aggressively pursued synergies between movies, television, and other products: "I want to be in the rights business in everything. . . . Rights are programs, programs are ideas, and ideas are value," he asserted in August 1983.[13] The main barrier to Diller's ambitions was Gulf + Western's overly diversified conglomerate structure. During the 1980s, under pressure from Wall Street, leaders of the entertainment corporations embarked on, as Adam Leaver puts it, "a quixotic search for corporate synergies that have proved elusive more often than not, resulting in a cycle of perpetual restructuring."[14] Gulf + Western divested itself of subsidiary companies unrelated to its entertainment holdings and formed partnerships with other media businesses. During 1986, Gulf + Western purchased three theater circuits for an estimated $300 million in an attempt to reinstate vertical integration.[15] Although the US Justice Department investigated, the US Supreme Court ruled that Gulf + Western, as well as MCA and Columbia, had not broken antitrust laws by purchasing theater chains.[16] The concentration of media ownership in the United States was facilitated by lax antitrust enforcement, media deregulation, and wider neoliberal agendas embraced by the Reagan administration.[17] Despite the relaxation of federal restrictions and Wall Street's support for corporate streamlining, the restructuring of Gulf + Western was a gradual and complex process set against a backdrop of management changes.

Hughes joined Paramount during a transitional period following the exodus of several senior executives. The sudden departure of Barry Diller, Michael Eisner, and Jeffrey Katzenberg—sometimes called "Hollywood's hottest stars"—from

Paramount caused a stir not only in trade publications but also in the mainstream press.[18] *New York* magazine dedicated a seven-page feature to the intrigue that surrounded "the liveliest Hollywood drama since *Indecent Exposure*."[19] Frank Mancuso emerged as chairman of Paramount. Gulf + Western's chairman, Martin Davis, stated that Mancuso's appointment was consistent with plans to make the corporation "a marketing driven company across the board."[20] Although Diller, Eisner, and Katzenberg were widely credited with engineering the studio's success in the early 1980s, Mancuso and Dawn Steel, Paramount's head of production, were instrumental in the development of strategies for the commercial exploitation of movies. Mancuso, who oversaw the distribution of Paramount's movies, had a reputation as "one of Hollywood's best marketing experts."[21] Steel, who had joined the studio as director of merchandising in 1978 and become head of production in 1980, played a central role the development of marketing tie-ins.[22] Evidently, with his background in advertising and proven ability to develop marketable movies, Hughes suited the approach championed by Paramount's new leadership. Moreover, his proclivity for modestly budgeted movies aligned with Mancuso's relatively conservative approach to production financing.[23]

Despite expectations to the contrary, Mancuso did not radically alter Paramount's business strategy and continued to pursue opportunities for cross-promotion between films and other media. According to Justin Wyatt, during this period "the [major studios'] attempts to maximize synergy between different media were matched . . . by the drive to focus and target moviegoers through the differentiated product of high concept."[24] A 1984 article in *New York* magazine explained how Paramount approached the business of moviemaking from this perspective: "The studio bases its choices less on the timeliness of the subject matter or the ability to attract big-name stars than on the concept—the story itself stripped of other considerations. A concept—or high concept, as its come to be known—refers to an idea that can be summarized in a sentence. And then sold to anyone over the age of seven."[25] There are varying assessments of the innovativeness of high concept and its influence on Hollywood cinema as a whole. Wyatt describes high concept as "perhaps *the* central development" within "post-classical cinema."[26] But as David Bordwell observes, relatively few films conform to Wyatt's definition of the high-concept style.[27] Wyatt also overstates the novelty of many high-concept marketing approaches. Long before the New Hollywood, studios sold movies to audiences by using bold imagery, stars, genre, and intertextuality. Even so, the term "high concept" gained currency during the 1980s, describing a particularly blatant, contemporary manifestation of Hollywood's long-standing pursuit of product differentiation and profit maximization.

During the mid-1980s, Hughes focused on tailoring his pictures to Paramount's high-concept marketing methods, building on his earlier explorations of the synergistic potential of teen movies at Universal. He deliberately narrowed the appeal of *Pretty in Pink* (Howard Deutch, 1986) and *Some Kind of Wonderful* (Howard Deutch, 1986) through a tighter generic focus on teenage romance. This niche appeal enabled Paramount to market the films very precisely, emphasizing themes, imagery, and star performers likely to appeal primarily to a target audience of teenage girls. Hughes also increased his control over the composition of the film's tie-in soundtracks, which earned him praise among critics and enabled him to cement his status as a mainstream tastemaker. Paramount harnessed the growing power of MTV as well as the films' distinctive branding to help sell both the movies and the soundtracks. Hughes conceived *Ferris Bueller's Day Off* (John Hughes, 1986) as a comedy with broad appeal, but the film was no less high concept in its engagement with the popular-cultural zeitgeist. Paramount capitalized on the film's contemporary feel, inclusive themes, and charismatic protagonist, positioning the film alongside *Top Gun* (Tony Scott, 1986) as one of the studio's potential summer hits of 1986. To explore Paramount's more bespoke approaches to the marketing and cross-promotion of Hughes's teen movies, I trace in this chapter each film's commercial exploitation alongside changes in the filmmaker's career.

Producer as Brand: Control and Collaboration

Through his deal at Paramount, John Hughes became part of an elite group of "creative producers" who wielded considerable influence over Hollywood cinema. Some of these producers, such as Steven Spielberg, were directors seeking greater autonomy; others were people who had previously held key positions at major media companies and who desired greater control and increased financial rewards for their roles in both the business and the creative aspects of production. In May 1985, the headline of an article by *Newsweek*'s David Ansen declared, "The Producer Is King Again": "Right now Hollywood is undergoing a power shift of enormous significance. The old-fashioned, creative producer is back, and he (and sometimes she) is a hot commodity. No mere check signer, this hands-on new producer models himself on the likes of Selznick and Dore Schary and Alexander Korda and Sam Spiegel, producers who put their imprint on a movie, producers whose names often surpassed the directors they hired and fired."[28] While Ansen overstated the extent of the transformation that had taken place, he nonetheless echoed a prominent discourse proclaiming the rise of the "creative producer" in the mid-1980s. Ansen positioned John Hughes alongside the likes of Don Simpson, Jerry Bruckheimer, Steven Spielberg, George Lucas, and Ivan Reitman. Significantly, Ansen argued that Paramount "set the model for a producer-dominated Hollywood: high-concept movies on tightfisted budgets."[29] Keen to sustain the impression that the studio granted its major producers considerable autonomy, Frank Mancuso asserted, "You have a rebirth of something that existed many years ago in the industry when the producer had a strong creative input and really put his stamp on [the movie]."[30]

Although certain decisions had to be negotiated with the studio funding the project, independent producers working under the package-unit system managed financing, labor, and the means of production for a movie.[31] Whereas some producers took a backseat once the package was assembled, more hands-on "creative" producers like Hughes also oversaw script development, casting, and the production process. Hughes's prolific output as a screenwriter meant it was no longer physically possible for him to direct each of his screenplays: "I generate more scripts than I can execute. I was rushed when I [directed] *Weird Science*, and I didn't want it to be that way again."[32] Consequently, Hughes forged a close working relationship with Howard Deutch, who was willing to surrender considerable creative control to the producer. Although Deutch occupied the director's chair on *Pretty in Pink* and *Some Kind of Wonderful*, Hughes retained his position as the dominant creative influence on these projects, through his screenplays, oversight of production, and careful selection of key collaborators, including the production designer John W. Corso and the costume designer Marilyn Vance. He also oversaw the development of the movies as "packages" that could be exploited in ancillary markets. By exerting his control over key elements of his projects in this way, Hughes was able to develop his signature product during his tenure at Paramount.

Pretty in Pink and the Art of Cross-Promotion

Hughes's first Paramount movie, *Pretty in Pink*, neatly matched the studio's interest in youth-oriented movies and cross-promotion between film and music. But Hughes and Molly Ringwald's account of the screenplay's inception implicitly denied any cynical motivation, and suggested instead that sharing the Psychedelic Furs' "Pretty in Pink" was part of their developing friendship.[33] Hughes claimed that once *Sixteen Candles* had wrapped, he "went home and wrote *Pretty in Pink* for Molly," taking inspiration from the song that Ringwald had brought to his attention.[34] He struggled to find a Hollywood studio willing to finance the project, because executives were skeptical that a girl-oriented movie would draw a substantial audience. "Female movies are not something that the town jumps up and down for," Hughes stated in a 1985 American Film Institute seminar. "They had this theory that boys make the purchase decisions . . . Tell it to Maybelline, y'know."[35] Hughes's association with Ned Tanen proved critical in getting the project into production. The filmmaker claimed that of the major executives in Hollywood, Tanen was "the only guy that's interested" in a "girl story."[36] By the time *Pretty in Pink* went into production, in 1985, the commercial success of Hughes's other teen movies and Ringwald's rapidly growing celebrity had no doubt eased any concerns that Paramount may have harbored.

The movie was Hughes's first collaboration with the director Howard Deutch, whose experience in music videos and movie trailers meant he was ideally suited to the project. Hughes served as executive producer on the movie, and Lauren Schuler received a producer credit as line producer. Hughes, who supervised production closely, ensured that the movie was shot in California, close to his new headquarters. This unexpected move by one of the Illinois film industry's main supporters generated conjecture in the trade press. Hughes claimed that he could not film *Pretty in Pink* in Chicago because the majority of the local production personnel he wanted to employ were unavailable, thanks to the increased popularity of Illinois as a film location.[37] Certainly, the city had a limited pool of experienced film technicians, and Hughes had always used a mixture of local crew members and technicians from Los Angeles.[38] Other factors also eroded the feasibility of Hughes shooting all his films in Illinois. There were no permanent soundstages in Chicago, and by the mid-1980s, residents of the city's suburbs were increasingly frustrated by the impact of increased film production, particularly on parking spaces.[39] Regardless, Hughes's decision seemed to tarnish his reputation in his home state. As *Back Stage* observed in August 1985, "Hughes's migration to the West Coast seemed a betrayal [of] the Chicago film community."[40] *Pretty in Pink* nonetheless retained the midwestern suburban aesthetic that was popular with Hughes's teenage audience.

Pretty in Pink's soundtrack, which was integral to its aesthetic, figured prominently in the promotional campaign devised by Paramount and A&M records. Hughes's reputation for developing commercially lucrative soundtracks prompted Paramount and A&M to give the writer-producer considerable control over the soundtrack album's musical content. The soundtrack featured a range of bands, most of them British

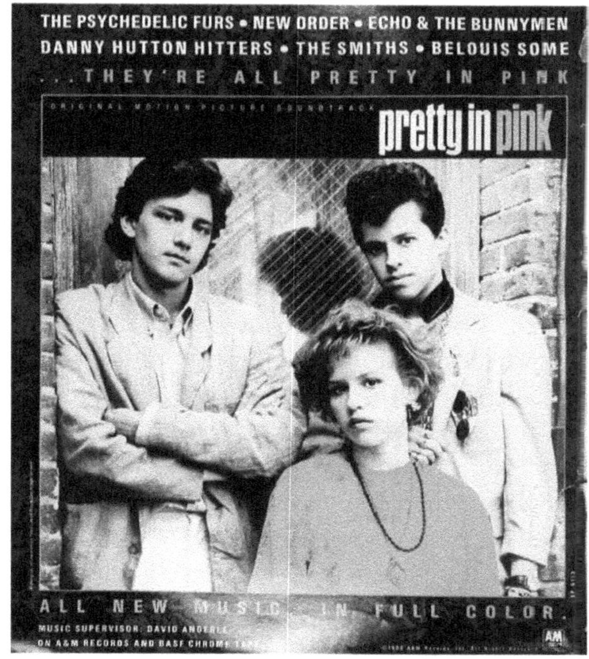

Figure 3.1. A&M Records advertisement for the *Pretty in Pink* soundtrack, *Billboard*, 15 February 1986, 2.

New Wave acts. The fact that none of the performers selected to feature on the album had scored a top 30 hit in the United States provided a clear indication of Paramount and A&M's confidence in Hughes's musical knowledge and his ability to popularize songs through his movies.[41] Before the album's release, A&M's vice president of marketing, Bob Reitman, insisted, "Hughes is really at the cutting edge of what's hip in music."[42] His new corporate partners were much more willing to pay for rights to songs than MCA/Universal. Only three of the artists on the album were signed to A&M: Orchestral Manoeuvres in the Dark (OMD), Jesse Johnson, and Suzanne Vega.[43] The trade press also seemed confident that the album would be popular with consumers. *Billboard*'s Brian Chin described the album as "an extremely solid specimen in a notably erratic field," adding, "Atypically, it elicits good efforts from everyone involved."[44] Impressed with the "shrewd" selections on the album, another *Billboard* reviewer predicted, "Barring box office disaster, this package should fare well indeed."[45]

In the buildup to *Pretty in Pink*'s release, Paramount worked closely with A&M to exploit fully the cross-promotional opportunities that the movie package provided. *Billboard*'s Sam Sutherland observed that "influencing A&M's massive effort behind the project is its prior experience with *Pretty in Pink* executive producer John Hughes," pointing to *The Breakfast Club*'s success in "both music and movie markets."[46] Instead of worrying about competition between the singles, A&M sought to capitalize on the buzz surrounding the film and its soundtrack and released three singles off the *Pretty in Pink* soundtrack within short succession. The label put out OMD's "If You Leave" first, focusing on "top 40 and adult contemporary" radio stations. A week later, it shipped New Order's "Shell Shock," which was aimed at "dance markets." Finally, A&M released the Psychedelic Furs' "Pretty in Pink" in the week of the movie's release.[47] The label also distributed a promotional twelve-inch EP, featuring the tracks by OMD and the Psychedelic Furs, to "AOR, progressive and college radio" stations.[48] A&M also paid for print advertising to support the release of the album. For instance, to stimulate interest among retailers, A&M took out a full-page advertisement on the inside cover of *Billboard* magazine on 15 February 1985.[49] The ad, which featured the album's cover art, stressed that the soundtrack featured "all new music." Both the album sleeve and the covers of the 45 and EP versions of OMD's "If You Leave" replicated the film's logo and central marketing image. The recordings thus provided promotional support for the movie as well as creating an additional revenue stream.

A&M's biggest promotional coup was in securing an "MTV Feature Presentation" for the "*Pretty in Pink* Premiere Party," which, stated an executive, "was a joint A&M and Paramount effort."[50] Aired the night before *Pretty in Pink*'s general release, the show provided one hour of free advertising for the movie, which was aimed squarely at MTV's target audience. A loosely organized collection of clips from the movie, interviews, and backstage footage, the show featured live performances by OMD, the Rave-Ups, and the Psychedelic Furs. In an interview, the Psychedelic Furs' lead singer, Richard Butler, was open about the band's reasons for participating in the movie's soundtrack and its promotion: "I'd like to think [the movie] was going to get us across to more people. And I think it will certainly do that."[51] John Hughes echoed this sentiment, stating, "I hope this video and the song and the film do for the Furs what *The Breakfast Club* and 'Don't You' did for Simple Minds."[52] Consistent with criticisms of MTV during this period, the veejays displayed a visible lack of professionalism and struggled to marshal the show's content. Slightly more structured, though somewhat trite, interviews with *Pretty in Pink*'s cast and crew were offset by a range of awkward, spontaneous chats with celebrities in varying states of inebriation. While Michael J. Fox, Judge Reinhold, and Dweezil Zappa lent their reasonably hip credentials to the proceedings, more mature celebrities, including Andy Summers from the Police, Jon Anderson from Yes, and the actress Teri Garr, seemed out of place. Michael Keaton, clearly aware of the event's orientation toward a youth audience, sarcastically joked, "This a fun party, and what I like is, it's not very trendy."[53] Although lacking finesse, the show encapsulated the strategies used to promote *Pretty in Pink* and aligned the movie with popular-cultural trends.

The music videos for "Pretty and Pink" and "If You Leave," which were featured in the MTV Premiere Party, were another important facet of the promotional strategy for *Pretty in Pink* and its soundtrack. Discussion of the videos distanced them from the already-hackneyed "music trailer" format and focused on their innovative approaches to linking the movie with the song. Wayne Isham, the producer of the "Pretty in Pink" music video, emphasized the effort that had gone into the video and how he chose to foreground the Psychedelic Furs' performance: "We've all seen a lot of movie-connected videos, and I wanted to do something different that would be fun to watch. Which is why we took twelve hundred pictures and animated them and hand colored them and projected them on weird structural shapes. . . . To me, of the utmost importance is the music, so I wanted to get the band in performance."[54] This new spin on the promotional music clip did not go unnoticed. *Billboard,* for instance, noted the video's novel "blend of still photographs of pink washes and patterns with footage from the film."[55] Clearly a much lower-budget affair, the music video for "If You Leave" focuses on OMD's performance. The video refers to *Pretty in Pink* through the occasional superimposition of images from the film and through painted portraits of the stars on a stylized set. OMD's Andy McCluskey explained, "I think that everybody is just about sick and tired now of seeing . . . the band, the film, the band, the film, just cut together. So we're trying to make more subtle references to the film."[56] MTV added the video for "If You Leave" to the channel's playlist at the end of January 1986, and "Pretty in Pink" in late February, providing important exposure for the songs and the movie.[57]

Paramount's promotional materials complemented the music-focused MTV-led strategy to publicize *Pretty in Pink.* The trailers reinforced the centrality of music to the film, as well as the romance plot and high school setting. One trailer intersperses scenes from the movie, primarily composed of close-up shots, with the scene of Duckie (Jon Cryer) dancing to "Try A Little Tenderness."[58] Another trailer, created for television, is edited much more rapidly and scored throughout by the Psychedelic Furs' "Pretty in Pink."[59] Similarly, *Pretty in Pink*'s poster neatly encapsulates its concept, using bold imagery and striking text to emphasize the teenage love triangle at the center of the story. Molly Ringwald receives star billing, consistent with the film's development as a vehicle for the young actress. Her distinctive hairstyle and pouting lips were instantly recognizable to her fans and, because of the circulation of her image in glossy magazines and on MTV, familiar to a growing number of consumers. The same image formed the template for print advertisements in major US publications, which were another part of Paramount's strategy to create "buzz" around the movie's release. The ads included excerpts from reviews that highlighted the film's "romance," "heart-warming" ending, "tender humor," and engagement with "real concerns," and described it as "a hip fairy tale."[60] Paramount thus varied the publicity enough to create a sense of novelty and dynamism while maintaining a cohesive identity for the film based on the soundtrack, the love story, and the stars.

Pretty in Pink benefited from the American press's rapidly growing interest in Molly Ringwald. Reporting on Ringwald's fledgling career during the release of *Sixteen Candles* and *The Breakfast Club* tended to position her alongside her costars. *People* magazine, for instance, profiled the actress alongside Anthony Michael Hall after the release *Sixteen Candles*, focusing on the teenagers' mix of sophistication and normality.[61] In the buildup to the release of *Pretty in Pink*, press coverage that focused solely on Ringwald's career and personal life increased considerably. Many articles positioned her as John Hughes's "muse." Without hinting at any impropriety, accounts of their meeting and relationship were often couched in quasi-romantic terms. The October 1985 issue of *Elle* recounted their meeting in a style befitting of a teen romance novel: "They clicked. He wore sneakers, had a great record collection, and wrote that script with Molly Ringwald's picture pinned over his typewriter."[62] Media interest in Ringwald continued to increase once the movie hit cinemas, but these reports placed a greater emphasis on the actress's career independent of Hughes. An article in *People* suggested that Ringwald's appearance in *Pretty in Pink* and her fan following confirmed her status as "a real star" who was "way ahead of the Brat Pack."[63] The eighteen-year-old actress, the report noted, had recently signed a contract with United Artists that gave her control over the development and production of her movies.[64] In one interview, Ringwald disclosed, "For me the teenage cycle is pretty much over. . . . I don't see myself working with John [Hughes] again. I want to do adult roles."[65]

Paramount released *Pretty in Pink* on 28 February 1986. The movie entered the weekly US box-office chart at number 2, earning a high per-screen average of roughly $9,000 across 827 screens, and peaked at number 1 the following week.[66] During its domestic theatrical release, the movie grossed over $40 million, against a production budget of $7 million, and ranked twenty-second in the annual US box-office chart.[67] Released the same week as the movie, the *Pretty in Pink: Original Soundtrack* album entered the Billboard 200 on 1 March 1986 at number 118 and peaked at number 5 on 3 May 1986.[68] It was the third-highest-selling soundtrack album and the fiftieth-highest-selling pop album of 1986, according to *Billboard*'s end-of-year charts.[69] Singles off the album also performed well. The Psychedelic Furs' rerecorded version of "Pretty in Pink" peaked at number 40 on the Billboard Hot 100, making it the band's most successful single in the United States.[70] But the biggest hit from the soundtrack was Orchestral Manoeuvres in the Dark's "If You Leave." Recorded specifically for the movie, the single peaked at number 4 on the Billboard Hot 100.[71] The success of *Pretty in Pink* at the box office and in the music charts confirmed that the partnership between Hughes Entertainment and Paramount showed significant commercial promise.

While *Pretty in Pink*'s concept and promotional campaign satisfied corporate agendas, Hughes maintained that his interest in popular music was genuine. In a 1986 interview with MTV, he refuted accusations that his use of music in movies was cynically motivated: "I don't look at the album as a marketing tool. Because if you do that, you're gonna fail. It's really betraying the music. When I approach a band, I wanna respect them and be respectful of their music."[72] Hughes's decision to focus on new music gave a certain amount of validity to his claims, and he emphasized the authenticity of the bands he had selected. For instance, he declared that he was glad that the Psychedelic Furs agreed to participate in the project, because "they're a band that hasn't compromised, and those kind of bands are getting harder and harder to find."[73] Critics and consumers clearly found this approach refreshing. Following the success of the album, *Billboard*'s Paul Grein remarked, "What makes *Pretty in Pink* unique among hit soundtracks is that it's not a star-studded package, but a collection of songs by new and developing acts."[74] Similarly, the *New York Times*' Stephen Holden credited the soundtrack with attempting to popularize "an idiom and musical attitude that until now have languished on the side lines of mainstream pop."[75] He concluded, "*Pretty in Pink* wants to define the new cutting edge of mainstream teenage pop taste."[76] J. D. Considine, a writer for *Musician*, a magazine aimed at rock musicians and fans, remained more skeptical about the movie's motives: "It relegates new music to the status of a fashion accessory. The combination of the hit-movie maker and nubile nymph Molly Ringwald is guaranteed to bring these bands their biggest audience ever."[77]

Paramount Home Video built on *Pretty in Pink*'s successes in the theatrical and soundtrack markets when it released the video to the rental market in October 1986, priced at $79.95.[78] During the early 1980s, Paramount had shown that it was willing to take risks in the home-video market and had already enjoyed some success with sell-through pricing with *Star Trek II: Wrath of Khan* (Nicholas Meyer, 1982), *Flashdance*, and *Raiders of the Lost Ark* (Steven Spielberg, 1981).[79] While *Pretty in Pink* was not a hit of the magnitude required to justify a high-volume sell-through release, Paramount Home Video managed the video's release carefully. For example, the distributor tried to stimulate retailers' interest with a full-page feature in *Billboard*, which cited the movie's box-office credentials and its status as a "music sensation."[80] Advertisements for the video release made use of the bold visuals from the movie's publicity materials and soundtrack packaging. The video's sleeve, designed to stand out in video stores, also encapsulated the key attractions of the movie. It featured the movie's distinctive logo and "A John Hughes Production" laid over the central image of the stars, with Ringwald highlighted in pink. Much like Hughes's Universal teen films, *Pretty in Pink* became a popular video rental.[81] It placed thirty-first in *Billboard*'s 1986 Annual "Top Videocassette Rentals" Chart.[82] The solid commercial performance of *Pretty in Pink* on home video, combined with the film's success at the box office and in the soundtrack market, acted as confirmation of Hughes's commercial insight and raised expectations for his next teen movie.

Making It a "Paramount Summer" with *Ferris Bueller's Day Off*

Released just four months after *Pretty in Pink, Ferris Bueller's Day Off* was a project very different from the Molly Ringwald vehicle. Directed by John Hughes and starring Matthew Broderick, the movie is a lighthearted comedy that follows the exploits of a charismatic high school senior as he skips school and spends the day in Chicago with his friends. Based on the film's "irreverent attitude, cast sassiness, tons of rock music and all the other expected ingredients," *Variety* predicted that it would be a "reasonable summer comedy hit for Paramount."[83] Whereas Paramount and Hughes had devised a well-honed niche marketing campaign for *Pretty in Pink*, the distributor cast a much wider net when publicizing *Ferris Bueller's Day Off*. The studio continued to court Hughes's established teenage following, supplying exhibitors with posters, stickers, and pin badges that featured a distinctive shorthand "FBDO" logo and the slogan "Leisure Rules," but tried not to limit the movie's reach. Broderick, who had built a profile as an accomplished actor with broad appeal since his 1983 Tony Award for *Brighton Beach Memoirs* and his leading role in *WarGames* (John Badham, 1983), dominated the film's publicity materials. In an effort to attract a wide audience, Paramount emphasized that *Ferris Bueller's Day Off* was purely a comedy. Advertisements in the *New York Times* featured quotations that called it "the year's funniest movie" and "the funniest film in years."[84] Another ad emphasized that despite the movie's PG-13 rating, *Ferris Bueller* was "a movie you can take the whole family to."[85]

In stark contrast with the complex cross-promotional strategy developed for *Pretty in Pink*, the studio did not release a soundtrack album for *Ferris Bueller's Day Off*, nor were there any official single releases. In his appraisal of the summer's hit movies, *Billboard*'s Steve Gett noted that "John Hughes did not jump on the soundtrack bandwagon" that year, and that just two films in the box-office top ten for the season lacked soundtrack releases.[86] Perhaps unsurprisingly, the filmmaker's commercial partners were dismayed by the absence of an album. Hughes later observed, "A&M was very angry with me over that; they begged me to put one out."[87] The filmmaker, however, felt that

Figure 3.2. As featured in . . .: the single sleeve for Yello's "Oh Yeah."

the movie's soundtrack was too eclectic to be commercially viable.[88] For promotional purposes, he compiled a single consisting of two songs for which he held the rights in the United States, "Beat City" by the Flowerpot Men and "I'm Afraid" by Blue Room. His company sent the 45 rpm single to his mailing list, which consisted of roughly 100,000 fans in 1986.[89] By rewarding Hughes's fans for their loyalty with a limited-edition artifact, this direct-marketing technique sought to stimulate word-of-mouth publicity for *Ferris Bueller's Day Off* among teenagers.

Although there were no official music tie-ins, record companies still piggybacked on the movie's success. According to *Billboard*, Polygram decided to "rush-release" the single "Oh Yeah" by the Swiss electro duo Yello after the film proved popular with audiences.[90] The packaging for the single clearly sought to capitalize on the song's association with the movie. The phrase "as featured in the hit movie *Ferris Bueller's Day Off*" appeared in bold print on the sleeve for the single release, and similarly, a promotional twelve-inch EP carried the label "featured in *Ferris Bueller's Day Off*." In addition, Capitol Records reissued the Beatles' "Twist and Shout" after the song appeared in both *Ferris Bueller's Day Off* and the Rodney Dangerfield vehicle *Back to School* (Alan Metter, 1986). The single peaked at number 23 on the Billboard Hot 100 chart and remained in the top 40 for seven weeks. Inclusion on the film's soundtrack also provided the British band Sigue Sigue Sputnik with extra publicity for EMI's mid-August 1986 release of its Giorgio Moroder–produced album *Flaunt It*.[91] Although Hughes's corporate partners did not profit directly from the music releases linked with *Ferris Bueller's Day Off*, the popularity of these recordings reinforced the impression that Hughes's movies could stimulate record sales.

Ferris Bueller's Day Off also featured within a larger publicity campaign designed to promote Paramount's brand and the studio's major releases. During early July 1986, Paramount released an advertisement that placed *Ferris Bueller's Day Off* alongside *Top Gun*, the studio's major summer blockbuster release. The ad bore the slogan "Make it a Paramount Summer!" as well as the studio's logo. The logo acted as a guarantee of quality, building on the reputation that the studio had developed earlier in the decade as well as on its status as one of the oldest studios in Hollywood. "Throughout its history," notes Paul Grainge, "Paramount has sought to exploit its trademark advantage as a major film distributor, using its logo to authenticate and differentiate its film product."[92] Paramount created a television advertisement promoting both films that told audiences how to experience them: "Take off with *Top Gun* . . . And take it easy with *Ferris Bueller's Day Off*."[93] These advertisements sought to give *Ferris Bueller's Day Off* the same "event" status as the Tom Cruise vehicle. They also served as a reminder that Paramount had contracts with Hollywood's leading producers: Don Simpson, Jerry Bruckheimer, and John Hughes. Although *Ferris Bueller's Day Off* never topped the domestic box-office chart, the film grossed roughly $70 million during its run, making it the tenth-highest-grossing movie of 1986.[94] At the end of the summer season, the *New York Times* proclaimed that "with *Top Gun* and *Ferris Bueller's Day Off*, Paramount is the unchallenged leader among the studios."[95]

Some Kind of Wonderful, Hughes Music, and Indie Ambitions

The founding of Hughes Music early in 1987 confirmed John Hughes's credentials as a major media-industry figure, with influence beyond the movie business.[96] According to the *Los Angeles Times*' Patrick Goldstein, MCA Records' decision to award the filmmaker a five-album deal and a custom label gave Hughes "unprecedented clout, not just as a filmmaker but also as a force in the music industry," and confirmed his status as "Hollywood's one-man entertainment conglomerate."[97] Although Hollywood executives were increasingly preoccupied with the cross-promotional opportunities offered by movie soundtracks, the deal between Hughes and MCA was highly unusual. As Goldstein observed, "It's practically unheard of for a filmmaker to have his own record company—but then it's equally unprecedented for a soundtrack, like *Some Kind of Wonderful*, to be largely populated with groups that have never been signed to a US record contract."[98] The Hughes Music deal not only reflected Hughes's standing within the music and film industries after his cross-promotional successes during the mid-1980s, but also recognized his status as a tastemaker.

Hughes did not conceive of Hughes Music as merely an outlet for his film soundtracks. When he founded the label, he stated that his long-term aspirations were for a legitimate stand-alone record company: "Right now, the films are a launch for the music. They drive the new label. But we'd like the label to eventually drive itself—and help establish a new generation of great bands."[99] In line with these ambitions, the filmmaker appointed Tarquin Gotch head of Hughes Music. Gotch had worked in the British record industry with artists such as Simple Minds, the Thompson Twins, the Stray Cats, Elaine Page, and the Beat (known as the English Beat in the United States).[100] During the mid-1980s, he managed a number of British acts that became popular in the United States, such as General Public, XTC, the Dream Academy, and the Beat. Gotch's wealth of experience in the music industry, personal contacts, and knowledge of contemporary performers was an invaluable resource for Hughes. Initially, his presence helped bolster the credibility of Hughes Music. Gotch told the *Los Angeles Times*, "We're trying to find fresh music, to break new ground and not rely on the same established stars."[101]

Hughes's and Gotch's musical knowledge was evident in

the content of the first album released on the Hughes Music label, *Some Kind of Wonderful: Music from the Motion Picture.* A review in *Fanfare,* "the magazine for serious record collectors," praised the album and noted "Hughes's impeccable musical tastes": "John Hughes continues to produce great soundtracks to his increasingly mundane teenage flicks. What's refreshing about *Some Kind of Wonderful* is that so little of the music (and so few of the artists) is familiar. This is probably the best assemblage of new artists and new music on a soundtrack album since last year's *Pretty in Pink,* also by Hughes."[102] The artists featured on the record were more obscure and less aligned with mainstream pop music trends than those on the *Pretty in Pink* soundtrack. The Jesus and Mary Chain, Pete Shelley (formerly of the Buzzcocks), and Stephen Duffy (cofounder of Duran Duran) were probably the best-known acts on the track listing. Working in a similar vein, Hughes developed a concept album for the Kevin Bacon vehicle *She's Having a Baby* (John Hughes, 1988), with the vinyl LP version divided into a "He" and a "She" side. The record consisted of excerpts of the film's score, by Stewart Copeland (former drummer for the Police), and a range of tracks performed by British artists, including Kate Bush, XTC, Everything but the Girl, Bryan Ferry, and Kirsty MacColl. Both albums were a continuation of Hughes's attempts to bring more marginal forms of pop music into the mainstream.

Neither of these albums was a hit of the same magnitude as the *Pretty in Pink* soundtrack, however. The *Some Kind of Wonderful* soundtrack peaked at number 57, and the *She's Having a Baby* album achieved a chart high of number 92 on the Billboard 200.[103] As had been the case on Hughes's earlier soundtracks, the artwork for the single and album releases of *Some Kind of Wonderful* and *She's Having a Baby* featured logos and promotional images for the films. But these "brands" lacked the appeal of Hughes's earlier efforts. The underwhelming box-office performances and short theatrical runs of both films meant relatively few people encountered the songs through the movies. Moreover, the unoriginal music videos devised for the main singles prevented them from standing out in a crowded marketplace.

Whereas the videos for "Don't You," "Pretty in Pink," and "If You Leave" avoided the standard music-trailer format, the music videos for "I Go Crazy" (from *Some Kind of Wonderful*) and "She's Having A Baby" offered little in the way of aesthetic novelty. Ultimately, both albums lacked the competitive edge required to succeed during the soundtrack boom of the mid-1980s, which, as Jeff Smith observes, "resulted in a glutted market" during peak release periods.[104]

The mismatch between Hughes's audience and the kinds of music on the soundtracks was, arguably, the biggest problem blighting the commercial prospects of the albums. First, the style of music on the *Some Kind of Wonderful* soundtrack was associated with college radio rather than mainstream radio stations and MTV, and so the album and singles received less airplay than had the songs on the *Pretty in Pink* soundtrack. Second, the notions of "cool" and "authenticity" surrounding alternative rock bands and their fans conflicted with the commercial objectives of the *Some Kind of Wonderful* soundtrack, which addressed a teenage female audience. As Norma Coates argues, "The female teenybopper, defined in opposition to the true, male, rock and roller, fan *or* artist, was discursively invented and subsequently naturalized as the binary opposite of the 'authentic' rock fan in the mid-1960s."[105] The late 1980s saw the resurgence of aggressively masculine rock bands that, suggests Doyle Green, sought to reclaim "hip . . . from the apparently 'feminine' clutches of New Pop groups."[106] The Jesus and Mary Chain, for instance, made deliberately offensive sexist comments in interviews, such as: "I want some woman to get down on her hands and knees, suck my knob off, buy me loads of drink, give me loads of drugs."[107] Even the presence of John Hughes's name could not fully resolve the tensions between the sensibilities of the bands on the *Some Kind of Wonderful* album and the filmmaker's target demographic.

Hughes's time at Paramount confirmed his status as one of Hollywood's leading creative producers. The formation of Hughes Entertainment in 1985 marked a milestone in Hughes's career as a producer; it increased his control over the development of his projects and the overall direction of his career. Thereafter, Hughes released all his movies through the company. From 1987 onward, he also ensured that the company's branding appeared on publicity materials, increasing its visibility and further encouraging audiences to view his releases as "John Hughes" films. While not all his teen movies were major box-office hits, they nonetheless showcased Paramount's marketing prowess and generated revenues in the soundtrack and home-video markets. Hughes's triumphs were part of a bigger success story for Paramount; the studio dominated the North American box office in both 1986 and 1987, beating all the other major studios by a convincing margin.[108] In assessing the studio's achievements in 1986, the *New York Times*' Geraldine Fabrikant asserted, "Besides being lucky, Paramount has capitalized on shrewd marketing moves and savvy production deals."[109] Among the key deals, Fabrikant highlighted Ned Tanen's "crucial contribution . . . in bringing John Hughes to Paramount."[110]

Perhaps Hughes and Paramount's greatest shared achievement was the refinement of cross-promotional marketing techniques that used recorded music and MTV to promote Hughes's movies and their soundtracks. The marketing campaign for *Pretty in Pink* was a tour de force, marking the pinnacle of Hughes's achievements as a creator of teen-oriented movies. As well as generating record sales, Hughes's cutting-edge soundtracks earned plaudits within the critical community and launched several bands into the American mainstream. His founding of Hughes Music in 1987 simultaneously confirmed his musical expertise and his elevated status within the film industry. Despite the hype that surrounded the creation of the label, Hughes's lofty ambitions never came to fruition. Hughes and Gotch's struggle to accomplish their goal of turning Hughes Music into an "indie" label was, in part, a product of the American record industry's changing focus "from record sales to rights exploitation."[111] Ironically, the industrial conditions that had supported Hughes's soundtrack successes in the mid-1980s and helped him acquire his own label made it extremely difficult for alternative rock bands to cross over to the mainstream during the late 1980s; by then, companies were reluctant to invest in heavily marginal genres. MCA passed on the first band that Hughes Music signed, Flesh for Lulu, because the label felt that the deal was too expensive.[112] In the end, Hughes Entertainment was a bigger priority for Hughes than Hughes Music, and during the late 1980s he largely abandoned the record label in order to focus his energies on film production.

As his status in the media industries increased, Hughes struggled to maintain the image of a youthful industry outsider. In the fall of 1986, Louise Farr of the Fairchild News Syndicate wrote a profile that highlighted inconsistencies within Hughes's celebrity image after his elevation to sophisticated studio mogul. She pointed to the expensive décor of the "Hughes building," notably a desk that was a "slab of grey marble" and a coffee table made of "fake cement upon which sit two massive plastic form rocks," as an indicator of his increasingly chic, Californian taste.[113] An accompanying picture of Hughes wearing a black Versace suit and sporting a fashionable haircut seemed to validate Molly Ringwald's accusation in *Time* magazine that he had "changed" since his move to Los Angeles and "started looking very GQ."[114] Hughes seemed aware that his increasingly urbane style distanced him from his teenage and Middle American audiences, and accordingly, he attempted to reinforce the normality of his lifestyle. He maintained, "I don't have a lot of industry pals. I don't go to Maui on people's boats and stuff."[115] In spite of the filmmaker's attempt to regulate his image, the presentation of Hughes as a Hollywood yuppie sat awkwardly in relation to the modest, midwestern, youthful image that he had cultivated earlier in the decade. Probably of greater consequence to Hughes's career prospects, however, were rumors that had started to circulate about his professionalism. Farr claimed that within the industry, he had acquired "a reputation for being prolific but somewhat difficult."[116] Somewhat predictably, Paramount's executives were willing to overlook accusations about Hughes's uncompromising management style as long as he continued to deliver profitable movies.

Thanks to his ability to create stories that nearly always connected with audiences, Hughes managed to maintain his reputation as "the guru of the teen movies" during the mid-1980s.[117] Not only did he successfully tap into a variety of trends in youth culture, Hughes became a bona fide tastemaker with, as Nina Darnton of the *New York Times* put it, "his finger on the pulse of teenage America."[118] The stars of his films—the so-called Brat Pack—grew in popularity and fame, boosting the films' commercial prospects. These attractive young stars developed a following that, as Timothy Shary notes, "was built upon wistful, tormented, and ultimately clean images of mid-'80s youth."[119] As I discuss in chapter 4, Hughes's Paramount teen films offered audiences an appealing combination of fashionable clothes, cutting-edge music, memorable dialogue, and engagement with themes that sought to capture the anxieties and worldviews of 1980s suburban teenagers.

CHAPTER 4

GENDER, GENERATION, AND COMING-OF-AGE IN 1980S AMERICA

By the late 1980s, there was a growing critical consensus that John Hughes had succeeded in developing a signature product, a specific type of film associated with his name. In a 1987 *New York Times* review, Janet Maslin proclaimed, "That Mr. Hughes did not actually direct *Some Kind of Wonderful* is almost beside the point. It was directed by Howard Deutch, who also did *Pretty in Pink,* but both films were written by Mr. Hughes and fully reflect the Hughes point of view."[1] Although critics acknowledged Howard Deutch's contribution to the visual aspects of *Pretty in Pink* (1986) and *Some Kind of Wonderful* (1987), they attributed authorship of most other aspects of the films to Hughes. In his review of *Pretty in Pink, Boxoffice*'s Jimmy Summers, for example, mused that Howard Deutch's direction "is probably why the movie seems much slicker technically" than Hughes-directed films, "but everything else is definitely from the Hughes factory."[2] Such widespread recognition of Hughes as the overriding creative force not only on *Pretty in Pink* and *Some Kind of Wonderful* but also on *Ferris Bueller's Day Off* (John Hughes, 1986) consolidated his reputation as a "teenpic maestro" and "the tastemaker of teendom" in the late 1980s.[3] Clearly, the attribution of primary authorship to Hughes was professionally advantageous to the filmmaker and commercially beneficial to Paramount, which was investing heavily in the John Hughes brand.

Compared with Hughes's Universal teen movies, the Paramount films are more overtly topical, particularly in their ruminations on social class and romance in mid-1980s America. Both *Pretty in Pink* and *Some Kind of Wonderful* are part of the larger "cycle of cross-class romances" within the teen movie genre that engaged with class issues in Reagan's America.[4] *Pretty in Pink* is a romantic drama that charts the trials and tribulations experienced by Andie (Molly Ringwald), a working-class high school senior, when she dates Blane (Andrew McCarthy), a sensitive but ineffectual rich boy. The film ends with Andie united with Blane rather than her working-class best friend, Duckie (Jon Cryer). *Some Kind of Wonderful,* released one year later, also centers on a love triangle, this one between Keith (Eric Stoltz); his working-class best friend, Watts (Mary Stuart Masterson); and a popular girl, Amanda Jones (Lea Thompson). The film, which concludes with Keith embarking on a romantic relationship with Watts, is often interpreted as, suggests Timothy Shary, "a class corrective to *Pretty in Pink.*"[5] While these romantic dramas are grounded by a certain sense of realism, *Ferris Bueller's Day Off* pushes to the limit the fantastical "anything can happen" feeling present in *Sixteen Candles* and *Weird Science.* The film cuts between three lines of action: a primary one involving the exploits of the affluent teen Ferris (Matthew Broderick) as he plays hooky, and two minor ones featuring Ferris's sister, Jeanie (Jennifer Grey), and the hapless dean of students at their high school, Edward Rooney (Jeffrey Jones). The movie entwines scenes of broad comedy, including slapstick, with moments exploring teenagers' feelings about their futures.

Through their emphasis on teenage romance and issues of acceptance, both *Pretty in Pink* and *Some Kind of Wonderful* follow in the footsteps of the teen movies that Hughes wrote and produced at Universal. Paramount highlighted *Some Kind of Wonderful*'s affinity with Hughes's previous work through press materials that positioned the film as "continuing to explore themes that have been addressed in such earlier John Hughes films as *Pretty in Pink* and *The Breakfast Club*."[6] In this chapter, I consider to what extent Hughes's Paramount teen films replicate the features of his earlier work and reflect on the ways that they develop, or deviate from, the teen movies he wrote and directed at Universal. Many of the stylistic departures in *Pretty in Pink* and *Some Kind of Wonderful* can, perhaps unsurprisingly, be attributed to Howard Deutch's music-video-inspired direction. Hughes was careful, however, to ensure that the movies could be identified as his work in other ways. Part of Hughes's talent as a producer, writer, and director was to harness the creativity of a small group of collaborators to help develop many of the visual elements that became closely identified with his teen movies and a style of filmmaking described as "Hughesian." These visual features work to support the films' narratives, whose considerable similarities can be traced back to Hughes's screenplays.

Toward a High-Concept Style

Despite narrative and thematic similarities, each of the films that John Hughes wrote and produced at Paramount has a distinct visual and aural identity, which facilitated marketing and branding. Howard Deutch's experience in working on music videos and movie trailers ensured that *Pretty in Pink* and *Some Kind of Wonderful* would offer a more sustained "MTV aesthetic," via glossy visuals, lively editing, and dynamic camera work. Throughout *Pretty in Pink* and *Some Kind of Wonderful*, Deutch makes greater use of fluid camera movement and longer duration shots than did Hughes, who preferred montage sequences composed of shorter static shots. The music video sensibility in these movies is further aided by the editing and the sound design. Richard Marks, the editor of *Pretty in Pink*, was a protégé of Dede Allen, who edited *The Breakfast Club*. Marks shared his mentor's appreciation of the relationship between sound and image, ensuring that editing and sound worked in harmony. *Some Kind of Wonderful* benefits from the skills of Bud Smith and Scott Smith, both of whom worked on

Flashdance. Thanks to the expertise of these editors, New Pop, New Wave, and college-rock songs are carefully integrated into sequences that work in tandem with the visual imagery to create particular effects.

The synthesis of Deutch's vibrant music-video style, Hughes's economical approach to storytelling, and Paramount's emphasis on high-concept movies is signaled from the very start of *Pretty in Pink*. The opening sequence encapsulates the film's narrative premise and establishes a visual style distinct from that seen in Hughes's directorial efforts. The Psychedelic Furs' "Pretty in Pink" starts as the opening shot fades in, reinforcing the movie's connection with the rock song. The montage that follows depicts a run-down area in a working-class neighborhood: dusty roads, a parking lot, run-down buildings, chain-link fences topped with barbed wire. Compared with the leafy suburban neighborhood shown at the start of *Sixteen Candles*, the gray, brown, and blue tones of the concrete, metal, and neglected buildings in *Pretty in Pink* suggest a harsher environment. The film's title appears as the camera pans left across some railroad tracks, in a visual representation of "the wrong side of the tracks." The juxtaposition of the words "Pretty in Pink" with the semi-urban milieu sets the tone for a story of individual triumph against a backdrop of drab conformity and class division. The text "Starring Molly Ringwald," emphasizing her star billing, appears as the camera comes to rest on a small suburban house with a pink car parked outside. Deutch then introduces Andie through a montage of close-up shots of her dressing for school, which gradually reveal the character's unique attire and Ringwald's distinctive features, including her iconic red hair and pouting lips. The final shot in the sequence, which shows Andie emerging from her bedroom in an eclectic ensemble, highlights the role that personal style plays in the film as well as the centrality of Ringwald's star image.

The opening of *Some Kind of Wonderful* likewise demonstrates how the film departs significantly from the style established in the films that Hughes directed and shows the continued development of Deutch's personal style. More elaborate and faster paced than the beginning of *Pretty in Pink, Some Kind of Wonderful*'s opening showcases Bud Smith and Scott Smith's high-energy style of editing. The rhythmic beats of Propaganda's "Abuse" and shots of the tomboyish Watts drumming help unify rapidly edited shots of the film's central characters. Close-ups of the working-class Keith laboring in a dirty auto shop are juxtaposed with shots of Amanda Jones kissing her rich boyfriend, Hardy, in her bedroom. The film then revisits the "wrong side of the tracks" metaphor from *Pretty in Pink,* but it takes on a different resonance. Keith walks along the tracks against a highly industrial backdrop and squares up to an oncoming freight train. Close-up shots show his neutral expression and lack of fear as the train approaches and allow for the display of Eric Stoltz's facial features. Keith playfully steps out of the way at the last minute, tapping the railroad cars as they go past. Whereas the railroad tracks in *Pretty in Pink* signal a boundary that Andie wants to cross permanently, Keith in *Some Kind of Wonderful* does not view them as a barrier and can move freely between the two spaces. As a young man, he has the means to achieve social mobility, should he choose that path. Thus, the film's opening sequence not only establishes the style of *Some Kind of Wonderful,* but also efficiently signals the characters' class backgrounds and their roles within the narrative.

While Hughes uses close-up shots sparingly in his Universal teen films, Deutch uses close-ups and extreme close-ups much more frequently in *Pretty in Pink* and *Some Kind of Wonderful,* adding to the films' narrative excess. Details highlighted in the mise-en-scène closely guide the audience's interpretation of the narrative and emphasize the characters' personalities through clothing and accessories. Deutch also favors prolonged close-up shots capturing performers' facial expressions, intended to heighten the emotional resonance of specific moments. As in melodrama and soap opera, this "excessive" approach to narration "leaves a residue of emotional intensity" and "serves as a form of punctuation" between loosely connected scenes.[7] Later in *Pretty in Pink,* for example, the montage sequence depicting Andie and Blane's breakup is punctuated by close-ups showing

Steff's and Andie's animosity toward each other, Andie's and Blane's discomfort and anguish, and Duckie's distrust of Blane and his anger at Steff. In keeping with the films' commercial aesthetic, close-up shots also serve to accentuate the stars' physical characteristics and performance traits. By creating discrete moments that slow the narrative, close-up shots of Ringwald and the films' other stars evoke images from the films' publicity materials and other paratexts. Thus, Deutch's widespread, characteristic use of close-ups in *Pretty in Pink* and *Some Kind of Wonderful* offers a conspicuous demonstration of how the aesthetic and commercial facets of the films are closely entwined.

Figures 4.1a–4.1d. Emotional intensity: close-ups of the stars of *Pretty in Pink*. *Clockwise from top right*: Molly Ringwald, Andrew McCarthy, James Spader, and Jon Cryer.

Hughes used *Ferris Bueller's Day Off* as an opportunity to expand his repertoire as a director, assisted by Tak Fujimoto, the film's cinematographer, and Kenny Ortega, the second unit director and choreographer. Although Hughes had already used staging and composition to good effect in *The Breakfast Club*, his collaboration with Fujimoto prompted a further exploration of space and distance in anamorphic widescreen. Hughes uses widescreen compositions to create a sense of scale and to emphasize the production values created by location shooting, as when the teenagers visit the Sears Tower and in the crowded scenes at the Chicago Mercantile Exchange, Wrigley Field, and the parade in downtown Chicago. These shots also create a strong sense of place in a movie that Hughes described as his "love letter to the city."[8] In other cases—for instance, during Jeanie's encounter with the juvenile delinquent (Charlie Sheen) at the police station—Hughes uses space within the frame to reinforce emotional closeness or distance between characters. The film's most noticeable staging of a widescreen composition comes in the sequence at the Art Institute of Chicago. The sequence opens with a whimsical shot of a chain of children crossing the screen, joined by Ferris, Sloane, and Cameron, followed by a montage of static shots of paintings and shots displaying deliberately staged, striking compositions that depict the actors in the space, motionless apart from a tender kiss between Ferris and Sloane. Hughes later described this as "a very self-indulgent scene," and it is arguably his most overt attempt to express his viewpoint through film style.[9]

Hughes continued to rely heavily on the creative input of his editors to shape the narrative and pace of his directorial efforts. In spite of his attempts to explore shot composition and staging further, the filmmaker still preferred static shots, using camera movement sparingly. As he had done on *The Breakfast Club*, Hughes shot a large amount of footage for *Ferris Bueller's Day Off* and then used the editing process to refine the structure, pace, and focus of the final movie.[10] His heavy reliance on the cutting room stemmed from his efforts to push his films into production as quickly as possible in order to capitalize on his other successes. While Hughes's claim that he wrote the screenplay for *Ferris Bueller's Day Off* in six days may have been an exaggeration, he clearly treated his screenplay as a flexible document rather than a finely polished piece of work forming a rigid blueprint for production. Paul Hirsch, the editor for *Ferris Bueller's Day Off*, speculated that Hughes favored stories set in one day and avoided costume changes in order to offer greater flexibility in postproduction.[11] Following test screenings, Hughes and Hirsch adjusted the sequencing of the scenes

Figure 4.2. At the Art Institute of Chicago: staging and composition in *Ferris Bueller's Day Off*.

featuring Ferris, Sloane, and Cameron in Chicago in order to retain the audience's interest and to make the parade the climax of the movie.[12] Providing numerous options for the editing process was, evidently, a prudent commercial move.

The visual style of *Pretty in Pink, Some Kind of Wonderful*, and *Ferris Bueller's Day Off* marks them simultaneously as outputs of Deutch's and Hughes's directorial efforts and as products of Paramount in the late 1980s. A Hollywood director may, as David Bordwell suggests, have a "distinct approach to narration," but he or she nonetheless operates within a specific paradigm.[13] As discussed in chapter 3, these movies can be positioned within a larger cycle of extremely commercial high-concept films produced during the mid- to late 1980s, in which Paramount was an industry leader. With regard to this period, as Justin Wyatt argues, "one can talk about the 'personality' of a Paramount film: the visual style, genre . . . and marketing approach."[14] Although the studio was not necessarily striving for uniformity in its productions, visual and thematic continuities recur in groups of movies released in roughly the same period. Unsurprisingly, given the studio's production agendas, the teen movies that Hughes created at Paramount demonstrate a far greater commitment to the logics of high-concept filmmaking than do his Universal films.

Popular music forms an integral part of the style and

narration of all three of Hughes's Paramount teen movies. Hughes and his music supervisor, Tarquin Gotch, carefully selected each track in order to compile a soundtrack that enhanced the narrative and style of the film.[15] Music is used in all three movies in much the same way as a classical score might have been, namely, to "provide characterization, embody abstract ideas, externalize thought, and create mood and emotion."[16] Deutch and Hughes also used music on the set to help establish a scene for the actors.[17] In teen films, the use of music often relates to a character's subjectivity or indicates an affiliation with a particular youth subculture, acting as a mark of authenticity. As Kay Dickinson astutely observes, "to certain audiences, the pop song amidst a film narrative is far from (purely) a disruptive cash-in and may, in fact, be more distinctly pertinent to their identity formation" than a conventional classical score.[18] Diegetic music provides opportunities for the characters to express themselves through song and movement, most noticeably in the dance scenes choreographed by Kenny Ortega in *Pretty in Pink* and *Ferris Bueller's Day Off*. Hughes's use of music was, therefore, not simply a crass attempt to sell records, but rather a fundamental part of the films' textual operations.

While Hughes's Paramount teen films have a distinct style, they stick closely to the same principles of visual storytelling deployed in *Sixteen Candles, The Breakfast Club*, and *Weird Science*. Working in harmony with the cinematography and editing, the mise-en-scène of Hughes's Paramount teen movies plays an integral role in supporting the narrative and emphasizes the contemporaneity of the worlds portrayed. John W. Corso's production design for *Pretty in Pink* and *Ferris Bueller's Day Off* continues to develop the generic codes present in Hughes's earlier films and creates a strong sense of time and place, locating the films squarely in mid-1980s Chicago. *Some Kind of Wonderful*'s production design, by Josan F. Russo, deploys the same visual markers of genre, such as teenage bedrooms, the high school, nightclubs, and shopping malls, but situates the film in California rather than the Midwest. Much of the set design and architecture locates the film in Los Angeles, most strikingly the iconic Hollywood Bowl, which figures prominently in a pivotal scene. The film's color palette is also discernibly different from that used in Hughes's other teen movies, featuring more warm colors and yellow tones, which complement cinematographer Jan Kiesser's use of sunlight. In many respects, then, while *Pretty in Pink* and *Ferris Bueller's Day Off* are anchored by the same midwestern suburban settings as those associated with Hughes's earlier teen films, *Some Kind of Wonderful* stands apart.

In Hughes's Paramount teen movies, fashionable clothes and accessories form a major part of the films' distinctive aesthetic and support the narratives' thematic focus on personal style and identity. Building on the highly codified representations of high school life in Hughes's Universal movies, *Pretty in Pink*, *Ferris Bueller's Day Off*, and *Some Kind of Wonderful* portray a diverse range of mid-1980s adolescent subcultures. The costume designer Marilyn Vance played a pivotal role in creating the looks of the high school factions in all three movies, as she had done on *The Breakfast Club* and *Weird Science*, undertaking extensive research into how real teenagers in Chicago dressed.[19] For decades, observes Amanda Ann Klein, teen-oriented cinema relied on the ability of producers to isolate "new, exciting, or scandalous" elements of contemporary youth culture and "translate these fragments into saleable filmic images."[20] Hughes's and Vance's talent for harnessing the appeal of quirky youth subcultures ensured that the films resonated with a target audience of suburban teenagers. As Janet Maslin noted in her 1986 review of *Pretty in Pink*, "Much of its energy comes from more madly contemporary touches: wild costumes . . ., wacko hairdos, classroom note-passing by computer."[21]

Style and fashion sense play a key role in the articulation of *Pretty in Pink*'s themes, signaling class affiliation and individuality. Andie and her best friend, Duckie, who are members of the "zoids," their high school's predominantly working-class faction, express their group affiliation through their unusual taste in clothes and obscure New Wave music. Both teenagers create wardrobes out of numerous retro items. Andie favors pinks and busy floral prints, and Duckie's style is heavily inspired by teddy boy and rockabilly looks. Cats, the zoids' nightclub, is populated by vibrant teenagers with striking hairstyles and eclectic clothes. Energetic performances from the Rave-Ups and Talk Back signal the club's authenticity; the bands' absence from the soundtrack album further accentuated their legitimacy. The "richies," the popular clique in *Pretty in Pink,* presided over by Steff (James Spader), dress in designer gear and, as *Time* magazine's Richard Corliss put it, "already know how to use the tyranny of style to ostracize the poor."[22] The rich boys, including Blane, don linen suits, and the girls wear outfits from high-end stores and frequently mock Andie's appearance. In an early scene, Steff's vindictive girlfriend, Benny (Kate Vernon), accuses Andie of buying her clothes from a "five and dime" and later comments, "Nice pearls; this isn't a dinner party." Throughout the film, the richies' dominance of the high school is signaled visually through the multitude of pastel-clad preppie youths. Through juxtaposition of the two groups, *Pretty in Pink* presents the diversity and do-it-yourself nature of zoid subculture as a form of resistance against the social supremacy and conformity of the richies.

Unlike Andie and Duckie in *Pretty in Pink,* Keith and Watts in *Some Kind of Wonderful* are not affiliated with a particular social group or subculture. While Andie and Duckie express their individuality through their flamboyant clothes, Keith shows his creativity through his art and in the décor of his bedroom, which, as Hughes's script explains, is "a shrine to art."[23] Filled with posters and postcards as well as Keith's own work, the bedroom points to Keith's need to retreat to a private, domestic space in order to express his true identity, away from the regulated spaces of male youth culture. Fittingly, when Keith finally admits to his father that he has no desire to go to college and is unpopular at school, he does so against the backdrop of his bedroom. Watts's bedroom is darker, grimier, and less curated than Keith's room. It is the polar opposite of Amanda Jones's pastel-hued, highly feminine bedroom, as well as those of Samantha in *Sixteen Candles* and Andie in *Pretty in Pink.* The space is dominated by Watts's drum kit and stereo. Posters for bands and musicians (including the Sex Pistols, General Public, and Jim Morrison) adorn the soundproofed walls. The only concession to childhood is a toy drum on a shelf. Whereas the characters' bedrooms in Hughes's other films conform to gender stereotypes, Keith's and Watts's bedrooms are places where they can retreat from the pressure to conform to gender norms in their high school and in wider society.

In many ways, *Ferris Bueller's Day Off* is markedly different from Hughes's other teen films. Unlike Hughes's other protagonists, Ferris Bueller has an easy confidence and manages to transcend the cliques within his high school. As the school secretary, Grace (Edie McLurg), points out, "Oh, he's very popular. . . . The sportos, the motorheads, geeks, sluts, bloods, wastoids, dweebies, dickheads—they all adore him. They think he's a righteous dude." Ferris's diverse tastes serve to reinforce his uniqueness. His bedroom is decorated with a selection of band posters (including, in a nod to Hughes's other teen movies, Simple Minds, the Rave-Ups, and Flesh for Lulu), British and American flags, and other quirky ephemera such as a moose head wearing a life preserver. The presence of a keyboard, a guitar, a stereo, a TV set, amplifiers, and a computer signal both his creativity and affluence. Ferris also owns an extensive wardrobe, including unusual items such as his printed sweater vest, and parades through nine outfit changes before he leaves the house. Despite his many overt assertions of individuality, Ferris is, in many respects, unknowable. Elizabeth G. Traube describes Ferris as "a creature composed entirely of surfaces" whom the audience knows "only through his artful stagings of self."[24] Ferris's chameleon-like ability to adapt and take on different personas in order to navigate a range of situations is key to his success.

Complex Femininities

By focusing on high school seniors, *Pretty in Pink*, *Ferris Bueller's Day Off*, and *Some Kind of Wonderful* present more nuanced characters than those in Hughes's Universal teen films and explore the personal trials and triumphs of young people on the cusp of adulthood. As discussed in chapter 2, the problems faced by the characters in *Sixteen Candles, The Breakfast Club,* and *Weird Science* are rooted in the present and confined to high school and the family. In contrast, the protagonists in Hughes's later teen films are conscious of their social status and the challenges that await them after graduation. Molly Ringwald as Andie, Matthew Broderick as Ferris, and Eric Stoltz as Keith represent, as Christina Lee suggests, "that transitory, but liminal, moment of optimism that the future holds unbounded potential before the disappointment of adulthood descends."[25] Moreover, the focus on older teenagers and young adults in *Pretty in Pink, Ferris Bueller's Day Off,* and *Some Kind of Wonderful* allows brief glimpses of more complex gender and sexual identities than the ones explored in Hughes's earlier work. Although there are virtually no crude references to sex, the cultural politics of sexuality is a subtext present, to a varying extent, in all three films.

Pretty in Pink's contradictory attitudes toward gender are most overtly demonstrated in the transformation of Iona, Andie's boss and confidant. The owner of an independent record store, Iona is outspoken and sexually liberated, and she has a unique sense of style. Although many teen films, suggest Shirley Steinberg and Joe Kincheloe, reinforce the "misogynistic belief that women are not able to form meaningful relationships with one another" and therefore must compete against one another, Andie and Iona's relationship is built on trust and mutual respect.[26] In many ways, Iona is a strong and, arguably, feminist role model for Andie. Yet she sheds much of her individuality in order to secure a relationship with Terrence, a yuppie pet-store owner who dresses in a linen suit. In her final scene, Iona wears a sensible blazer and admits to Andie, "I look like a mother." Although Iona's embrace of traditional gender norms is presented as an active choice, it nonetheless reduces her eccentric clothes and feisty attitude to a phase, limiting the transgressive power that she possessed in earlier scenes. Although the film celebrates the zoids' subculture, *Pretty in Pink* also suggests that marginal identities often have to be sacrificed, by women at least, in order to move into adulthood and achieve a meaningful romantic union.

In keeping with the fantasy thread running through Hughes's work, Andie, the film's heroine, does not have to make the same compromises as her older friend does. As the *New York Times*' Janet Maslin observed, "In keeping with the spirit of the times, she gets to have it all."[27] Following her confrontation with Blane—in which she remarks, "You're ashamed to go out with me. You're afraid. You're terrified your goddamn rich friends won't approve"—Andie resolves to go to the prom alone. In a montage sequence scored by New Order's "Thieves Like Us," she makes her own prom dress. The dress is a statement of her individuality and resilience. As Andie explains to her father, "I want them to know they didn't break me." The outfit, a mixture of "fragmented pop couture from various eras," notes Christina Lee, not only articulates Andie's "self-determinism and agency" but also shows how teenagers can harness the transformative and subversive potential of popular culture.[28] On arrival at the prom, Andie is embraced by Duckie, and they face their peers together. Shortly after, the film concludes with Andie reunited with Blane, who finally stands up to Steff and tells Andie: "I always believed in you. I just didn't believe in me. I love you . . . always." Thus, Andie gets her man while retaining her personal integrity, her unique sense of style, and her best friend.

Even by the romance genre's standards, *Pretty in Pink*'s Cinderella conclusion is noticeably undermotivated. In fact, Hughes changed the ending at Paramount's request after negative audience responses at test screenings. In an earlier draft of Hughes's screenplay, Andie originally rejected an apology from Blane, and the film concluded with Andie and Duckie dancing together "without shame or concern for what anyone thinks."[29] This celebration of friendship between the two outsider characters seems more consistent with the structure and concerns of the narrative. While the heightened fantasy world of *Sixteen Candles* can sustain a fairly superficial attraction, *Pretty in Pink*'s more realistic setting demands greater adherence to character psychology. This convenient resolution of the protagonist's dilemma is characteristic of Hollywood's "utopian" impulse.

This narrative strategy, as Richard Dyer notes, relies on the "management" of contradictions created by "the gap between what is and what could be."[30] The film's stylized ending and constant blurring of the boundaries between realistic scenes of teenage life and MTV-ready moments, encapsulated by the final scenes at the prom, encourage the audience to view the ending as "escapist" entertainment. In fact, by showing Duckie break the fourth wall, with a surprised look to the audience, Deutch seems to acknowledge the ending's implausibility explicitly.

In its fraught attempts to balance commercialism with coherent storytelling, *Pretty in Pink* offers a salient demonstration of the often conflicting pressures that shape commercial cinema. According to Deutch, Hughes understood that the "Cinderella" ending would alter the political message of the film, but proceeded because the union of Andie/Ringwald and Blane/McCarthy seemed to be what the audience wanted.[31] Although love crosses the social divide in *Pretty in Pink,* the movie's ending does little to challenge social hierarchies and instead tries to unite the different high school factions.[32] Although Blane risks rejection by his high school peers, he does not have to sacrifice his wealth or wider social status to join with Andie. Timothy Shary argues that the movie implies "that young women want men with money and will reject men more loyal and better suited to them to achieve that financial-romantic goal."[33] From a narrative perspective, however, Andie's rejection of Duckie has little to do with his social status. Although she is clearly fond of him, Andie does not express feelings beyond friendship at any point, responding to his grand romantic gestures with either laughter or irritation. While it may have been what certain audiences desired, a romantic union between Duckie and Andie would have been inadequately justified.

The dilemmas faced by the more empowered teenage girls in *Some Kind of Wonderful* point to the shifting discourses that surrounded femininity in the late 1980s. Amanda Jones is more complex than the popular girls in *Sixteen Candles* and *Pretty in Pink.* She embodies what Hilary Radner dubs the "new femininity of the single girl," in which the woman's "capital is constituted by her body and her sexual expertise, which she herself exchanges."[34] By flirting with an unattractive driver's education teacher to escape detention, Amanda shows she has learned to exploit the power she possesses as an attractive, sexually active female. Although she later claims that she simply fears being alone, popularity and access to an affluent lifestyle seem to motivate her tolerance of Hardy's possessive demeanor. In fact, she seems to enjoy playing power games with Hardy, using her sexuality as a weapon, prompting Watts to observe shrewdly, "Obviously, she gets off on it." Whereas Hughes's earlier teen films tend to marginalize sexually active teenage girls, *Some Kind of Wonderful* redeems Amanda. In a scene at the Hollywood Bowl, she finally articulates her feelings. When Keith accuses her of using him to get back at Hardy, she points out that he is a hypocrite. She tells him, "You're using me to pay back every guy who had more money and more power than you. Paint it any color you want. It's still you using me." Ultimately, Amanda is presented as a victim of a culture that allows men to treat her as an object, and her actions are, therefore, a pragmatic response to her situation.

Unlike Amanda, Watts refuses to comply with norms of femininity, and by the standards of both the teen film and 1980s Hollywood cinema, she is an unlikely romantic lead. Her tomboyish appearance and demeanor inevitably raise questions about her sexual orientation. In an early scene in the film, Duncan asks Watts, "How long have you been a lesbian?" He explains, "You have a little bit too much up front to be a guy, so you must be a lesbian." In a later interaction, a boy called Ray tells her that "a lot of guys" think that she is "confused" but that she "radiate[s] this sexual vibe." Her response articulates her feelings clearly and evokes mainstream feminist discourse: "Ray, this is 1987. Did you know that a girl can be whatever she wants to be?" Watts's refusal to conform to gender norms poses *Some Kind of Wonderful*'s biggest challenge to traditional ideas of femininity. Through her acceptance of Keith's gift of a pair of diamond earrings, argues Timothy Shary, Watts takes her "first steps toward a presumably more feminized role" and the "attainment of heterosexual romance," moving away from "her apparent lesbian destiny."[35] Although Watts's nonnormative performance of femininity does not necessarily equate with lesbianism, the film's ending tries to counter any doubts about her sexual orientation and reinforces the view that heterosexual romance is what teenage girls desire. Despite this narrative resolution, *Some Kind of Wonderful* offers brief glimpses of alternative, less passive visions of teenage femininity.

Alternative Masculinities

Unlike his rich peers, *Pretty in Pink*'s Duckie performs an unconventional masculinity, underpinned by his subcultural tastes. His rockabilly-inspired look asserts his rejection of the affluent masculinity embodied by Blane and Steff. Early in the film, his taste in music and his belief in "old-fashioned" romance is revealed when he exclaims, "They just don't write love songs like they used to" while fast-forwarding through a mixtape. In an excessive display of romantic sentiment, Duckie dances to "Try a Little Tenderness" for Andie and Iona. His exaggerated movements and lip-syncing to Otis Redding's soulful, gospel-influenced vocals suggest an effort to demonstrate the intensity and sincerity of his emotions for Andie. At the same time, his performance is an attempt to compensate for his lack of sexual power.[36] Unable to compete with Blane's wealth or handsome looks, Duckie has to resort to a more demonstrative performance of his own brand of unconventional masculinity and enact, as Michael D. Dwyer suggests, "a display of cultural capital" in which he signals his musical knowledge.[37] While the audience is encouraged to find this spectacle endearing, Andie clearly finds Duckie's actions irritating. Although the film celebrates alternative tastes and performances of gender, it is plain that Andie craves a more conventional romantic partner. Unlike the female characters in the film, however, Duckie does not have to change in order to secure a mate. In an implausible turn of events, he pairs off with one of the attractive conventional girls at the prom.

Keith in *Some Kind of Wonderful* is distinct from Duckie and

Figure 4.3. Alternative style: Duckie (Jon Cryer) dances for Iona (Annie Potts) and Andie (Molly Ringwald) in *Pretty in Pink*.

the geeks in Hughes's earlier films. Through his passion for art and penchant for eyeliner, he embodies an ostensibly "alternative" masculinity. At the same time, his job as a mechanic and his low-key, grungy dress sense, as well as his infatuation with Amanda, ensure that he conforms to certain norms of hegemonic masculinity. *Some Kind of Wonderful*'s focus on a teenage boy produces a more active, individualist ethos than the sort found in Hughes's other teen romances. Whereas Samantha in *Sixteen Candles* and Andie in *Pretty in Pink* are largely motivated by and defined through their romantic liaisons, the romance in *Some Kind of Wonderful* merely forms part of Keith's transition into manhood. Paramount's press materials described the movie as "one young man's struggle to be his own person, to withstand the pressures placed on him by family and friends."[38] Although Keith has greater autonomy than Hughes's female protagonists, the nuclear family nonetheless figures centrally in *Some Kind of Wonderful* as a site of both conflict and support.

For the film's narrative emphasis and character development, Keith's relationship with his father, Clifford, is as important as the teenagers' romantic entanglements. Seemingly ignorant of his son's ambition to be an artist, Cliff wants Keith to study business at college and be "the first guy in this family who didn't have to wash his hands after a day's work." This father-son relationship becomes an important focal point for an exploration of social mobility and personal aspirations. When Cliff discovers that Keith has emptied his college fund, he confronts his son, demanding, "Where's the fucking money, Keith?!" Stoltz's physicality and vocalization in the argument that follows evoke James Dean's excessive, angst-ridden performance in *Rebel Without a Cause*. Whereas Jim Stark's father lacks masculine power, Cliff in *Some Kind of Wonderful* remains a tough but compassionate patriarch. In both films, the characters' inability to communicate meaningfully points to a generational divide. In the 1980s movie, generational differences between Cliff and Keith shape their attitudes toward masculinity and success in Reagan's America. The baby-boomer father is clearly invested in the idea of upward social mobility through individual hard work, a belief that was appearing increasingly untenable by the late 1980s. In this context, Keith's rejection of this dream, suggests Christina Lee, "marks a radical political agenda to live in the Now."[39]

The politics of working-class identity not only shape Keith's relationship with his father, but also underpin his friendships and alliances at school. The rich teenagers in *Some Kind of Wonderful* are much the same as their counterparts in *Pretty in Pink*. The film's antagonist, Hardy, and his friends wear flashy clothes, drive expensive cars, and socialize at the mall and at parties. The working-class youths are generally shown socializing at a live-music venue and engaging in creative hobbies. In *Pretty in Pink*, the working-class zoids' resistance to the rich clique is largely symbolic, but in *Some Kind of Wonderful* the working-class students physically enact their revenge on the rich kids. Keith forms an unlikely alliance with Duncan, a leather-clad Hispanic youth, and his gang, which is composed of a mixture of white, Hispanic, and black "delinquents." The basis for the young men's friendship is Duncan's appreciation of Keith's artistic talent as well as class solidarity. The arrival of Duncan and his friends at Hardy's party is a literal attack on affluent white privilege. Whereas *Pretty in Pink* suggests the faint possibility of reconciliation between social groups, through Andie and Blane's union, *Some Kind of Wonderful* suggests class boundaries cannot be crossed without characters compromising their integrity.

In stark contrast to working-class Keith and Duckie, Ferris Bueller personifies, as Chris Jordan puts it, "a Reagan-inspired philosophy of succeeding through careful manipulation of self-image and interpersonal relations with others."[40] Aided by his privilege as a young white middle-class man, Ferris is able to influence others and, notes Catherine Driscoll, shows a keen awareness of "how to perform different and at times contradictory images of youth."[41] To dupe his parents, he plays the innocent and vulnerable child, making cutesy faces and adopting childlike speech. He takes an entirely different approach in an upscale restaurant, using his understanding of assertive middle-class adult behavior to convince the maître d' that he is "Abe Froman, the Sausage King of Chicago." Of all the adolescent protagonists in Hughes's films, Ferris is most playful and yet, in some ways, the most aware of the rules of the adult world. His privilege and savoir faire are most clearly signaled through the film's use of direct address. Ferris frequently breaks the fourth wall to talk to the audience, sharing his life philosophies and commenting on the action of the film. R. L. Rutsky and Justin Wyatt argue that these digressions slow the plot progression by allowing Ferris to engage in extended displays of self.[42] *Ferris Bueller's Day Off* does not, however, abandon conventional Hollywood storytelling entirely. Ferris's asides are, as Michael Moffat argues, a crucial component of the film's narrative structure.[43] The movie is therefore not a significant departure from Hughes's character-led, efficient approach to storytelling.

In *Ferris Bueller's Day Off,* Hughes continues to explore the relationship between teenagers and their parents. William J. Palmer describes *Sixteen Candles* and *Ferris Bueller's Day Off,* along with *Risky Business,* as representative of "the rebellion of the eighties teen generation against their yuppie parents' attitudes and things."[44] Certainly, in *Ferris Bueller's Day Off,* Cameron's rebellion against his father is presented as justified, given the emotional neglect the boy has suffered. Several scholars have construed his angst as Oedipal aggression, derived from a seemingly universal impulse.[45] Whereas Leger Grindon echoes Palmer's interpretation, arguing that the father's reverence for his prized Ferrari emblematizes Cameron's parents' prioritization of wealth and prestige over their child's well-being.[46] Taking out his anguish on the car, Cameron shouts, "Who do you love? You love a car, you son of a bitch!" Ferris's parents are also affluent yuppies—his father works in advertising in Chicago, and his mother is a real estate agent—with an upscale home, but Chris Jordan is wide of the mark when he asserts, "The movie takes Ferris's careerist parents to task for their negligence."[47] Much like Samantha Baker's parents in *Sixteen Candles*, Tom and Katie Bueller may have flaws, but they are not neglectful of their children. Both parents check on Ferris during the day, and Katie prioritizes retrieving her daughter from the police station over a property deal. Moreover, although the film ridicules Ferris's parents for their gullibility, they are not the only adults whom the teenager dupes.

Ferris Bueller's status as a romanticized figure representing the exuberance and potential of white male suburban youth is most clearly encapsulated in his performance of "Twist and Shout" on top of a parade float in downtown Chicago. As the teenager dances and lip-syncs to the Beatles' cover of the song—originally recorded by the black R&B groups the Top Notes and then the Isley Brothers—the whole crowd, including large groups of African Americans, joins in an ecstatic moment of celebration. Michael Moffat asserts that although "this climax is fantasy," Ferris "demonstrates an ability often valued in the American democratic ethos: to bring together, to de-alienate, otherwise estranged or potentially estranged groups."[48] Ferris's ability to lead the diverse, multicultural crowd in a celebratory rendition of the Beatles' hit is, however, an overt demonstration of the character's privilege. As Michael D. Dwyer astutely observes, the scene "represent[s] a defense *against* difference, and affirmation of cultural insiders like Ferris and their ability, or privilege, to 'transcend' race and 'just have fun.'"[49] As an affluent young man, Ferris can be celebrated for his maverick status and can perform a seemingly inclusive whiteness that obscures social divisions in American society. Thus, the parade scene illustrates how Ferris Bueller enjoys the advantages of white privilege.

Ferris's exploits undermine the idea of young people as subject to adult and institutional control, but only to a limited extent. The film mocks authority figures, most notably the teacher Edward Rooney, a typically comical teen film "villain" who does not pose a genuine threat to the characters.[50] In its portrayal of increasingly implausible triumphs over adult authority, the movie is to some extent "a fantasy of teen omnipotence."[51] This fantasy is, however, of limited duration, occurring in a clearly demarcated time period, allowing for only temporary subversion of the social order.[52] Vicky LeBeau contends that *Ferris Bueller's Day Off* is "a key example of a cinema that colludes with a representation of youth rebellion as nothing more than a series of tricks and revels in parental and personal wealth and status."[53] On the one hand, by depicting Ferris as an individualistic hero, the film celebrates the triumph of white male privilege. He is also the only character who breaks the fourth wall and, thereby, transcends the restrictions of classical narrative. On the other hand, the film satirizes American society's willingness to accept the words and actions of affluent white men. This subtle critique is woven through the scenes involving Jeanie Bueller, who is constantly dismissed by the same adults who venerate her brother. Through the course of the day, "what she learns," argues Janet Staiger, "is that neither her parents nor schoolmates recognize her obedience as meaningful in opposition to Ferris's charm and charisma."[54] The film's parallel narrative structure thus allows for divergent interpretations of Ferris's ability to manipulate the adult world.

Hughes's time at Paramount showed that through the roles of screenwriter and producer, he could still retain textual "ownership" of core aspects of films that he did not direct. He had accrued enough power within the film industry to control the realization of his screenplays, which was his original motivation for becoming a director. By entrusting directing duties to carefully selected people, he could not only increase his prolific output, but also strengthen his overall brand. Despite clear differences in their directorial styles, both Hughes and Deutch shared a commitment to visual storytelling and to capturing the ephemeral tastes and preoccupations of mid-1980s suburban youth. Moreover, both directors were clearly amenable to using their skills to service a wider "industrial expressivity," by adopting a self-conscious, overtly commercial style that reflected Paramount's agendas during this period.[55] *Pretty in Pink, Ferris Bueller's Day Off,* and *Some Kind of Wonderful* are not the products of a sole author. Multiple people and entities shaped the films and benefited, to varying degrees, from their success. Nonetheless, continuities between these movies and Hughes's earlier films at Universal encourage interpretations of these films as "John Hughes" movies.

Although hip music and eccentric teenage fashions were the most marketable and topical aspects of Hughes's Paramount teen movies, they do not function simply as commercially motivated adornments. Music forms an integral part of the overall aesthetic and narrative logic of the films. Popular music tracks score key scenes and montages in all three films, and these musical moments enable and reflect narrative progression. Working in conjunction with music, clothing and accessories play a similarly crucial role in the narratives' explorations of identity, relationships, and belonging. This emphasis on characters' appearances is typical of many high-concept films of the mid-1980s, in which, observes Justin Wyatt, "issues of style or image become crucial to the functioning of the characters and the development of the narrative."[56] Hughes's teenage characters often choose to distinguish themselves or conform to social expectations through their personal style, and consequently, personal transformations have considerable narrative resonance.

John Hughes's late-1980s teen films offer mixed, arguably contradictory, messages about gender, class, and privilege in Reagan's America. Andie, Iona, Watts, and Amanda (along with Samantha, Allison, and Claire in Hughes's Universal teen films) are presented as psychologically complex characters who offer perceptive insights on events. As Barbara Jane Brickman observes, *Sixteen Candles, The Breakfast Club, Pretty in Pink,* and *Some Kind of Wonderful* "foreground the concerns of the female teen in a nuanced way that was rare in the genre."[57] Their gender and class, however, still heavily influence their actions, and they have far less freedom and agency than their male counterparts. Significantly, while they embody certain feminist traits, these are often compromised in order for the characters to achieve a romantic resolution. Like their adult-oriented equivalent, the "New Romances," these films acknowledge societal change but work to contain "any 'threat' of female independence" by placing women in traditional heterosexual partnerships.[58] Similarly, *Some Kind of Wonderful* and, to a lesser extent, *Pretty in Pink* work to "recuperate" potentially queer characters through heterosexual romance. This ostensibly conservative narrative strategy does not, however, eradicate the residue of complex representations of masculinity and femininity present in the films.

All of Hughes's teen films contain elements of fantasy, most notably romance against the odds and resistance to adult control. Through contained moments of adolescent wish fulfillment, Hughes's teen films offer at most a fleeting rebellion against the status quo. The films' limited critique of the American class divide did not go unnoticed by critics; Pauline Kael's review of *Pretty in Pink* noted that a growing number of 1980s movies shared the "fantasy theme of love bridging the gap," without offering "any kind of realistic or political context."[59] Hughes tends to critique characters' attitudes toward wealth and privilege, rather than their affluence per se. Steff in *Pretty in Pink* and Hardy in *Some Kind of Wonderful* are villains because of their preoccupation with status and material possessions, as well as their sleazy attempts to use their privilege to treat Andie and Amanda as objects. Similarly, Cameron's parents in *Ferris Bueller's Day Off* are rebuked for prioritizing ostentatious displays of wealth over the well-being of their son. Overall, the challenges faced by Hughes's teenage characters position middle-class identity as both the norm and the ideal in suburbia.[60] During the late 1980s and early 1990s, as I will discuss in chapters 6 and 8, Hughes began to focus more on affluent protagonists, sidestepping many of the social issues encountered in his teen films.

By the mid-1980s, Hughes had developed a reputation as the "king of an entire genre, however inconsequential and small."[61] To do this, he had, by his own admission, begun to rely too heavily on the same tried-and-tested formulas for his teen movies.[62] Following the release of *Ferris Bueller's Day Off*, critics began to suggest that the Hughes's work lacked originality. *Variety*'s reviewer proposed that Hughes had "run out of fresh things to say about his beloved high-schoolers" and that the tropes in his films had "become clichés in their own time."[63] Similarly, *Boxoffice*'s Kris Turnquist dismissed *Some Kind of Wonderful* as "an assembly-line special, constructed out of junked parts from earlier movies," and suggested that "Hughes has overdrawn his own creativity account."[64] *Some Kind of Wonderful*'s disappointing box-office performance seemed to confirm that Hughes needed to reorient himself both creatively and commercially. There was, nonetheless, mileage left in the formulas that the filmmaker had devised and refined during the mid-1980s. The film cycle is "capable of resonating again with audiences," notes Amanda Ann Klein, "as long as the familiar icons, formulas, conventions and themes" are reinvigorated and "deployed in a new way."[65] In the years that followed, Hughes's body of work provided an enduring reference point for portrayals of American adolescence on screen. By 1987, however, the writer-director-producer was ready to branch out beyond the teen films that had defined his career to date.

CHAPTER 5

SOLID FAMILY FARE

Universal (1988–1990) and Warner Bros. (1987–1993)

After *Some Kind of Wonderful*'s disappointing box-office performance, Hughes moved away from the teen-film genre. Attempting not to alienate his teenage following, he declared, "I hate to say I'm moving beyond anything, because I don't want to denigrate that work or that audience."[1] His next release through Paramount was *Planes, Trains & Automobiles* (John Hughes, 1987), a screwball road movie about two men trying to return home for Thanksgiving, starring Steve Martin and John Candy. During production, Paramount increased the resources and freedom granted to Hughes, demonstrating how, in 1980s Hollywood, major studios rewarded directors who had strong commercial records.[2] It was his most expensive movie to date, with a production budget of almost $30 million, which exceeded the industry average and was particularly high for a comedy, leading one reporter to describe the movie as "[Ned] Tanen's most expensive vote of confidence in Hughes."[3] Fortunately for Hughes and Paramount, *Planes, Trains & Automobiles* performed well during the 1987 holiday season, particularly throughout Christmas week.[4] During its run in American theaters, the movie grossed roughly $49.5 million, making it the twenty-first-highest grossing movie of 1987.[5] Although the costs of production eroded

Paramount's profit margin, the R-rated comedy confirmed that Hughes could write, direct, and produce films that appealed to a wider audience than his teen movies did.

Rumors that Hughes was planning to leave Paramount for a new deal with Universal began to circulate in late July 1987, before the release of *Planes, Trains & Automobiles*.[6] The *Los Angeles Times* claimed that Ned Tanen, one of Hughes's closest allies at Paramount, and Dawn Steel, Paramount's president of production, were often in conflict, and both were frustrated by their managerial and administrative responsibilities.[7] The departure of Tanen seemed likely to diminish Hughes's influence at the executive level. And after the lackluster box-office performance of *Some Kind of Wonderful*, studio executives expressed concerns that his films were "becoming too expensive to remain profitable."[8] Although Hughes remained with Paramount for the release of *Planes, Trains & Automobiles* and *She's Having a Baby* (John Hughes, 1988), it was unclear whether his relationship with the studio would continue. Publicly, at least, Paramount executives seemed confident that Hughes would continue to work with the studio. A spokesperson told *Variety* that he had three or four scripts under way and would, it was hoped, direct a movie for the studio in the summer of 1989.[9] Yet when Universal officially announced a new deal with Hughes, the *Los Angeles Times* suggested that the news confirmed recent "rumors of a falling-out" between Hughes and Paramount after conflict over the distributor's release strategy for *She's Having a Baby*.[10] The studio had shelved the movie, which wrapped in late 1986, and had forced Hughes to focus on *Planes, Trains & Automobiles* because of the threat of a Directors Guild of America strike in mid-1987.[11] Hughes later claimed that by postponing the release of *She's Having a Baby* until February 1988, the studio had sacrificed the promotional momentum generated by his teen films.[12] While major studios could exert control over filmmakers, Hughes's exit from Paramount illustrated the perils of this overbearing approach.

During April 1988, Hughes signed a multipicture development and production agreement with Universal, which was eager to renew its partnership with Hughes, despite the seemingly acrimonious nature of his departure from the studio a couple of years earlier. Universal had struggled at the box office in the mid-1980s, lagging behind the industry leaders, Paramount and Warner Bros.[13] Tom Pollock, chairman of the MCA Motion Picture Group, cheerfully announced the filmmaker's "homecoming" in a press release: "I am delighted that John Hughes is returning to Universal. . . . Very few filmmakers today can create and oversee a motion picture from concept through release with the talent of John Hughes and his company."[14] The contract specified that Hughes would "write, direct and produce a minimum of two films" in addition to producing two of his scripts, and it permitted him to work in Chicago rather than Hollywood.[15] Crucially, the contract was nonexclusive, giving the filmmaker the freedom to develop and release projects through other studios. The deal prompted *Premiere* magazine's Terri Minsky to assert, "Hughes has power in Hollywood, the power to make any movie he wants, when and where he wants."[16] While this was an exaggeration, Hughes had quickly secured an enviable amount of power, thanks to his prolific output, relatively consistent box-office performance, and strategic approach to working with major studios.

During the mid-1980s, by specializing in teen film and working exclusively with Universal and then Paramount, Hughes was able to develop a standardized product. As detailed in this chapter, his career from the late 1980s onward was more varied, shaped by both his and the major studios' efforts to replicate his earlier successes and tap into industry trends. As he attempted to make a name for himself beyond the teen market, Hughes formed alliances with multiple studios, reflecting both his ambitions for Hughes Entertainment and his elevated status within Hollywood as a writer, producer, and, to a lesser extent, director. Accordingly, this chapter examines the commercial aspects of his projects with Universal and Warner Bros. during the late 1980s and early 1990s. Throughout this period, Hughes experimented with ways to attract a broader audience, focusing his attentions on comedies with cross-generational appeal. In a 1996 interview, Hughes claimed that he "just stumbled" into making family films, insisting, "It was all accidental, my career was not planned in any way . . . I went from teen-king to kid-meister."[17] Whether or not his shift in focus was intentional, the continuities between his movies, along with his pragmatic approach to developing films that met audience demand, enabled him to adopt a serial production model.[18] This risk-management strategy hinged on reworking and adapting the successful elements of his earlier projects, gradually reorienting his career and the John Hughes brand.

The Rise of Family Entertainment

Hughes began his transition into cross-generational entertainment through vehicles for comedians—a prevalent trend in Hollywood cinema since the late 1970s. The studios had built movie packages around the former stars of *Saturday Night Live* (NBC, 1975–) and its Canadian counterpart, *SCTV* (syndicated, 1976–1981; NBC, 1981–1984), as well as around major stand-up acts of the time, looking to capitalize on both the popularity of "boomer humor" and the performers' fame. The box-office success of *National Lampoon's Animal House* (John Landis, 1978), in particular, gave the studios confidence to invest in movies starring the likes of John Belushi, Chevy Chase, Dan Aykroyd, Bill Murray, Steve Martin, John Candy, and Rick Moranis.[19] Hughes had already shown an aptitude for writing this form of comedy. As noted in chapter 1, he began his writing career at *National Lampoon* magazine, and his two breakthrough hits as a screenwriter were *National Lampoon's Vacation* (1983), starring Chevy Chase, and *Mr. Mom* (1983), starring Michael Keaton. Hughes's earlier commercial achievements and his experience of writing for the major comedy stars of the period therefore informed his decision to return to this style of comedy in the late 1980s. The challenge would, however, be to ensure that the films had wide appeal and fit with the American film industry's changing commercial priorities.

By shifting his focus to family films, Hughes and his distributors, Universal and Warner Bros., capitalized on wider industry agendas, particularly in the areas of theatrical exhibition and home video. During the late 1980s, the major film distributors pressured theater owners to make their facilities more family friendly by focusing on cleanliness, customer service, and, as Charles Acland puts it, the provision of "total entertainment."[20] Consequently, new multiplex cinemas often became the central hubs of new "lifestyle centers."[21] These family-friendly sites housed restaurants and stores as well as venues for other leisure activities such as bowling and laser tag. Faced with growing competition from these multiplexes, many independent theaters invested in their facilities, too.[22] These modernized spaces, suggests Acland, sought to "replace the unruliness of teenagers with a brand of bourgeois civility."[23] The incentives for movie theaters to attract more affluent family audiences were heightened by the 1989–1990 recession. During 1991, the dollar value of cinema admissions fell to under $1 billion for the first time since 1976.[24] Exhibitors, whose share of box-office receipts had declined to just 40 percent by 1991, were hit hardest.[25] As well as losing out on ticket sales, theaters saw falls in revenue from their concession stands, which accounted for as much as 90 percent of the profit at some theaters.[26] Thus, the rebranding of theaters as family spaces, added to the growing pressure to increase not only ticket sales but also sales of popcorn, candy, and other treats, fueled a demand for contemporary family entertainment.

Hughes's cross-generational movies enabled his distributors to take advantage of changes within the home-video market too. By 1991, over three-quarters of American households with a television set also owned a VCR.[27] Despite theaters' attempts to modernize, Americans were spending more money on renting and buying videos than on attending the cinema. For families, in particular, renting a video was more convenient and much cheaper than going out to see a movie. Despite home video's impact on theatrical attendance, Universal, Warner Bros., and the other major Hollywood studios had to engage strategically with this hugely popular entertainment technology. During the late 1980s, they set up specialist divisions dedicated to handling the marketing and distribution of video titles, and thereby significantly increased their market share. By August 1991, the major film studios accounted for over 90 percent of the wholesale video business, with Warner Home Video, FoxVideo, and Buena Vista Home Video leading the market.[28] Despite this dominance, suggested *Billboard*, the major studios were "struggling to energize a sluggish rental market" and had achieved only "mixed success in the sell-through business."[29] Consequently, during the early 1990s, the major studios experimented with a diversity of approaches to pricing and marketing home videos. As discussed in this chapter, MCA's and Warner Bros.' release strategies for Hughes's movies demonstrated how the studios gradually refined their distribution and marketing methods, showing an increased dedication to "family entertainment."

The Great Outdoors (Howard Deutch, 1988) was the first movie Hughes released through Universal after his departure from Paramount. The film starred John Candy and Dan Aykroyd as two feuding brothers on vacation together with their families. *The Great Outdoors* continued the development of Candy's professional relationship with Hughes, with whom he had worked closely on 1987's *Planes, Trains & Automobiles*. Arguably the bigger star, Aykroyd had appeared in several major comedy hits and had known Candy for over a decade. The two comedians had worked together at Second City in Toronto in the early 1970s, and both had appeared in the movies *1941* (Steven Spielberg, 1979) and *The Blues Brothers* (John Landis, 1980). In directing *The Great Outdoors*, Howard Deutch built on his previous collaboration with Hughes on *Pretty in Pink* and *Some Kind of Wonderful*. Universal considered Hughes, Deutch, Candy, and Aykroyd to be a promising mix of talent, likely to reap rewards at the box office, and agreed to a budget of over $25 million.[30]

MCA struggled to make *The Great Outdoors* a cohesive commercial package, demonstrating that the corporation could no longer implement the niche cross-promotional strategies that had been profitable in the marketing of Hughes's teen films. MCA tried to capitalize on audiences' familiarity with Aykroyd's earlier work by tying the soundtrack album, somewhat tenuously, to another Universal hit, *The Blues Brothers. The Great Outdoors* album features several tracks performed by the Elwood Blues Revue, a band that Aykroyd had recently formed for a world tour based on the Blues Brothers' act. By using the movie's album to promote his other projects, Aykroyd was deploying a strategy typical of stars in the New Hollywood; it was not unusual for major performers to prioritize their personal brand over the demands of a film's producers.[31] The soundtrack nonetheless generated publicity for the film. Wilson Pickett and Aykroyd performed the main single, "Land of a Thousand Dances," live at the Atlantic Records fortieth-anniversary concert on 14 May 1988 at Madison Square Garden, roughly a month before the film's release. The official music video, which featured Pickett and Aykroyd as well as clips from *The Great Outdoors,* was on Active Rotation on MTV before the film's release in June 1988. Although the musical recordings did not crack the *Billboard* charts, the accumulation of promotional images and activities across media for the soundtrack release for *The Great Outdoors* created a "a vortex of publicity" for the film.[32] This broad approach to cross-promotion was a significant departure from the increasingly precise methods that had been used to market Hughes's teen films.

Luckily for Hughes and Universal, Aykroyd and Candy added significantly to the commercial prospects of what turned out to be a mediocre movie. Reviews were generally negative, but some critics applauded Candy's efforts to make the most of the material. Peter Smith of the *St. Petersburg (FL) Times,* for example, stated, "*The Great Outdoors,* Hughes's latest extrusion from his script factory, has almost nothing to recommend it, save a lovely performance by John Candy, one of the most likable actors anywhere."[33] Consistent with Universal's investment in the production, the studio gave *The Great Outdoors* a wide opening on its theatrical release. While not a major hit, the movie performed reasonably well, despite competition from the family-oriented comedies *Big* (Penny Marshall, 1988) and *Who Framed Roger Rabbit* (Robert Zemeckis, 1988). During its domestic run, *The Great Outdoors* grossed over $41 million.[34]

The movie may not have met expectations, proving to be less than the sum of its parts, but it showed both Hughes and Universal that a more refined version of the comedian vehicle had the potential to reap commercial rewards.

Uncle Buck (John Hughes, 1989) benefited from a more obvious fit between star and role, making it appear to be a less cynical attempt to capitalize on a comedian's star power. Unlike the more generic lead roles in *The Great Outdoors*, Hughes wrote the part of Buck specifically for Candy. The movie was mutually beneficial for the filmmaker and actor because it offered Candy an opportunity to develop his on-screen persona further and allowed Hughes, as a producer, to capitalize on the actor's comic talents and growing appeal. As well as moving into leading roles in films, Candy was working on a number of side projects, including a syndicated radio show, *Radio Kandy*, and an NBC cartoon, *Camp Candy* (1989–1992). These endeavors all reinforced the actor's likability and everyman credentials. Candy's promotional interviews for *Uncle Buck* helped emphasize his close relationship to the role by explaining how he and Hughes had collaborated on the development of the movie.[35] Candy also suggested that he and the filmmaker shared the same outlook: "We're very similar in a lot of ways—our sense of humor and the way we view people and situations. . . . He's got a good feel for a kind of middle-American audience."[36] Hughes, who had experienced some negative publicity in the late 1980s, certainly benefited from his star's generous appraisal of his work and his efforts to sell *Uncle Buck* to a broad audience.

Critics underestimated both Candy's star power and the overall appeal of *Uncle Buck*. Predicting that the movie was "unlikely to hold its theaters for a long run," *Variety*'s reviewer was underwhelmed by its "sitcom humor as well as sentimentality" and described the film's climax as "a transparent attempt at audience manipulation."[37] The *New York Times*' Vincent Canby said that the "good sitcom idea" at the film's core led to "results [that] are sometimes funny and, in the way of small-screen entertainment, so perfectly predictable that one could mail in the laughs."[38] Hughes, he mused, "may be the first auteur of television-style entertainment."[39] This negative reception was, and remains, typical of critical responses to popular comedies. As Sam Friedman argues, critics often seek to distance themselves from "the ordinary, undiscriminating comedy consumer" by presenting "mainstream" appeal in comedy as an aesthetic weakness.[40] The film may have been "inoffensive multiplex piffle" and "acceptable family fodder," as *USA Today*'s reviewer Mike Clark put it, but that was, by and large, what the film was supposed to be.[41] Released on 16 August 1989 on over 1,800 screens, *Uncle Buck* topped the domestic box office in its opening week, pushing another family-focused Universal movie, *Parenthood* (Ron Howard, 1989), into second place.[42] Hughes's movie stayed at number 1 in the United States for four weeks and grossed over $66.7 million domestically and $12.5 million in foreign markets, making it the eighteenth-highest-grossing film in the United States, and the twentieth highest worldwide, in 1989.[43] *Uncle Buck* thus provided both Hughes and Universal with a much-needed box-office hit and confirmed Candy's status as a major star.

Hughes's comedian-focused projects were not restricted to his work for Universal. After signing a multipicture deal with Warner Bros. in 1987, he developed *National Lampoon's Christmas Vacation* (Jeremiah Chechik, 1989), starring Chevy Chase.[44] The filmmaker's leading role in the conception of the project reflected his growing clout in Hollywood. Whereas *National Lampoon* and Warner Bros. had simply hired Hughes as a screenwriter on the first two *Vacation* movies, by 1989 he was in a position to assemble the movie package himself and produce it through his company. Hughes received $1 million for the script, which he based on his *National Lampoon* story "Christmas '59," and a producer's fee of $750,000.[45] He also secured a budget of $27 million from Warner Bros.[46] This was slightly above the industry average of $23 million, signaling the studio's confidence in the project.[47] Hughes hired Chris Columbus as the director, but he soon withdrew from the project, and

Jeremiah S. Chechik, who had previously directed TV commercials and music videos, took the helm. While some of the movie was shot on location in Colorado, the majority of the production took place on a soundstage in Los Angeles, which made for an uneventful shoot. Whereas Hughes often took an active role in his earlier productions, his busy schedule and the distance from Chicago meant the writer-producer delegated day-to-day production duties to Tom Jacobson.[48]

The publicity for *Christmas Vacation* relied heavily on the star power of Chevy Chase, who had already appeared as Clark Griswold in two earlier installments of the *National Lampoon Vacation* series. Warner Bros. downplayed *Christmas Vacation*'s association with *National Lampoon* in an attempt to target family audiences, which might be deterred by *Lampoon*'s reputation for mature humor. The trailer emphasized the film's thematic focus on family as well as its Christmas setting and broad slapstick humor. Critical reception, which was somewhat mixed, reflected this shift away from the more adult-oriented, satirical humor of the earlier *Vacation* films. Although some critics felt that the franchise was tired, they conceded that *Christmas Vacation* largely succeeded as a lightweight mainstream comedy. The *New York Times*' Janet Maslin mused, "Fatigue is in the air," and remarked, "The screenplay . . . by John Hughes makes no pretense at being anything other than a disjointed collection of running gags."[49] Arguing that the lack of narrative allowed Chase to exhibit his skills as performer, *Screen International*'s reviewers ventured, "Chase's band of loyal fans will be happy with *Christmas Vacation,* as will followers of Hughes's suburban angst."[50] Released during the 1989 holiday season, the film excelled at the domestic box office, topping the chart for two weeks and grossing over $71 million during its run, despite its limited shelf life as a Christmas movie.[51] Although the movie significantly benefited from Chevy Chase's star turn, as well as a strong supporting cast, it nonetheless affirmed, along with *Uncle Buck*, that Hughes could write and produce, as *Variety* put it, "solid family fare."[52]

Warner Bros. and *Curly Sue*

Despite the success of *Christmas Vacation,* Warner Bros. was unwilling to give Hughes free rein on his productions. During preproduction on his next major movie, *Home Alone* (Chris Columbus, 1990), the studio instructed him to cut $2 million from the film's $18 million production budget.[53] Warner Bros.' demands occurred against a backdrop of major changes to its parent company's corporate structure and business strategy. When Warner Communications Inc. announced its plans to merge with the publisher Time Inc. in March 1989, it prompted *Variety* to proclaim, somewhat optimistically, that the deal nurtured "the explosive power of perfect synergy."[54] The "megamerger" between Warner Communications and Time concluded in 1990, following a bidding war with Paramount and several legal battles.[55] The newly formed conglomerate's holdings included HBO, Warner Cable, DC Comics, *Life,* and *Fortune,* as well as *Time* and Warner Bros. Although *Batman* (Tim Burton, 1989) offered a tantalizing glimpse of how the new corporation could harness cross-promotion and sell movies across multiple formats, the Time-Warner merger was slow to produce any major results. An unsuccessful movie could have negative consequences for numerous divisions within the conglomerate, prompting Warner Bros. to invest somewhat cautiously in new films and to defer exploiting a movie in certain markets until it was a proven success.[56] Hughes's mid-budget comedies did not fit with the studio's new global, multiplatform ambitions. Confident in his expertise and status within the industry, Hughes refused Warner Bros.' request to cut *Home Alone*'s budget and took the project to 20th Century Fox. Unfortunately for Warner Bros., *Home Alone,* which I will discuss in chapter 7, became one of the highest-grossing movies of all time.

Hughes's relationship with Warner Bros. changed radically after he signed a major multipicture deal with 20th Century Fox in 1991. Although *Home Alone*'s success surprised everyone in the industry, passing on one of the highest-grossing movies of all time was an embarrassment for Warner Bros., which, suggested *Variety*'s Charles Fleming, had acquired a reputation as "the stodgiest, most traditional studio in town."[57] While *Home Alone* was dominating the box office, the studio's chairman and CEO, Robert Daly, conceded to *Variety*, "Obviously, we wish we had the movie," but claimed that the studio had a strong relationship with Hughes, calling him "a terrific filmmaker."[58] The studio was optimistic about its next Hughes release, *Curly Sue* (John Hughes, 1991), a comedy-drama about a nine-year-old homeless girl and her guardian. Shot in Chicago during late 1990, the movie was very different from Hughes's earlier comedies, and its box-office prospects were by no means certain. As I will show in chapter 6, the film was more an adult-oriented drama than a child-oriented comedy. Moreover, the film's adult stars, Jim Belushi and Kelly Lynch, lacked the widespread fame of Steve Martin, Dan Aykroyd, and John Candy.

Warner Bros. was forced to take a strategic approach to the 1991 release of *Curly Sue* in order to maximize theatrical revenues. The distributor opened the movie on 1,634 screens four weeks before the highly competitive Thanksgiving weekend.[59] Although the movie grossed only a "mediocre" $5 million in its opening week, the distributor increased its advertising expenditures because attendance increased in the second week and the movie generated "favorable exit interviews," consistent with the film's positive test screenings.[60] Helped by Warner Bros.' unusual strategy, *Curly Sue* became "one of the few movies to grow in the modern day market without adding screens," and as *Variety* noted, it developed "word of mouth and hit perception."[61] In a press release publicizing the movie's box-office surge, a studio executive stated, "We think that, as with John Hughes's other films, this one appeals to people of all ages and offers a family entertainment experience."[62] This embrace of "family entertainment" reflected a noticeable shift in studios' priorities, given their avoidance of the "family" label during the previous decade. The movie topped the domestic box office during its third week of release but struggled once competition for family audiences increased in late November and December.[63] Across its domestic theatrical run, *Curly Sue* grossed over $33 million, placing it forty-first on the 1991 annual chart.[64] Although the movie was not a major hit, the film reinforced the perception that Hughes's films could build audience interest after the opening week and, crucially, maximize revenue through family appeal.

Warner Home Video, which was the rental-market leader at the time, priced *Curly Sue* (at $94.99) for purchase by video stores rather than consumers, but showed confidence by shipping over 250,000 copies during the first month of release, April 1992.[65] In an attempt to increase sales volume, the distributor also included *Curly Sue* in a promotion that offered a case of Milk Duds candy to stores that purchased more than twenty-five copies.[66] Despite Warner Bros.' efforts to boost sales of the video, it was only a moderate success. *Curly Sue* spent eighteen weeks on *Billboard*'s "Top Video Rentals" chart and placed thirty-first on the annual chart.[67] This performance may not have met Warner Bros.' expectations, but North America was not the only video market it targeted. By the early 1990s, in line with Time Warner's ambitions to become a global company, Warner Home Video had expanded its reach significantly, and the distributor released *Curly Sue* on video in numerous international markets, including the United Kingdom, Germany, Spain, Finland, the Netherlands, Poland, and Japan. Notably, the UK video's sleeve emphasized that the movie was "from John Hughes, the creator of *Home Alone*," asserting the filmmaker's international status as a creator of popular family comedies.

Universal and *Beethoven*

Hughes's relationship with Universal deteriorated after the release of *Uncle Buck*. As part of an ambitious plan to significantly increase the studio's output, Universal had slated two Hughes films for 1990, both of which he would write and direct, and one of which he would produce.[68] The filmmaker left Universal in late 1990 without realizing these projects, claiming that a major factor in his departure was Universal's decision to sell the rights for an *Uncle Buck* TV show to CBS without consulting him.[69] After Hughes left, the studio retained the screenplay for *Beethoven* (Brian Levant, 1992), a family comedy about a St. Bernard. The filmmaker agreed to the deal on the condition that his identity remain confidential. He later told a reporter, "I cannot endorse [a] picture that I'm not going to have any say in."[70] Consequently, Universal credited the final screenplay to "Edmond Dantès" (the title character in *The Count of Monte Cristo*) and Amy Holden Jones, although, as the *New York Times'* Caryn James observed, "It is an open secret that *Beethoven* and *Home Alone* share the same creator."[71] Seeking a high-profile name to attach to the project, Universal persuaded Ivan Reitman, one of Hollywood's most successful comedy directors and producers, to be executive producer on the film. MCA's press release announcing the start of production in May 1991 emphasized Reitman's involvement and his previous family hits, including *Ghostbusters* (1984), *Twins* (1988), and *Kindergarten Cop* (1990), noting that "his films have grossed in excess of $2 billion at the box office."[72] While Reitman's involvement was an asset, the success of *Beethoven* ultimately hinged on whether its story and overall concept would appeal to a wide audience.

Universal was surprisingly confident about *Beethoven*'s commercial prospects, releasing it across 1,688 screens in April 1992, despite the lack of major stars or presold source material. The studio's decision to use a wide release for a mid-budget, seemingly unremarkable family film was extremely unusual. The major Hollywood studios typically reserved expensive, high-profile release strategies for big-budget movies in order to reduce the risks created by substantial investments.[73] The studio timed *Beethoven*'s release carefully, premiering it during an off-peak period when there was very little competition for family audiences. Steven Spielberg's *Hook* (1991) and Disney's *Beauty and the Beast* (1991) were the only other family-oriented films in the box-office top twenty, and both movies had been in cinemas for over four months. Although 20th Century Fox released *FernGully: The Last Rainforest* (Bill Kroyer, 1992) a week after *Beethoven* debuted, the environmentally conscious animation struggled to achieve broad appeal. While these factors created favorable conditions for *Beethoven*'s debut in theaters, the family audience would dictate its commercial fate.

Universal's investment in the release paid off, and *Beethoven* grossed $57 million in its domestic theatrical run, making it the sixth most successful PG-rated film of 1992, doing so despite a lack of critical consensus on the movie's potential to appeal to adults as well as children.[74] Roger Ebert, who did not particularly enjoy the film, mused, "If I were under the age of 14 and had not already seen all of those earlier animal movies, I might well have enjoyed *Beethoven* more. It's the kind of clever, innocuous family entertainment that's always in short supply."[75] In contrast, the *New York Times*' Caryn James declared, "It has enough energetic charm to keep parents' attention focused on the screen."[76] The family comedy's broad appeal was not restricted to North America, and it grossed over $90 million internationally, making it the sixteenth-highest-grossing film of 1992 worldwide.[77] Such was the film's success that in 1993 *Variety* referred to *Beethoven* as a "kiddie bonanza" that, alongside *Home Alone*, was "paving the way" for the major studios' growing focus on "family fare."[78]

MCA/Universal Home Video's careful handling of *Beethoven*'s video release during the summer of 1992 showed how lucrative nonblockbuster family films could be in the sell-through market. MCA priced *Beethoven* at $24.98 and shipped approximately three million videocassettes, which had a wholesale value of $40 million.[79] *Video Week* suggested this was an unusual move, asking, "Why sell-through for [a] live-action title whose box office is well under [the] usual $100 million benchmark?"[80] The strategy was potentially risky, but MCA developed a high-profile campaign to exploit the limited competition for the family market.[81] The distributor was even willing to forgo a promotional partner in order to release the video during the lucrative summer season.[82] The marketing for *Beethoven* on video reflected MCA's increasingly sophisticated approach to promoting its releases. By 1992, the value of the US home-video market was $3.8 billion, but distributors had to compete for audiences' attention.[83] Whereas "direct advertising was an afterthought" for much of the 1980s, as Frederick Wasser notes, in the early 1990s distributors became more

Figure 5.1. "Your Best Friend This Sell-Through Season": advertisement aimed at retailers for *Beethoven* on video, *Billboard*, 1 August 1992, 81.

strategic in their marketing of sell-through video releases.[84] When marketing *Beethoven* on video, MCA targeted three groups: mothers, grandmothers, and children.[85] In addition to female-oriented publications such as *People* and *Woman's Day*, the company focused on magazines aimed at parents, including *Parents* magazine and the *TV Guide* spin-off *Parents' Guide to Children's Entertainment*, as well as the children's comic *Disney Adventures*.[86] MCA also targeted a wider audience through advertisements on cable and broadcast television during the Thanksgiving period and the buildup to Christmas.[87]

Despite the varied methods used to publicize *Beethoven* on video, marketing materials consistently emphasized its attractions for children by focusing on the distinctive St. Bernard and the film's slapstick comedy. MCA was evidently less concerned about the movie's appeal to adults, hoping instead that they would buy the video as a gift for children. Consequently, the distributor positioned *Beethoven* carefully within a narrow retail context. In an advertisement targeted at retailers, MCA described the video as "your best friend this sell-through season" and offered a variety of point-of-purchase materials, including "Beethoven-sized standees," posters, and activity booklets.[88] Increasing new releases' visibility in retail spaces had become a priority for major studios by the early 1990s. That said, MCA executives claimed that competition from other family-oriented videos, such as *Beauty and the Beast* and *Hook*, presented a commercial advantage.[89] The firm's vice president of marketing, Andrew Kairey, stated, "We will benefit rather than compete against it because of the added floor traffic."[90] This symbiotic relationship between video releases demonstrated how the Hollywood studios' interests became aligned around the family film trend. MCA also used *Beethoven*'s release to sell catalogue titles, offering a $5 rebate if consumers purchased selected family videos, including the *Back to the Future* trilogy, *Kindergarten Cop*, *King Ralph* (David S. Ward, 1991), and *Holiday Inn* (Mark Sandrich, 1942).[91] MCA's investment in the promotion of *Beethoven* paid off: sales of the video exceeded three million units in the United States.[92] As well as helping fuel the family-film production trend, the theatrical and home-video success of *Beethoven* further strengthened Hughes's reputation within the industry, even though many audiences knew nothing of his creative contribution to the movie.

Warner Bros. Family Entertainment and *Dennis the Menace*

When Warner Bros. officially launched its Family Entertainment banner in May 1991, *Variety* suggested the move was symptomatic of "industry-wide awareness that survival in the 1990s may be a matter of creating wholesome, family-oriented entertainment."[93] In the late 1980s and early 1990s, conservative political and religious groups publicly criticized Hollywood for not making enough films suitable for families. The American Family Association and the Christian Film and Television Commission mounted campaigns that chastised the entertainment industry for exposing children to inappropriate content. Warner Bros. and the other major Hollywood studios were reluctant, however, to attribute their increased focus on the family market to political considerations. As *Daily Variety* noted, "[Warner Bros.] sources hastened to add that shouldn't be seen as a concession to mounting criticism in the press and on Capitol Hill that Hollywood fare has gotten too violent."[94] Hollywood executives claimed instead that their focus on a cross-generational audience made sound business sense. The journalist Bernard Weintraub agreed with this assessment, suggesting that concerns about the US economy "led studios to look for scripts meant to lure the widest possible audience, meaning families."[95] At the same time, *Variety* cautioned that "family movies are not instant moneymakers" and suggested that the trend might be short-lived.[96]

A "John Hughes Production," *Dennis the Menace* (Nick Castle, 1993) was the first Warner Bros. Family Entertainment film. The movie was in the production pipeline before the creation of the studio's family entertainment division. In July 1991, the studio confirmed that Hughes would "produce" and "creatively supervise" a movie based on Hank Ketcham's *Dennis the Menace* comic strip.[97] The deal, several months in the making, hinged on Hughes's involvement in the Warner Bros. project, with Spielberg and Universal allegedly Ketcham's second choice.[98] Securing the film rights for such an iconic American character was a testament both to Hughes's post–*Home Alone* status as a creator of global family entertainment and to the powerful combination of Hughes Entertainment and Warner Bros. Confirming that *Dennis the Menace* would launch the Warner Bros. Family Entertainment brand, a senior studio executive stated that the movie "embodies the spirit and the appeal of our new label."[99] He added, "John Hughes has given movie audiences many films where timeless humor crosses all age boundaries and presents a world in which families, and especially kids, are celebrated."[100]

Convinced of the commercial potential of a movie written and produced by Hughes and based on a well-known character, Warner Bros. invested heavily in both the production and promotion of *Dennis the Menace*. Seeking to capitalize on the residual publicity of *Home Alone*'s tremendous success, Hughes and Warner Bros. mounted a highly coordinated marketing campaign that began during the preproduction phase. Hughes Entertainment launched a nationwide talent search to find the boy to play Dennis, which attracted considerable public attention. According to the *Chicago Tribune*, parents sent over twenty thousand audition tapes to Hughes Entertainment, through which a Los Angeles casting company then sifted.[101] Hughes claimed to have viewed three hundred tapes before selecting the final short list of ten boys, who appeared at a press conference at the end of June 1992.[102] The winner of the contest, six-year-old Mason Gamble, had the same blond hair, pale skin, chubby cheeks, and precocious demeanor that the leading child star Macaulay Culkin possessed in his younger years. Helpfully for Hughes and Warner Bros., Gamble was an unknown performer whom they could mold to the role.

While *Dennis the Menace* was still in postproduction, Warner Bros. hired Anthony Goldschmidt, one of Hollywood's leading graphic designers, to create the film's distinctive branding and to develop a big-budget marketing campaign.[103] Responding to an increasingly congested family-entertainment marketplace, Warner Bros. and its marketing partners aimed to give *Dennis the Menace* a certain prestige to distinguish it from lower-budget family films.[104] Although Mason Gamble played a key role in the film's promotion, publicity materials emphasized the studio's investment in the production by focusing on the movie's elaborate sets, spectacular set pieces, and the supporting adult cast of Walter Matthau, Joan Plowright, Christopher Lloyd, and Lea Thompson. Despite this evocation of prestige, certain aspects of the movie's promotion remained unashamedly commercial. Consistent with wider industry strategies, Warner Bros. secured several promotional tie-ins for *Dennis the Menace*, focusing on food and drink products popular with preteens. The deals with Nestlé candy, Crush beverages, Hires Root Beer, and Sun-Maid raisins created additional publicity for the movie, as well as helping the brands target children.[105] The use of Gamble's image to sell these products occurred in the midst of an ongoing debate about the increasingly pervasive use of fictional characters and celebrities to market often-unhealthy products to children. For Warner Bros., the benefits of the tie-ins clearly outweighed the risk of negative publicity, although such blatant commercialism was at odds with the "quality" line adopted in most of the film's publicity.

Thanks to assertive marketing and an appealing combination of presold elements, *Dennis the Menace* was "easily one of the summer's most anticipated movies."[106] In fact, Warner Bros.' marketing blitz was more typical of that for a blockbuster release than for an average family film, demonstrating the increased stakes for makers of family films in the post–*Home Alone* era. The studio's investment in both production and marketing could not prevent negative reviews, however. The majority of critics focused their concerns on the level and nature of "violence" in the film and on the film's sinister villain, Switchblade Sam, whom Roger Ebert described as "dirty, threatening, and scary."[107] Audiences nonetheless attended the film in significant numbers. *Dennis the Menace*'s total domestic gross of roughly $51 million was respectable, but it was not a hit of the same magnitude as the *Home Alone* films, which Hughes released through 20th Century Fox. Warner Bros. nonetheless claimed to be pleased because the studio had expected the film's appeal to be "more limited."[108] This claim seems somewhat disingenuous, considering the studio's expenditure on the production and its positioning of the film in the marketplace. Fortunately for the studio and Hughes, the movie performed well overseas, pointing to a substantial global audience for American family entertainment. In a year when Hollywood's international box-office revenues exceeded domestic revenues for the first time, *Dennis the Menace* grossed $66 million internationally, bringing the movie's worldwide gross to over $117 million.[109]

Warner Bros. then used *Dennis the Menace* to help build the profile of the studio's fledgling Family Entertainment label in the home-video market. In May 1993, the chief of Warner Bros., Robert A. Daly, proclaimed, "We believe that Warner Bros. has, both in its libraries and in its current and future programming capabilities, a valuable heritage on which to develop entertainment and entertainment-related products for children and families."[110] The movie was part of a regular release roster that saw Warner Bros. launch a new sell-through Family Entertainment video every two months, supported by "an aggressive multimillion dollar marketing campaign that includes advertising on all four TV networks and cable, rebates and coupons for other Warner products, and free collectibles."[111] According to *Billboard*, Warner Bros.' strategic approach to marketing *Dennis the Menace* and its Family Entertainment brand were part of a wider trend of video distributors launching "family oriented sell-through lines with ambitious, Disneyesque marketing campaigns."[112] For example, the company packaged its videocassettes in plastic clamshell cases rather than cardboard sleeves. The use of more durable packaging, an approach pioneered by Disney, presented the video as a collectible item that could withstand children's repeated handling. By focusing on the higher-quality aspects of its brand, Warner Bros. sought to distance itself from companies producing cheap children's entertainment.

Warner Bros. Home Video's branding strategy for *Dennis the Menace* and other family titles traded heavily on the studio's long-standing reputation. The Warner Bros. Family Entertainment logo featured a tuxedo-wearing Bugs Bunny alongside the WB shield. In a press release, the studio explained that it was "inspired by Warner Bros.' long history of popular media products for the enjoyment of children and families."[113] This was consistent with how major studios use their logos, observes Paul Grainge, "to associate themselves with cinema's past and experiential pleasures in the present."[114] One advertisement announced, "The newest name in family entertainment is an old friend," alluding to Warner Bros.' history in the entertainment business, and advised retailers, "To Make Big Bucks Look For Bugs Bunny In His Tux!"[115] The Family Entertainment brand also gave Warner Bros. yet another opportunity to repackage films from its extensive library. The rebranding of older movies

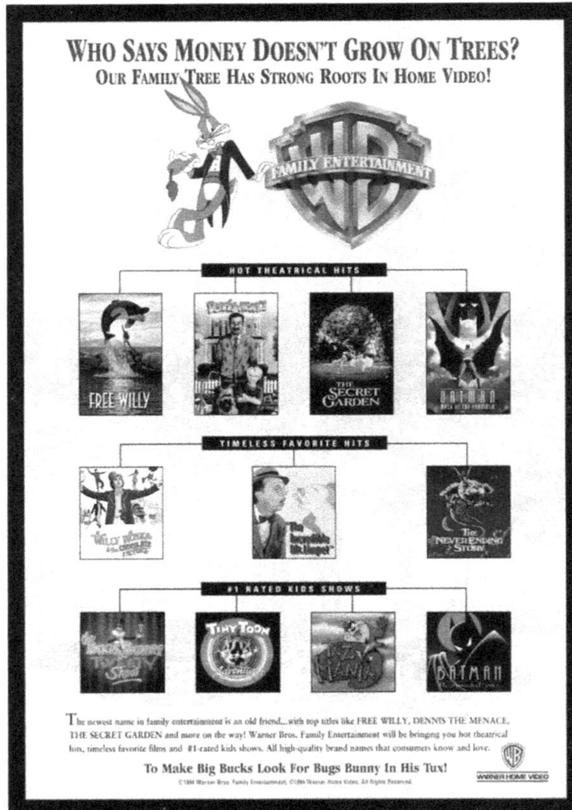

Figure 5.2. Warner Home Video's family tree: advertisement aimed at retailers, *Billboard*, 19 February 1994, 85.

as "timeless favorite hits" for the whole family reflected the major studios' focus on, as Barbara Klinger puts it, "revitalizing old properties within contemporary taste markets" by "giving them new sellable, historical identities."[116] Another advertisement, which included *Dennis the Menace* and *Curly Sue*, told parents, "Bugs Bunny and the Warner Bros.' shield are a symbol of high quality entertainment for all the family" and featured a variety of "carefully selected" old and new video releases.[117] This rebranding of *Curly Sue* as a classic and the positioning of *Dennis the Menace* as a future classic drew on the nostalgic aesthetics of the movies and was consistent with the prestige emphasized in the films' original marketing.

Warner Bros. extended *Dennis the Menace*'s brand across a

range of ancillary markets, in keeping with Time Warner's wider strategy to maximize the profitability of "filmed entertainment." The corporation created Warner Bros. Family Entertainment to produce synergies that spanned "film, video, television, animation, recorded music, consumer products, theme parks, live entertainment, and interactive media."[118] As an Associated Press article noted, it was "more than just a label for new films": it was "a way to distinguish products that can be cross-marketed."[119] The merchandising campaign for *Dennis the Menace*, which targeted boys between four and twelve years old, encompassed clothing, accessories, board games, and stationery.[120] Warner Bros. contracted Ocean Software, which had created numerous video games based on movie and TV licenses, to develop a *Dennis the Menace* game for the Super Nintendo Entertainment System (SNES), the Nintendo Game Boy, and the Commodore Amiga.[121] Ocean offered a $5 rebate to consumers who purchased the videocassette as well as the game, demonstrating how ancillary products could cross-promote each other.[122] Surprisingly, Warner Bros.' branding was absent from the video game's packaging, and instead, the Hughes Entertainment logo was featured prominently. The connection between Hughes and the *Dennis the Menace* game was reinforced in a cover story in *SNES Force* magazine, which included a three-page feature on the game and a two-page article positioning Hughes as the creative force behind the movie.[123] The coverage illustrated how Hughes's adaptation had reinvigorated the cultural and commercial value of an established character, endorsing his credentials as one of Hollywood's leading creators of family entertainment during the early 1990s.

Although Hughes had acquired a significant reputation within Hollywood and had successfully built his brand around the teen film, his name alone was not a major selling point in the wider, more competitive marketplace. Consequently, his late-1980s comedies, *Planes, Trains & Automobiles*, *The Great Outdoors*, *Uncle Buck*, and *National Lampoon's Christmas Vacation*, harnessed the star appeal of Steve Martin, Dan Aykroyd, John

Candy, and Chevy Chase to mitigate some of the risks created by the filmmaker's move away from teen movies. Casting a star, as Paul McDonald notes, not only deploys the performer's individuality as "a means of product differentiation and product assurance" but also "immediately imports a known set of meanings from other films."[124] *Uncle Buck* arguably marked the zenith of this approach, with Hughes and Candy both working to ensure a strong symbiosis between performer and role. Adopting a perspective shared by many other critics, *Boxoffice*'s Jim Kozak proclaimed: "As designed by Hughes and embodied by Candy, Buck is a grand, classic creation."[125] The box-office success of both *Uncle Buck* and *Christmas Vacation* confirmed, within the space of a few months, that Hughes could develop comedies with broad, cross-generational appeal. Star power was by no means a predictor of hit status, however, as the mediocre box-office performance of Universal's *The Great Outdoors* demonstrated.

While none of the movies that Hughes released through Universal and Warner Bros. in the late 1980s and early 1990s could match the commercial performance and cultural impact of his 1991 hit *Home Alone*, they played an important role in the development of his brand as a filmmaker after his move away from teen films. How Universal and Warner Bros. positioned his films in the theatrical and video markets reflected their wider corporate agendas as well as their growing investment in family entertainment and Hughes's career progression. The relative creative freedom that Warner Bros. gave Hughes on *Curly Sue* was a by-product of his elevation to Hollywood's top tier after the global box-office success of *Home Alone*. Warner Bros.' decision making also seemed to reflect the major embarrassment caused by the studio's refusal to fund *Home Alone*. Its increased deference to Hughes's instincts suggested that studio executives were wary of making the same mistake twice. As *Curly Sue*'s box-office debut demonstrated, however, Hughes's involvement did not guarantee an immediate theatrical hit. Warner Bros.' careful management of the film's release showed that the distributor played a crucial role in maximizing box-office returns. Similarly, Warner Bros.' strong presence in the increasingly crucial home-video market helped maximize the revenues generated by *Curly Sue* on video.

Warner Bros.' decision to place Hughes at the center of its Family Entertainment brand in the mid-1990s not only demonstrated the studio's belief in the commercial value of family films but also provided confirmation of the successful reorientation of Hughes's brand from teen to family audiences. Warner Bros. positioned *Dennis the Menace* as a major release, supported by an elaborate publicity campaign and a sizable production budget. As I will discuss in chapter 6, the package that Hughes assembled and the style of the film, which he closely supervised, reinforced the studio's efforts to present it as both an upscale contemporary family film and a piece of nostalgic Americana. *Dennis the Menace* also clearly fit within Warner Bros.' plans to use family films to further develop ancillary markets. The fact that the character of Dennis was an established brand provided reassurance at a time when the risk of unprofitability made Hollywood studios cautious about licensing products for unknown films.[126]

The Hughes Entertainment and Warner Bros. partnership also suggested the importance of "brand values" when publicizing family-oriented products. As Hughes moved into family-film production, he repeatedly asserted his affinity with Middle America by highlighting his midwestern roots and his status as a family man. Although he received some negative press regarding his professional behavior during the early 1990s, interviewers consistently presented him as an average man who "exudes wholesome, conservative, family values."[127] Responding to criticism that he peddled "movie-length TV shows off an assembly line," Hughes professed, "I'm a guy who walks around malls that writes movies for other people who walk around malls."[128] The filmmaker maintained a certain level of consistency across his family films during the early 1990s by recycling and reworking particular narrative tropes and themes. As I will show in the next chapter, Hughes and his collaborators deployed their stylistic and narrative strategies to create a frequently nostalgic vision of family life that reinforced "traditional" values while acknowledging certain changes in American society. These changes, and the issues they raised, were typically explored through a mixture of comedy and sentiment. Crucially, the movies delivered a predictable set of pleasures to cross-generational audiences, with Hughes's name and the Hughes Entertainment brand acting as guarantees of a certain level of quality in an increasingly diverse family-entertainment marketplace.

CHAPTER 6

PRESSURES OF PARENTHOOD AND FANTASIES OF CHILDHOOD

John Hughes conceived of the majority of his movies of the late 1980s and early 1990s as family films. Heather Addison proposes that the family film is "a broad category of films designed to appeal to children."[1] Peter Krämer, however, differentiates between the children's film ("films made specially for children") and family films ("those films aimed at both children and their parents") but notes that "there is considerable overlap between the categories."[2] The family-adventure trend of the 1980s played a key role in cementing this distinction. Rather than trying to target children and adults separately, Noel Brown notes, these blockbuster movies relied on "largely undifferentiated modes of address" that assumed "audiences of all ages may be engaged by similar, but specific, patterns of fantasy."[3] Blockbusters such as *E.T.* (Steven Spielberg, 1982) and the *Indiana Jones* series (Steven Spielberg, 1981–1989), emphatically demonstrated the commercial rewards that this textual strategy could generate. In the subsequent decade, Robert C. Allen argues, the use of the term "family film" shifted from designating "films addressed exclusively at children" to indicating those with cross-generational appeal.[4] Hughes's movies of the late 1980s and early 1990s clearly fit within this revised definition of the family film.

Hughes explained in interviews that he felt a movie had to hold the interest of both adults and children in order to be a genuine family film.[5] Creating cross-generational appeal was, however, a difficult balancing act. Pressures to appeal to adults' and children's interests led to variations in the textual concerns and primary address of Hughes's family films. His late-1980s movies, *The Great Outdoors*, *Uncle Buck*, and *Christmas Vacation*, rely primarily on an undifferentiated address to avoid alienating adults, who constituted the comedians' main fan base. Children still constituted most of the audience for family films, however, meaning that elements designed to appeal to adults typically had to work alongside more child-friendly content.[6] Hughes's early-1990s films discernibly shift toward a dual address that tries to engage adults and children separately. *Curly Sue* offers a mix of child-oriented action and comedy alongside a romantic comedy plot aimed at adults. *Beethoven* and *Dennis the Menace* focus their attentions on entertaining younger and preteen children, primarily through comedy and cuteness, but still feature relatively developed adult characters who are often experiencing professional and parenting dilemmas. Hughes's work thus shows the breadth and flexibility of the family film genre.

Hughes's creative contributions to most of his late-1980s and early-1990s films were as screenwriter and producer or executive producer. As with his teen movies of the 1980s, there are clear thematic consistencies between the films, similarities that encouraged associations with Hughes's wider body of work. Family unity, childhood, and American suburban life—concerns that had been at the core of Hollywood family films for decades—are thematic preoccupations of his movies. Hughes's family films engage with the genre's key themes in different ways, responding to cultural changes and wider trends in Hollywood cinema. Although they negotiate social changes, as Noel Brown observes, family films nonetheless tend to "nostalgically and defiantly evoke utopian family ideals."[7] Consistent with Richard Dyer's observations on entertainment in general, the utopian sensibility of family entertainment is rooted "in the feelings it embodies."[8] The emotions associated with family and childhood in Hughes's movies are linked with ideological values and with more general expectations about family films, such as the happy ending. As Brown suggests, "Almost all family films attempt to elicit pleasurable emotional responses in audiences, especially feelings of comfort, reassurance, and even happiness."[9]

With their heart-warming resolutions that celebrate family unity, Hughes's family comedies are prime examples of the genre's conservative tendencies. Through their representations of childhood and families, Hughes's family films participate in wider debates in American mainstream and political culture. During the early 1990s, argues Andrew Hartman, Republicans remained anxious that "the America of the conservative imagination was dead or dying," despite their dominance of the political sphere throughout the previous decade.[10] They believed themselves to be fighting, as the Republican Patrick Buchanan put it in 1992, a "cultural war" that was a "war for the soul of America."[11] "Family values" became a key battleground in this ideological conflict. President George H. W. Bush's aspiration to make American families "more like the Waltons and less like the Simpsons"—said in a speech at the same national convention where Buchanan delivered his "culture war" jeremiad—echoed conservatives' nostalgic view of America's past in its celebration of a traditional, white, patriarchal family that remained stoic in the face of extreme hardship. The ideal of the nuclear family seemed increasingly distant, however, from the realities of American life. The divorce rate in America climbed during the 1970s and 1980s, leading to changes in the constitution of families and their living arrangements.[12] In addition, the feminist movement had shifted women's expectations of marriage and their domestic situations, as well as their wider roles in society. Hughes's representations of families, whether by accident or design, engaged with these social and cultural contexts and, therefore, the politics that underpinned them.

The Pressures of Parenthood

Hughes tackled family dynamics in his teen movies, in both comical and dramatic ways, albeit from a teenage perspective. In those films, the family provides a realistic backdrop to the suburban characters' lives but remains a moderately stable entity against which the teenagers must define themselves. As he moved away from teen films in the late 1980s, Hughes started to place greater emphasis on the family as a whole and on the relationships between parents and preteen children. In doing so, he was revisiting themes and tropes explored in his earlier screenplays for *National Lampoon's Vacation* and *Mr. Mom*. Hughes's first two postteen movies, *Planes, Trains & Automobiles* and *She's Having a Baby*, which were primarily addressed to adults, present the family from the father's perspective. In the case of the former, the protagonist, Neal Page (Steve Martin), is a beloved husband and father driven by his desire to return home to his wife and three children. His white upper-middle-class family, which lives in a large house in a highly affluent Chicago suburb, primarily serves a symbolic function. The film's idealized vision of family life reflects Neal's status and successful pursuit of the American Dream. Toward the end of the movie, his wife and children are glimpsed in hazy cutaway shots while sitting at the dinner table, immaculately dressed, awaiting the return of their patriarch. In contrast, his companion, the traveling salesman Del Griffith (John Candy), lacks both a family and a home. The conclusion of the film, which shows Neal welcoming Del into his home, confirms that the "traditional" family and the nostalgic values attached to it are to be celebrated.

The Great Outdoors, *Uncle Buck*, and *National Lampoon's Christmas Vacation* represent a clear shift in Hughes's screenplays toward stories that are *about* families, rather than simply featuring families. Much like his earlier movies, these films focus on fathers or, in the case of *Uncle Buck*, an uncle turned father figure. Consistent with the marketing logics that shaped the productions, the performances of the star comedians (Dan Aykroyd, John Candy, and Chevy Chase) are brought to the fore, with ample opportunities for them to parade their specialized traits and strengths as performers. Displays of the comedians' skills are often shown in scenes that emphasize the men's childlike qualities and tendencies to abandon civilized behavior, suggesting that fatherhood is less about innate ability and more about the acceptance of certain responsibilities and constraints. The sibling rivalry and class differences between Roman (Aykroyd) and Chet (Candy) in *The Great Outdoors* fuel numerous comic situations as the men revert to their childhood roles. They are forced to reconcile their differences and to embrace their adult obligations when Roman's twin daughters fall down a mine shaft and a bear attacks the cabin with their families inside. In contrast, *Christmas Vacation* suggests the overzealous embrace of fatherhood can unleash comic mayhem. The pressure that Clark Griswold (Chase) puts on himself as a father to create "the most fun-filled old-fashioned family Christmas ever" fuels his descent into anarchic irrationality.

Fatherhood thus proved a fertile source of comic possibilities for Hughes as he moved away from the teen film. In her review of *Christmas Vacation*, the *Washington Post*'s Rita Kempley remarked, "John Hughes . . . definitely has a way with the foibles of parenthood. Whether it's *Uncle Buck* or *Mr. Mom* or the booby-footed Clark, Hughes has found an irresistible formula in fatherly ineptitude."[13] *Uncle Buck* was a turning point in Hughes's work, offering glimpses of how intergenerational family dynamics can create humor, especially when precocious preteen children are involved. Buck (Candy) has deliberately avoided adult responsibilities while indulging in adult vices, including drinking, smoking, and gambling. As his girlfriend Chanice (Amy Madigan) wearily explains, "Buck's a man who wants to remain a boy forever." Buck's reluctance to talk down to children and his ability to share their sense of fun allows his preteen nephew and niece, Miles (Macaulay Culkin) and Maizy (Gabby Hoffman), to become more fully realized and significant characters than children in Hughes's earlier films. Candy's performance is key in facilitating these comic incidents, signaling the importance of the interplay between the adult and child performers on screen. Moments such as Miles's interrogation of his uncle and the conversations he shares with the children in the car highlight the comic potential of interactions between children and adults. Hughes proceeded to mine this rich seam of humor in his early-1990s family films.

Curly Sue stands apart from many of Hughes's family

films because it centers on a single-parent family. The homeless drifter Bill (Jim Belushi) has assumed the role of primary caregiver for Sue (Alisan Porter), despite possibly not being her biological father. Such a portrayal of a lone father figure was uncommon in the Hollywood family film, even though nearly a quarter of American children were being raised in single-parent households during the early 1990s.[14] *Curly Sue* does not advocate for the single-parent family, however. Instead, the narrative centers on the creation of, as Warner Bros.' publicity put it, "a real family."[15] Much like *Pretty in Pink*, *Curly Sue* presents the single-parent family as dysfunctional. Bill fails to conform to the dominant societal view of fatherhood because, despite the love and emotional support he gives Sue, he struggles to act as a provider. Although his joblessness would have been credible in the context of the early-1990s recession, the narrative suggests that he is unemployed by choice. Only once Bill has committed to working for a living can he become Sue's father. Fatherhood in Hughes's earlier films is an unquestioned norm, but in *Curly Sue* it is contested terrain, reflecting wider debates concerning masculinity and the role of fathers in contemporary families.

Reflecting the complex discourses surrounding fatherhood in the early 1990s, George (Charles Grodin) in *Beethoven* has to sacrifice his business ambitions in the interests of family unity but nonetheless retains his patriarchal authority. The relationship between George and his family gives *Beethoven* much of its structural logic. His character arc concerns not simply developing a bond with the dog, but also his pursuit of his family's respect and affection. His family is largely oblivious of his efforts to walk, feed, and clean up after their slobbering St. Bernard. Instead, George's anger and frustration at the dog are a source of comedy. Although he works hard to give his wife, three children, and large dog a middle-class lifestyle, his family is unsympathetic to his struggles. The father's pursuit of success in business is, in fact, disrupting family life, as he dedicates more of his time to work and expects his wife to join him. Despite his attempts to impose control, George lacks authority and masculine power for most of the film. When he punches a man and then jumps through a widow during the film's climax, his children are impressed at how "awesome" he is, and his wife says, "I've never found you more attractive." George finally proves that he can protect his family and embody a more physically aggressive form of masculinity. *Beethoven* therefore suggests that a modern father needs to be both strong and sympathetic to his family's needs.

In *Dennis the Menace*, it is Mr. Wilson who assumes the role of patriarch, allowing the movie to showcase Walter Matthau's talents. Mr. Wilson embodies a more traditional form of masculine authority than Dennis's permissive father (Robert Stanton), who remains peripheral to the narrative. The elderly man's fraught relationship with Dennis (Mason Gamble) allows for an exploration of paternal feelings and responsibility, and of the heartbreak of involuntary childlessness. In a touching scene between Mr. Wilson and his wife, it transpires that they had always wanted children. A rare orchid that he has maintained for forty years represents a diversion from their inability to have a child. When Dennis distracts a crowd awaiting the orchid's ten-second bloom, Mr. Wilson angrily tells the boy that the orchid "means more to me than you ever will" and says, "I don't want to see you. I don't want to know you." When Dennis runs away following this confrontation, the elderly man realizes that he cares for the boy and that his priorities were confused. Mr. Wilson's newfound enthusiasm for caring for the boy after they are reunited marks a new chapter in the older man's life. *Dennis the Menace*'s resolution suggests that children provide adults, no matter how old, with a sense of purpose and meaning.

Parenthood and child care are nonetheless gendered issues in Hughes's movies. As the focus of his family films shifted to children, motherhood became a more prominent narrative trope. Mothers in Hughes's earlier films remain at the margins of the narrative, perhaps with the exception of *Mr. Mom*, which shows a woman returning to work. Women tend to exist primarily as mothers to teenagers and children or as wives to hapless men. Little consideration is given to the mothers' motivations or to the possibility that motherhood is a heterogeneous experience shaped by personal decisions and external pressures. But the trope of balancing child care and family with work later became a central narrative concern in several of Hughes's films, including *Beethoven, Curly Sue,* and *Dennis the Menace*. By the early 1990s, women's work-life challenges were an increasingly relevant issue because over half of women with children under ten were employed outside the home.[16] These films probe "the problem of 'choice' for women either between motherhood and a career or to take the plunge and try to have it all," described by Imelda Whelehan as "one of the most confused themes in postfeminist discourse."[17] The characters' varied attitudes toward their careers and families reflect the muddled and often contradictory perspectives that surrounded motherhood and work at the time.

Curly Sue's Grey (Kelly Lynch) is presented as a steely, driven lawyer whose dedication to her career has led her to neglect her relationships and dismiss the possibility of having a family. In an early scene, she pressures a woman into divorcing her husband, telling her: "If you want sympathy, you won't get it here. If you want emotion, I'm not an emotional person." As she bonds with Sue and weathers a series of crises, Grey undergoes a transformation from childless yuppie to mother—a common trope in 1980s and 1990s Hollywood cinema. She also falls in love with Sue's homeless guardian, Bill. Such cinematic romances reflect a wider set of postfeminist discourses, argues Diane Negra, and "regularly include a retreatist epiphany in which the professional woman comes to realize that the self she has cultivated through education and professionalization is in some way deficient unless she can rebuild a family base."[18] Reflecting her emotional awakening to the importance of motherhood, Grey sheds the masculine traits she has adopted to succeed in business and shuns her power suits and severe hairstyle for a more relaxed, "motherly" look. Significantly, when Grey resigns her job to spend more time with her new family, Hughes's screenplay makes it explicit that her embrace of a more traditional domestic life is redemptive. Her boss tells her, "You got your value system all screwed up somewhere along the line." To which she replies, "It was screwed up before."

Figures 6.1a and 6.1b. From career woman to mother: Grey (Kelly Lynch) in *Curly Sue*.

Beethoven, which Amy Holden Jones cowrote, asserts that a mother's decision to stay at home and raise her children is in the family's best interests. Alice Newton (Bonnie Hunt) repeatedly expresses doubts about returning to work at her husband George's rapidly expanding business. Consistent with wider societal discourses, *Beethoven* frames child care as a woman's issue, although it was, and remains, a major societal issue in the United States.[19] Alice's fears are confirmed when, while under the supervision of an adult babysitter, her youngest child, Emily, nearly drowns. By returning to the workplace and delegating her child care responsibilities, the mother put her child in mortal danger. In response to the babysitter's suggestion that the children need "a little discipline," Alice says, "What these children need is their mother." Her guilt prompts her to return to her role as a homemaker. After their unsuccessful attempt to woo some yuppie investors, Alice says to her husband, "If I had been home instead of helping you impress those morons, Emily wouldn't have fallen in the pool. . . . I'm not reentering the workforce." Conveniently, the family's affluence means she can choose to remain at home. Although *Beethoven* presents Alice Newton's decision to remain a stay-at-home mother as an active choice, her maternal guilt and her insistence that children should be looked after by their mother appeal directly to conservative visions of motherhood.

Whereas *Beethoven* presents working and motherhood as incompatible, *Dennis the Menace* acknowledges that the family's financial situation forces the mother, Alice Mitchell (Lea Thompson), to return to work. Consistent with a wider trend in the Hollywood family film, the movie suggests that she is capable of adequately nurturing her child while pursuing a career.[20] The director, Nick Castle, still makes it clear, through close-ups of her pained facial expressions, that she would rather stay at home with her son and that she feels guilty for leaving him with the Wilsons. This distress echoes that of Alice Newton in *Beethoven* and contrasts starkly with Grey's enthusiastic pursuit of a high-powered career in *Curly Sue*. Unlike the Newton children in *Beethoven*, Dennis is safe and properly cared for while under the supervision of his neighbors. Moreover, Alice Mitchell does not blame herself for Dennis's disappearance, nor does the film link his behavior with her return to work. In fact, the movie suggests that mothers can be assets in the workplace. Alice demonstrates a talent for real estate development, despite her yuppie colleague Andrea's hostility toward her as a working mother. Her experience as a parent enables her, much like the mother in *Mr. Mom*, to offer unique insights into consumer behavior. Moreover, Alice can pursue her career because the company agrees to keep her on a local project and offers to set up a day care center at the office. *Dennis the Menace* therefore provides a utopian solution to Alice's problems rather than meaningfully addressing the difficulties faced by women in the workplace. The film therefore exemplifies Hughes's use of fantasy in family films as a way to resolve widespread and challenging social issues on an individual level.

Fantasies of Childhood

The representations of children in *Curly Sue*, *Beethoven*, and *Dennis the Menace* were produced and consumed against a backdrop of major ideological battles over childhood that were enmeshed with political debates on the state of the American family. During the late 1980s and early 1990s, conservatives weaponized childhood innocence, claiming that minors needed to be protected from myriad threats, including progressive politics, drugs, and popular culture. At the same time, Republicans were calling for children who committed crimes to be tried as adults.[21] Progressives, with different priorities, used discourses of innocence to critique the encroachment of commerce into childhood. This pervasive notion of the child as innocent, argues Henry Jenkins, strips children of their agency and "presumes that children exist in a space beyond, above, outside the political."[22] Similarly, the universalizing nature of representations of childhood, Jacqueline Rose observes, "conceals all the historical divisions and difficulties" in which children are implicated.[23] Although Hughes and his collaborators avoided making blatant pronouncements about childhood, his family films confirm innocence as a shared ideal in American culture while simultaneously acknowledging that children are social beings with a certain degree of agency.

Curly Sue portrays the fragility of childhood innocence through its precocious protagonist, who has not been protected from economic or social realities in recession-era America. Nine-year-old Sue is a miniature adult with street smarts and a fairly cynical worldview. Like Addie in *Paper Moon* (Peter Bogdanovich, 1973), Sue pretends to be a naive young girl in order to scam adults out of money by manipulating their perceptions of childhood innocence. At the same time, Sue possesses many tomboyish traits, which she perhaps developed to help her survive on the streets. Her parents have abandoned her, and she thus lacks "the luxury of being femininely passive, delicate and naïve."[24] The film presents her precocity as a symptom of her dysfunctional social situation and as something beyond the limits of "normal" girlhood. Scenes of Sue experiencing hardships, including sleeping in a shelter, along with the revelation that she is illiterate, suggest that she needs to be protected from the harsh reality of the streets and given an education. Moreover, Sue's cuteness, which Hughes emphasizes throughout the film via close-ups, signals her innate innocence and speaks to an adult desire to protect and cherish the child. After establishing that Sue needs "rescuing" from her current situation, the film in its second half focuses on integrating her into an affluent heterosexual family, thereby reinstating her innocence.

Innocence and its precariousness take on a gendered resonance in *Curly Sue*. The film's opening sequence suggests that Sue hankers after a life that will allow her to express her femininity. Scored by Georges Delerue's highly sentimental music—all strings and flutes—a montage of close-ups shows Sue's hands as she plays with the contents of her bag, which is decorated with an assortment of ribbons, swatches of fabric, and badges. Her personal treasures include spinning tops, an empty pink party popper, plastic bangles and necklaces, a scarf, sequins, and a variety of small plastic toys. This insight into Sue's private world supports Grey's claims that the girl has a right to a proper childhood and that Bill's use of the child in his scams is ethically questionable. By the film's conclusion, Sue has been transformed from a tomboyish con artist, clad in a tank top and trousers held up by suspenders, into a regular middle-class girl who goes to school and wears pantyhose. Michelle Ann Abate argues that during the 1990s, "pretty tomboyism" ensured that displays of femininity counteracted the active traits associated with tomboys.[25] This representational shift ended the tomboy's association with marginal racial and sexual identities in cinema, reclaiming her for the mainstream.[26] Sue loses many of her active traits, but appears happy to receive the material comforts that her adoptive mother provides and willing to comply with the rules she had previously broken. At the end of *Curly Sue*, Sue's girlhood has been reclaimed as well as her childhood.

Hughes suggested that *Dennis the Menace* is "about incidents, really wonderful observations about family life and life at five years old."[27] His decision to focus on a younger child allows the movie to sidestep some of the anxieties that surround the representation of older children in films such as *Curly Sue* and *Beethoven*. Making Dennis younger, observes Filipa Antunes, "ensures the child conforms to notions of innocence and vulnerability from the start," rather than requiring the film to directly affirm these values through the narrative.[28] Dennis and his friends are much more innocent and naive than the preteens in *Curly Sue* and *Beethoven*, and they therefore appeal to adults' visions of an ideal childhood. For example, when Dennis and his friends discuss where babies come from, they conclude that a minister and a doctor install a baby through the woman's "belly button." *Dennis the Menace* offers a much more sentimental and nostalgic view of childhood than Hughes's other family films do. The world that Dennis and his friends inhabit is an extremely idealized space. The children play alone in the woods, where they use tools and paint to fix up a tree house without adult assistance. One evening the neighborhood kids play hide-and-seek in the street. Such representations contrast with the reality of many childhoods in the early 1990s, a period when children's play became increasingly regulated, directed, and contained.[29]

Dennis the Menace also presents a highly gendered view of suburban American childhood. The film signals this overtly through the children's clothes, interests, and behavior, which hark back to the postwar era. Dennis's striped T-shirts and overalls and Joey's cowboy hats and Cub Scout uniform reflect their fondness for active, outdoor play. Margaret likes highly feminine flouncy dresses and playing house. Unlike the comic strip and the TV show, the 1992 *Dennis the Menace* film downplays anxieties surrounding boyhood and masculinity. Henry

Jenkins observes that the 1950s–1960s version of Dennis "spoke to boys and their fathers about shifting conceptions of gender, about male fears about a loss of heroic status, the adoption of greater childrearing responsibilities, flight from domestic containment, and anxieties about the formation of gender and sexual identities."[30] Instead of engaging with these tensions around boyhood and masculinity, Hughes's movie invokes an imagined time when "boys were boys" and children's gender roles were more clearly delineated. In a conversation with Joey and Margaret, Dennis suggests, "Men have better things to do than looking after babies." Margaret replies, "Like what? Play golf and drink beer?" Dennis, whose understanding of manhood has clearly been shaped by an engagement with "boy's" popular culture, explains, "No. Having wars, driving cars, shaving, cleaning fish."

Dennis the Menace deliberately frames five-year-old Dennis's mischief as entirely without malice. Anticipating criticism of the slapstick violence in the film, Hughes claimed, "His pranks basically come out of innocence."[31] The character of Dennis fits within a tradition of the "good bad boy," who, Leslie Fielder suggested, symbolizes "authentic America, crude and unruly in his beginnings, but endowed by his creator with an instinctive sense of what is right," and whose innocence offsets his boisterous behavior.[32] The loose structure of the first half of *Dennis the Menace*, with its freestanding comic incidents, reflects Dennis's spontaneity and playfulness. The boy's attempts to solve problems in logical ways create many of the gags, and he rarely shows awareness that his actions could have negative consequences. In an early scene, he shoots an aspirin down Mr. Wilson's throat with a slingshot because he thinks his neighbor is sick. In another scene, Dennis squirts Mr. Wilson's nasal spray all over the bathroom, so he replaces it with mouthwash. He then realizes the mouthwash bottle is empty, so he fills it with toilet cleanser. As well as being the main source of comedy in the movie, these scenes help establish Dennis's boisterous nature, innocence, and innate goodness, rendering his actions in the film's slapstick climax as playful rather than malicious.

Children are not as central in *Beethoven* as in the movies that Hughes produced and released through Warner Bros., because the father, George, is the protagonist. Thanks to their strict upbringing, George's children are peculiarly wholesome and compliant. But the narrative suggests that this overbearing approach to parenting has limited the confidence of the two older children and distanced them from their peer groups. Compared with her classmates, the older sister, Ryce, is naive and often childlike, despite being a young teen. She dresses conservatively in skirts, turtleneck shirts, and cardigans, frequently adorned with floral prints. Even her crush on a boy is presented as largely innocent. Ted, a preteen, still sleeps in his parents' room when he has nightmares, and the other boys bully him for being a nerd. Both Ryce and Ted struggle socially because of their inability to meet gendered adolescent norms. They do not have to change their behavior radically, however; their issues are resolved, in a relatively sitcom-like fashion, through interventions by Beethoven, the dog. In this tiptoeing around issues related to adolescence and gender, *Beethoven* illustrates the difficulties of representing older children in PG-rated family movies aimed particularly at preteen audiences.

Suburban and Small-Town Utopias

Hughes's tales of American families typically unfold against the backdrop of affluent suburban neighborhoods, which are presented as places of comfort and security and the ideal locations for family life. A "timeless" visual style complements this emphasis on the suburban idyll. This contrasts with Hughes's teen films, which use carefully curated costumes, props, and settings to create a fresh, contemporary feel. This shift in visual style is especially visible in *Dennis the Menace*, with its marked adoption of an overtly nostalgic aesthetic that celebrates the small town as an authentically American space. The imagery of the small town and the associations it invites were several decades in the making, but became a potent national symbol during the 1980s and 1990s. Ronald Reagan's presidential campaign advertisements relied on the evocation of a mythical

small-town America, offering viewers a heady mix of nostalgic Americana, optimism, and patriotism. These commercials "sold an experience" of America, observes Erica H. Seifert, that many Americans found comfortingly familiar, although few of them lived in such idyllic surroundings.[33] The small town, suggests Ryan Poll, "is a complex national form that blurs the boundaries between fantasy and reality, ideology and history, counterfeit and original, general and specific, fiction and non-fiction."[34] Hughes's family films are implicated in this shared but somewhat illusory vision of the "real America."

While ostensibly set in the present day, *Dennis the Menace*

Figures 6.2a–6.2d. Small-town America: the opening shots of *Dennis the Menace*.

is a wistful fantasy of small-town life set in an extremely affluent, predominantly white neighborhood in Chicago's North Shore. The movie's affectionate portrayal of suburban life was due in part to Hank Ketcham's influence over how his comic strip characters should be presented on-screen. The cartoonist's insistence that no profanity be used around women or children, for example, led Walter Matthau to joke to *Variety*, "This movie is 'family values' all the way down the line."[35] In a promotional interview, Hughes explained his vision for the film: "It's very familiar, it's very simple, it's small-town life. It isn't necessarily American small town. It's life in a village. It's where you know everyone. You know your neighbors and trust your neighbors, rely on your neighbors, and they rely on you. And I think that's kind of fading away, and it's strange that this does seem like a far-off place, but in fact it was once common.[36] *Dennis the Menace* thus reflects a desire to return to an imagined American past. The movie opens with a shot of a deer grazing in the woods below a tree house. The sequence that follows includes shots of the tranquil countryside surrounding Dennis's town, a decidedly Capra-esque Main Street, and, finally, two large houses in a leafy suburban neighborhood. The film, as *Boxoffice*'s Mari Florence noted, suggests "a fondness for a time gone by, an era of simplicity," and relies heavily on borrowing and adapting "elements of accumulated popular culture."[37] This was a deliberate aesthetic choice. The press kit for the film explained: "The filmmakers strove to present a sense of timelessness in the film by showing a mixture of familiar objects that set the story in 1992, but don't look deliberately contemporary."[38] This use of intertextuality and the reworking of tropes are typical of how many popular films during the 1980s and early 1990s created "ahistorical nostalgic spaces" instead of faithfully re-creating the past.[39]

In many respects, *Dennis the Menace* embodies a postmodern sensibility through its deliberate use of intertextuality to create a sense of what Fredric Jameson refers to as "pastness."[40] Although the pre–World War II small town acts as a major reference point, Jim Bisell and David Willson's production design and Bridget Kelly and Ann Roth's costume designs allude to a variety of historical periods. In its inclusion of styles from the 1950s and 1960s, the movie invites associations with the television series *Dennis the Menace* (1959–1963), which was rerun on cable channels during the early 1990s and became familiar to baby-boomer parents and their children. Dennis's mother's style is inspired by the 1950s; Alice Mitchell sports a wavy, bleached blond hairstyle and often wears A-line dresses made from fabrics associated with the period. The look also recalls

Thompson's most famous role, Lorraine in *Back to the Future*, adding a further layer of intertextual association. At the same time, recognizably modern features such as telephones, plastic toys, and contemporary cars suggest that the movie is not set in the past. The diegetic music also makes it difficult to position the film in a specific period. Music from the 1990s is noticeably absent. Mr. Wilson is associated with music that was popular in the 1940s, including James Young's "Whatcha Know Joe" and the Glenn Miller Orchestra's "A String of Pearls." The Orlons' 1962 single "Don't Hang Up" scores a montage of Dennis's parents calling every babysitter in town. In its evocation of nostalgia from numerous periods, *Dennis the Menace* not only attempts to suggest timelessness, but also seeks to appeal to a wide age range—from grandparents to small children.

Beethoven's depiction of affluent suburban life draws on a set of images similar to those in *Dennis the Menace*, even though Hughes had no involvement in the former film's production. The Newtons' suburban neighborhood features Colonial-style houses with manicured green lawns, set back from wide tree-lined streets. The small town is surrounded by lush countryside untouched by urban sprawl. Its pleasant, picture-book Main Street includes a traditional bakery, a barber, a toy store, a pet store, and a firehouse. When Beethoven escapes from his enclosure, smiling members of the community greet the dog with gifts of food, reflecting Main Street's dominant cultural status as, states Ryan Poll, "an avowed space of benevolence, authenticity, and community."[41] This familiar iconography can serve a range of purposes, but in family entertainment it typically suggests more abstract ideas involving community, family, and American identity. The similarities between the setting of *Beethoven* and those of Hughes's other movies illustrate how a set of images relating to suburbia and the small town was widespread in American cinema and culture at this time.

Even when Hughes briefly abandoned the suburban setting in favor of downtown Chicago in *Curly Sue*, he used the location to stress the link between the family, childhood, and suburbia, as well as to reinforce the film's overall messages concerning childhood and parenthood. The urban environment inhabited by homeless Sue and Bill is dirty, cold, and potentially dangerous. Scenes of the pair walking through blizzards, loitering in alleyways, and sleeping in a homeless shelter show that the inner city is not a suitable place to raise a child, and confirm that Sue needs to be rescued from her current situation. Doug Kraner's production design contrasts this vision of poverty with Grey's excessively privileged lifestyle. Her spacious apartment, situated in a period building, is tastefully decorated and filled with expensive furniture and accessories, including a grand piano. Her immaculately organized kitchen contains highly curated bourgeois food. Grey's urban home thus reflects her prioritization of her career and material wealth over romantic relationships and motherhood. After Sue, Grey, and Bill become a family, the film's closing sequence unfolds in their new suburban neighborhood as they arrive at Sue's school in a large family car and wave good-bye to their contented daughter on her first day. Suburbia, suggests the conclusion of *Curly Sue,* is still the most appropriate place to settle down as a family.

External Threats to the Family

In *Beethoven* and *Dennis the Menace,* criminals who breach the suburban idyll and pose a danger to the middle-class family trigger the events that lead to the films' violent slapstick climaxes. Both films therefore affirm another prevalent conservative discourse: that the biggest threats to suburban family life come from outside, rather than inside, the family. To no small extent, the confrontations between main characters and clearly defined "bad guys" allowed the movies to replicate the narrative formula that helped make *Home Alone* wildly successful. While it may have been a prudent commercial move, this approach stimulated a debate around the levels of slapstick violence in the films. *Entertainment Weekly,* for example, asked, "Is *Beethoven* too violent?" and suggested the "kids movie" might "be too much for some families to handle."[42] In contrast, the *New York Times*' Caryn James tried to ease parents' fears, suggesting that "the film's comic tone promises everything will turn out all right, largely because of its cartoonish danger."[43] *Entertainment Weekly*'s film and video reviewers also condemned *Dennis the Menace*'s "complacent kiddie brutality" and "lurid violence."[44] Downplaying such criticisms, Hughes stated, "I'm not gonna ask you to bring your kids to see my movie if I wouldn't bring my kids. If it isn't appropriate for mine, it certainly isn't going to be appropriate for yours."[45] While the violence in these films proved divisive, it nonetheless plays a significant role in how the films tackle the apparent dangers that the villains embody.

In its choice of villain, a sinister vagrant named Switchblade Sam (Christopher Lloyd), who arrives via the railroad, *Dennis the Menace* hints at the potential for members of the underclass to infiltrate middle-class communities and homes. Consistent with the representational strategies used in *Dennis the Menace*, the villain's status as an outsider is signaled overtly. Sam's dirty, unkempt appearance and his cigarette smoking indicate that he does not meet the standards of suburban life. His lack of personal hygiene contrasts with the cleanliness of Dennis, who is shown splashing about in the bathtub on more than one occasion. While Switchblade Sam is Hughes's creation, his choice of a drifter as the antagonist in *Dennis the Menace* is consistent with the attitude that Hank Ketcham's comic strip displayed toward people who did not fit into the suburbs. Lynn Spigel argues that in the comic strip, "these misfits were drop-outs (always single men) who served no purpose in the social maintenance of family life."[46] Consistent with the viewpoint adopted in several of Hughes's screenplays, the film moves beyond simply suggesting that Sam is unsuited to the suburban environment and positions him as a threat that needs to be neutralized.

Dennis the Menace goes to great pains to establish Switchblade Sam as a thief. Numerous scenes show him stealing handbags and burglarizing houses to steal jewelry and other personal items. On several occasions, Sam watches children without their parents' knowledge. Shortly after his arrival in the town, he swaggers along the backyards on Dennis's street, trampling flowers and blowing cigarette smoke into the clean air. He looms over a small boy, who is shirtless, watching him as he plays with an apple on the other side of a white picket fence. The brief interaction that follows suggests that Sam's interest is in the apple, which he jabs out of the child's hand with his switchblade. In a later scene, Sam loiters by a playground and watches children play on the swings while their mothers' backs are turned. A point-of-view shot suggests he is primarily interested in a purse attached to a stroller, but the other shot compositions in the sequence emphasize that his activities are clandestine. In these and other sequences, the cinematography and editing position Sam as a voyeur, but the action and dialogue deny that he is a pedophile. Nonetheless, there is some merit to James Kincaid's argument that the film has a "child molester" subtext.[47] These moments in the film raise the specter of pedophilia in order to deny it. As the *Washington Post*'s Rita Kempley put it, "A child molester? Not in a Hughes movie."[48]

While Switchblade Sam's motives remain ambiguous, the climax of *Dennis the Menace* clearly indicates that the threat he poses to suburban life should be dealt with robustly. Following an altercation with Mr. Wilson, Dennis runs away. As he rides his bicycle through the misty and eerily lit woods, he is grabbed by Sam, who suddenly jumps out from the shadows. The tramp tells Dennis that he is his "hostage," which the boy assumes is a game. In the scenes that follow, Dennis ties Sam up, feeds him a large quantity of baked beans, knocks him unconscious, and sets him on fire. As with the incidents involving Mr. Wilson, the gags are set up by Dennis trying to solve specific problems rather than intending to injure his kidnapper. Dennis makes Sam eat the beans so that they can find the key to the handcuffs, which he dropped in the cooking pot, and he covers Sam with a blanket so that he will not get cold, but accidentally drags it across the open fire. By keeping the boy's innocence intact, the film disavows any particular agenda for the slapstick violence wrought by Dennis. Nonetheless, at the end of the film, Sam is paraded, bloodied and bruised, in front of the neighborhood to the cheers of the assembled children and adults. *Dennis the Menace* leaves little ambiguity about whether the homeless man deserves his painful fate.

Figure 6.3. Thief or voyeur? Switchblade Sam (Christopher Lloyd) lurking in *Dennis The Menace*.

Characteristic of *Beethoven*'s even more simplistic narrative and worldview, the film's choice of villain is more functional. The antagonist is a corrupt veterinarian, Dr. Varnick (Dean Jones), who performs experiments on animals, aided by his two incompetent henchmen, Vernon and Harvey. A modern take on the "mad scientist," Varnick dresses like a typical family vet but has a sinister smile, and his large spectacles distort his maniacal eyes. The director, Brian Levant, uses techniques from the horror genre, such as low angle shots and uplighting, to accentuate Varnick's creepiness, particularly when he threatens animals. This exaggerated presentation of an obvious villain contrasts with that of Switchblade Sam, whose ambiguous motives are a source of anxiety and whose mere presence disrupts a small-town paradise. Varnick's downfall is depicted in a highly cartoonish way, in keeping with his larger-than-life portrayal as a villain. After the vet kidnaps Beethoven, George and the family rescue the dog just as Dr. Varnick is poised to shoot him in the head. Multiple syringes containing brightly colored sedatives fly through the air and stab Varnick in the chest. The movie's conclusion confirms that Varnick and his accomplices, who were attacked by a mob of dogs, survived their injuries and were sent to prison for their crimes. This ending not only provides reassurance for children in the audience, but also underscores the moral message of *Beethoven* and confirms that the justice system has dealt with the criminals robustly.

Hughes began his transition away from teen movies and toward family films by focusing on the trials and tribulations of contemporary fatherhood. Besides allowing him to create movies that benefited from the star power of Steve Martin, John Candy, Dan Aykroyd, and Chevy Chase, this approach enabled him to shift the thematic focus of his movies onto family dynamics. Fatherhood in these films is not a natural state, but is instead linked with the acceptance of responsibilities that limit a man's personal freedom and more childlike tendencies. As the films' ambivalent representations of fathers suggest, the maintenance of family life is a struggle and a conscious choice. The narratives all work to ensure that these men mature and that they focus on their children and wives. They also often feature fathers displaying their masculinity by, for example, facing up to wild bears, threatening unruly teenage boys, and dominating other men. With the exception of Neal Page's family in *Trains, Planes & Automobiles*, all the suburban families in Hughes's late-1980s and early-1990s movies are sites of conflict, even if they are framed comically. Through the narratives' focus on reuniting families, the underlying message in these films is that family unity is a desirable state lying at the core of suburban American life.

During the 1990s, Hughes increased the emphasis on children in his films. Consequently, they display a greater narrative engagement with concepts of innocence and the shaping of childhood by social and cultural forces. While the narrative of *Curly Sue* gives Sue a certain degree of agency, it also shows that she needs rescuing from her dire circumstances and, significantly, that she can experience a proper girlhood only if she is raised in an affluent nuclear family in the suburbs. In contrast, *Beethoven* noticeably glosses over how children are affected by their social environment and, instead, frames all three Newton children as innately innocent. Similarly, *Dennis the Menace* sidesteps any concerns about contemporary childhood and instead goes to great lengths to suggest Dennis's innocence. Whether this seemed plausible to audiences is less certain. *Boxoffice*'s Mari Florence, for example, argued that the original Dennis's innocence "cannot be translated to present-day or understood by Dennis' '90s contemporaries."[49] Dennis's naiveté is significant because the filmmakers use it as an alibi for the slapstick violence against Switchblade Sam. To sustain this illusion, the film's conclusion makes it clear that Dennis has not been negatively affected by his experiences. Even after his abduction, he is still the same happy and mischievous boy that he was at the start. Through these differing representations of childhood, Hughes's Universal and Warner Bros. family films demonstrate that children's innocence needs to be shored up in the family film rather than taken for granted.

As Hughes focused increasingly on children, his films engaged more with motherhood and its significance. *Curly Sue* uses the creation of a reconstituted nuclear family to address the apparent breakdown of traditional American family values and issues of poverty during the early 1990s. By structuring the narrative around Grey's gradual shift to a more maternal role and by framing her choices as empowered, the film disavows any overt condemnation of her earlier, career-oriented choices. Nevertheless, by implying that true fulfillment can come only from being a mother and a wife, *Curly Sue* reinforces conservative values. *Beethoven* goes a step further in its advocacy for traditional gender roles, implying that Alice Newton's return to work endangered her children's lives. Finding this conservative representation of motherhood jarring, "like a rotten apple dropped into a bag of Halloween candy," the *New York Times*' Caryn James asked, "Who is responsible for sneaking in its insidious social message?"[50] While the screenplay was cowritten with Amy Holden Jones, who had a significant role in shaping the movie after Hughes's departure from Universal, the underlying sentiment is not distant from that expressed in Hughes's other family films. Although *Dennis the Menace* does not punish Alice Mitchell for her return to work, her guilt is a key theme, and her professional identity is linked with her role as a mother.

While Hughes's early-1990s family films engage with a variety of cultural discourses on parenthood, childhood, and the family, the families in question are white, affluent, and headed by heterosexual parents. This "ideal" family is common to many Hollywood movies of the period.[51] Although both *Uncle Buck* and *Curly Sue* feature alternatives to the traditional family, these films conclude by showing a reformed and functional nuclear family. Social problems affecting families in the United States in the early 1990s, such as poverty, unemployment, inequality, inadequate provision of child care, and child abduction, are alluded to in these movies. More often than not, however, the narrative resolutions of Hughes's Universal and Warner Bros. family films reinforce conservative ideologies concerning children and the family. Through their reliance on spectacle and the stimulation of emotion, family films, as Peter Krämer notes, "offer themselves as a temporary relief from the real-life problems which their stories focus on but can never solve."[52] While Hughes's Universal and Warner Bros. family movies thus offer glimpses of the realities of family life, they ultimately retreat to reassuring fantasies of unity and stability played out in an idealized suburbia. As I will detail in chapter 8, this fantasy of the ideal American family runs through Hughes's 20th Century Fox family films, too. Starting with *Home Alone*, his Fox movies marked a major turning point in his filmmaking and arguably represented the commercial pinnacle of his career. Hughes's Universal and Warner Bros. movies nonetheless helped lay the foundations for his move into family films and, as the 1990s progressed, acted as a barometer for his status in the American entertainment industry.

CHAPTER 7

FAMILY FILM FRANCHISES

20th Century Fox (1989–1997)

Released by 20th Century Fox in November 1990, *Home Alone* (Chris Columbus, 1990) "stunned Hollywood executives by laying to waste every huge-budget action blockbuster and sure-fire sequel aimed at the movie-dense Christmas season."[1] Written and produced by John Hughes and directed by Chris Columbus, the family comedy starred the child actor Macaulay Culkin as a nine-year-old who has to protect his house from invasion by two burglars after being accidentally left at home during the holidays. *Home Alone* combined Hughes's observational humor and festive sentiment with large doses of broad, slapstick comedy. A strong adult cast, including Joe Pesci, Catherine O'Hara, John Heard, and Daniel Stern, and good production values helped elevate the movie above the level of most family-oriented fare. Against a production budget of $18 million, the movie grossed over $285 million in its domestic theatrical run and remained in theaters for over thirty weeks.[2] It grossed a further $190 million overseas, making it Hughes's first film to demonstrate major international appeal.[3] No one in the industry, including Hughes and his collaborators, predicted that the mid-budget family comedy would be a major box-office hit. *Home Alone*'s considerable worldwide earnings transformed both Hughes's career and Hollywood's view of family entertainment during the early 1990s.

Hughes immediately sought to capitalize on his box-office credentials and his reputation for "speed and diligence" in order to obtain a new, lucrative contract with one of the major Hollywood studios.[4] After two months of dialogue and a "bidding war" between News Corporation's 20th Century Fox and Sony Corporation's Columbia Pictures, Hughes signed a non-exclusive seven-picture deal with Fox in mid-April 1991.[5] *Home Alone* was a decisive factor in negotiations; by the start of April 1991, the movie had already grossed $250 million at North American theaters, and it was predicted to generate over $350 million worldwide.[6] Securing a contract with Hughes became a major goal for Fox. Even News Corp.'s chairman, Rupert Murdoch, was involved in the process, alongside the studio's chairman, Joe Roth.[7] The deal with Fox, valued at over $200 million, made Hughes one of the highest-paid and most powerful filmmakers in Hollywood.[8] According to *Screen International*, the pact entitled him to fees totaling between $11 million and $12 million, excluding payments for participation.[9] Given that most top-end producers during this period received fees of around $500,000 per picture, such large sums of money demonstrated how highly Fox valued Hughes.[10]

Hughes occupied an especially privileged position in Hollywood during the early 1990s. For one thing, the costly deal between Hughes and 20th Century Fox appeared to contradict prevailing industry attitudes and business strategies. The major studios and their parent companies faced renewed financial pressures during this period, especially because the mergers of the late 1980s had burdened them with considerable debt. Fox was no exception, and both the trade press and mainstream newspapers dedicated extensive coverage to News Corporation's financial situation.[11] Most of the studios claimed that they were reluctant to enter into major deals with filmmakers due to "cost-cutting," especially following the commercial underperformance of several movies created by highly paid filmmakers, such as *Bonfire of the Vanities* (1990, Brian De Palma), *Revenge* (1990, Tony Scott), *Alice* (1990, Woody Allen), and *Avalon* (1990, Barry Levinson).[12] Industry commentators remained skeptical, however, that the studios were pursuing genuine reform; one *New York Times* report suggested that "Hollywood's new austerity seems to be more rhetoric than reality."[13] Hughes's deal with Fox demonstrated the lengths to which the major companies would go to secure filmmakers who could create movies with global, cross-generational appeal. Referring to Hughes's new contract, the *Los Angeles Times* commented, "If the age of the Hollywood mega-deal is really over, 20th Century Fox Film Corp. apparently hasn't heard the news."[14]

After *Home Alone*'s exceptional success, Fox and the other major studios were, as *Variety* put it, "frantically searching for the next 'little comedy' with colossal attraction."[15] Comedies were, however, a relatively risky enterprise. As *Variety* pointed out in June 1991, they were difficult to develop, often unsuccessful abroad, and lacking in prestige.[16] Consequently, Hollywood executives favored investment in established comedy filmmakers, which meant that Hughes, along with the likes of the producers Ivan Reitman and the Zucker brothers (of *Airplane!* fame), found himself in high demand. Even investing in well-known names did not guarantee success, as Hughes's own track record showed. The Ed O'Neill vehicle *Dutch* (Peter Faiman, 1991), written by Hughes and released by Fox in July 1991, starkly illustrated the dangers of overinvesting in a comedy. With a $20 million budget, the film, more adult oriented than the usual Hughes family fare, flopped domestically and had "almost no foreign potential," making it a "total write-off."[17] As Hughes's other box-office triumphs and failures showed, the family comedy market remained unpredictable. Fox nonetheless remained convinced of Hughes's commercial acumen. Moreover, the incentives for investing heavily in movies with potential cross-generational appeal extended beyond the box office. Hughes's family films suited wider corporate agendas, particularly American firms' attempts to acquire "family-friendly" reputations.

Whether by luck or design, the early 1990s marked the culmination of Hughes's strategic pursuit of creative control and commercial power within the US film industry. His deal with 20th Century Fox led to the creation of the most expensive and highly publicized movies of his career, *Home Alone 2* (Chris Columbus, 1992), *Baby's Day Out* (Patrick Read Johnson, 1994), and *Miracle on 34th Street* (Les Mayfield, 1994). 20th Century Fox's heavy investment in these films stemmed from more than just its confidence in Hughes's abilities as a screenwriter and producer; the studio also wanted to quickly exploit the emerging family entertainment trend. Production cycles, as Amanda Ann Klein observes, "exist to capitalize upon the success of a particular cinematic formula," and their commercial exploitation therefore hinges on the ability to release films rapidly.[18] Consequently, Fox deferred to Hughes's instincts and granted him a high level of autonomy, allowing Hughes Entertainment to steer production. The filmmaker was thus able to achieve a certain degree of uniformity across his family films. But this also led to spiraling production and marketing budgets as Hughes and Fox sought to differentiate his films in a crowded marketplace and surpass his previous hits.

Family Entertainment: Sell-Through Video and Merchandising

Family entertainment fit with 20th Century Fox's ambitions at the start of the 1990s. After the company's purchase by Rupert Murdoch's News Corp. in 1985, Fox wanted to become a leading entertainment company in an increasingly globalized marketplace. Despite a few major hits, such as *Aliens* (James Cameron, 1986), *Big* (Penny Marshall, 1988), and *Die Hard* (John McTiernan, 1988), the film studio had struggled to make an impact at the US box office during the late 1980s, lagging behind Paramount, Warner Bros., and Disney.[19] The studio nonetheless provided News Corp., which had a foothold in over fifty countries, with content and brands it could sell worldwide. Consequently, synergy was an integral part of Fox's corporate strategy during the 1990s, even though the formula for successfully exploiting films in a range of markets frequently remained elusive. Fox became increasingly preoccupied with the branding of films and the repurposing of them in a range of contexts. The simple concepts and striking imagery typical of family films, as well as the traditional "values" associated with the genre, fit within these commercial agendas. As Paul Grainge observes, "Family entertainment has been at the forefront of Hollywood's contemporary industrial strategies and branding efforts."[20] But it was not until *Home Alone* became a major hit that the studios began to consider live-action family comedies as potential global brands with significant commercial prospects beyond their American theatrical distribution.

During the early 1990s, the major studios focused on shifting the home-video market from rental to sell-through. According to *Billboard*, "key sell-through ingredients" included "wide kid appeal, comedy, and repeatability."[21] Hughes's family films had these features in abundance, making them strong candidates to be sell-through releases and appealing prospects for major corporations. FoxVideo, a Fox subsidiary founded in 1991, supported the video releases of Hughes's 20th Century Fox family films with ambitious marketing and distribution strategies. Through FoxVideo, the studio moved toward a strategic approach to marketing films in a global marketplace and disrupted some of the orthodoxies of the home-video business. Mirroring the studio's increasingly elaborate marketing campaigns for theatrical releases, the video distributor expanded advertising exposure and stimulated sales in sophisticated ways. During the early 1990s, FoxVideo aggressively pursued tie-ins for family and child-oriented videos, securing deals with food and beverage manufacturers, toy companies, and numerous other corporations looking to connect with families and young consumers. These influential promotional partners gravitated toward sell-through releases, further encouraging FoxVideo to adopt this pricing strategy.[22]

The home-video release of *Home Alone* in August 1991 signaled FoxVideo's ambitions for Hughes's movies. The distributor developed an extensive publicity campaign, prompting *Billboard*'s Paul Sweeting to remark that "the size of the promotion and the multiple sponsors come as a surprise."[23] FoxVideo secured contracts with Pepsi and American Airlines to develop tie-ins and provide additional publicity, making it the first movie on VHS to have multiple sponsors.[24] FoxVideo, Pepsi, and American Airlines, whose pooled marketing budgets came to an estimated $25 million, developed a coordinated marketing campaign that promoted both the movie and their products.[25] Pepsi, the videotape's primary sponsor, positioned the *Home Alone* tie-in as the climax of the "Pepsi Summer Chill Out" promotion, which included a nationwide contest with $74 million in prizes.[26] Pepsi spent $40 million on advertising for the promotion, $16 million of it on television advertisements for the *Home Alone* tie-in specifically.[27] The company funded a $5 rebate on the video for consumers who bought a two-liter bottle of soda, and supplied display materials for the *Home Alone* tie-in to forty thousand retail outlets.[28] American Airlines provided gift certificates for family-travel discounts and featured advertisements for the video in its in-house publications and in-flight videos.[29] In exchange for their promotional support, the sponsors' logos were featured prominently on the video's packaging, and the videotape began with a thirty-second commercial for Pepsi and a ten-second "tag" for American Airlines.[30] Fox, Pepsi, and American Airlines all benefited from the exposure created by cross-promotion of the *Home Alone* video.

In addition, FoxVideo recognized that family entertainment suited the changing retail environment for home videos in the 1990s. The market leaders Blockbuster, Walmart, and Kmart made no secret of selecting product lines to attract a notional "family" audience and offend as few people as possible. From the outset, Blockbuster placed considerable emphasis on its family-friendly policies. In 1988, Blockbuster instituted its trademarked "Youth Restricted Viewing" program, which both required store clerks to demand to see the IDs of young people trying to rent R-rated movies and enabled parents to block their children from renting movies in certain categories.[31] The corporation refused to stock X-rated movies or pornography and, in January 1991, confirmed that its stores would not carry videos with the NC-17 rating.[32] To sustain its family image, Walmart

Figure 7.1. Relive the fun: flyer advertising *Home Alone* on video.

was, as Barney Warf and Thomas Chapman note, "notoriously vigilant about 'protecting' consumers from products the management deems offensive, a strategy in keeping with the conservative campaign to 'protect family values' in the United States."[33] In 1992, Walmart and Kmart, too, decided not to stock NC-17 videos. Consequently, Fox and the other Hollywood studios were highly conscious that family-oriented videos rated G or PG would "gain better placement in a Kmart, Target, or Wal-Mart."[34] This awareness incentivized 20th Century Fox's continued investment in family films, including Hughes's movies, and led FoxVideo to factor these retailers' priorities into video release strategies.

FoxVideo's retail strategies for the *Home Alone* video reflected the growing importance of supermarkets and nationwide rental chains and the diminishing influence of independent retailers. To encourage stores to buy *Home Alone* in bulk, and in an attempt to regulate how the product was sold, FoxVideo offered retailers a "pre-pack floor display" that featured the movie's branding and included free posters for consumers.[35] To create buzz, FoxVideo embargoed sales of the video until its national release date of 20 August 1991 and "affixed large warning stickers" to that effect to shipping boxes.[36] But some retailers ignored the embargo, claimed *Billboard*, and released the video early in order to gain an advantage over their competitors.[37] Blockbuster used its substantial resources to undercut competitors' prices. The chain ordered large quantities of the *Home Alone* video and sold them at $17.95 a copy. If consumers used the Pepsi rebate, they could effectively purchase the tape for $12.95.[38] Smaller outlets could nonetheless profit from *Home Alone* because the video's low price allowed them to acquire a large quantity of rental stock.[39] In the two years following its release, American consumers purchased more than eleven million copies of *Home Alone* and, according to FoxVideo's estimates, rented the video almost nineteen million times.[40]

The burgeoning licensed-products market provided further opportunities for Fox and Hughes Entertainment to profit from the success of Hughes's family films. Although licensed products based on movies were potentially risky investments, the promotional benefits were significant for toy manufacturers, whose marketing resources were a tiny fraction of those of the major Hollywood studios. The success of tie-in toys hinged on several factors, including the film's theatrical performance, the timing of the toys' release, adequate availability of the toys, and the inherent appeal of the toys. Even if a movie was a box-office hit, toy manufacturers had to confront, as Janet Wasko puts it, "the real difficulty of translating film fantasy into popular products."[41] One medium that seemed particularly promising, in this respect, was video games. During the early 1990s, Hollywood executives showed greater interest in game tie-ins for major movies, and video game manufacturers expressed a renewed desire to collaborate with Hollywood.[42] Following a series of high-profile congressional hearings on video games in 1993, game companies such as Nintendo were particularly motivated to bolster their family-friendly credentials. The purchase of licenses based on Hollywood family films was an expedient way to for them to demonstrate their commitment to family entertainment. With these business incentives in mind, after the success of *Home Alone*, a range of companies approached Fox to purchase licenses for products linked to Hughes's family films, most notably *Home Alone 2*.

Kiddie Slapstick: *Home Alone 2*

Speculation about a sequel to *Home Alone* began in March 1991, when the project's fate was closely tied to Hughes's contract negotiations with the major studios. Once Fox had finalized Hughes's deal, the studio secured Macaulay Culkin's commitment to the project. Fox reportedly promised the child star a fee of $5 million for the movie and 5 percent of the film's adjusted gross.[43] In what the *New York Times* described as "an unusual show of zeal," Fox hired the same cast and crew that had worked on the original, "virtually down to the last gaffer and grip."[44] The entire central cast remained the same, although some experienced character actors joined the ensemble, including Tim Curry, Brenda Fricker, and Eddie Bracken. Chris Columbus returned as director, Julio Macat as cinematographer, Raja Gosnell as editor, Freddie Hice as stunt coordinator, John Williams as composer, and Jay Hurley as costume designer. John Muto, the production designer on *Home Alone*, was the most senior member of the original team who did not return for the sequel. The similarities between *Home Alone 2* and its predecessor were not limited to the cast and crew, however. In a November 1992 article, Hughes explained that in order to satisfy his audience, he deliberately constructed a narrative that was very similar to that of *Home Alone*: "I had to make a story using the same characters in the same situation with the same antagonists."[45] Thus, Hughes and Fox ensured that the sequel replicated many of the elements that had presumably contributed to the original movie's success.

Fox supported *Home Alone 2*'s theatrical release with an extensive marketing campaign. The studio secured over $20 million of promotional support from corporate partners, which matched the studio's marketing budget.[46] The primary corporate sponsors were American Airlines and Coca-Cola, both of which wanted to expand their appeal to American families. American Airlines, which is featured prominently in the movie, provided additional advertising and promotions, including discount vouchers for family flights. Coca-Cola built a campaign around Sprite in an attempt to "reinvigorate the brand and put Sprite's romance with moms and the family back on track."[47] Harnessing the appeal of the film's preteen star, Coca-Cola paid Macaulay Culkin over $1 million to appear in a thirty-second commercial for Sprite.[48] The Plaza Hotel, another major product placement in *Home Alone 2*, supplied contest prizes, too.[49] Similarly, the *New York Times* and Bloomingdales supported giveaways.[50] Other promotional partners included Scholastic books and Hardee's and Roy Rogers fast-food restaurants. In addition to using these brands to increase the visibility of *Home Alone 2*, 20th Century Fox promoted the film through divisions within News Corp. The Fox network and Fox's regional TV channels aired "The Making of *Home Alone 2*" shortly before the movie's release, as well as featuring TV spots advertising the film. FoxVideo also included a trailer for the movie on the video of *FernGully*. *Home Alone 2*'s publicity campaign thus demonstrated Fox's efforts to capitalize on synergies within News Corp., as well as on lucrative corporate partnerships.

The level of hype surrounding *Home Alone 2* ensured that expectations were high when the film debuted in November 1992 on over 2,200 screens in the domestic market. Although reviews were mixed, the movie took in $31 million in its opening weekend.[51] During its domestic run, *Home Alone 2* grossed over $173 million and ranked second on the 1992 US box-office chart, after Disney's *Aladdin*.[52] Fox was not, however, solely focused on the domestic market, and consistent with the studio's global ambitions, it released *Home Alone 2* in numerous countries in January 1993. The movie performed very well in Europe, topping the charts in Denmark, France, Germany, Finland, Norway, Sweden, and the United Kingdom. It was also a hit in Australia, Japan, Brazil, and South Africa. *Home Alone 2*'s popularity with overseas audiences was such that its international gross of over $185 million exceeded its domestic earnings.[53] *Home Alone 2*'s box-office success, while not quite of the same magnitude as the original's, validated Fox's substantial investment in the movie and in Hughes's production contract.

Expectations were high when FoxVideo released *Home Alone 2* on video in late July 1993. The distributor mounted a large promotional campaign timed to coincide with summer vacation, and developed bespoke promotions for Target stores and Toys "R" Us.[54] A $16 million advertising campaign supported the release, with sponsorships by American Airlines, Quaker Oats, Mattel's Aviva Sports, and Tiger Electronics. Quaker ran a *Home Alone 2*–themed television advertising campaign. It also featured the movie on fifteen million cereal boxes across the United States and offered a $5 rebate on purchase of the videocassette if consumers showed a receipt for Life cereal.[55] Aviva Sports and Tiger Electronics "tagged" the video in commercials, and American Airlines advertised it in its in-flight magazine and promotional materials.[56] Vouchers for American Airlines family flights and Aviva Sports' toys were enclosed in the videocassette packaging, along with a flyer for Tiger's toys.[57] Commercials for Quaker's Life cereal and American Airlines are featured at the beginning of the tape, in addition to an ad for the soundtrack albums for both *Home Alone* films. Anticipating high demand, FoxVideo shipped 7.5 million videocassettes, worth an estimated $135 million wholesale.[58] Although the video's suggested retail price was $24.98, some stores offered the video for less than $15.[59] Despite being released amid a "flood of family-oriented titles," the video topped *Billboard*'s sales chart for seven weeks and remained in the top 40 for over thirty weeks.[60] *Home Alone 2* was also a popular rental video, peaking at number 3 on *Billboard*'s rental chart during its twelve weeks in the top 40.

Whereas the first *Home Alone* was not heavily merchandised, the box-office potential of *Home Alone 2* enabled Fox to secure numerous licensing and tie-in agreements with major companies. Newspapers noted that thirty-five companies intended to produce 80–100 products using the branding from *Home Alone 2*.[61] Many of these products were fairly typical branded items such as T-shirts, watches, key chains, posters, and bed linens. Fox also issued licenses for Nintendo, Sega, and PC games. Nintendo secured rights during the movie's production and developed its versions of the video game for the Nintendo Entertainment System, Super Nintendo Entertainment System, and Game Boy, whose release was to coincide with the movie's. Far more innovative, and controversial, was the incorporation into the action of *Home Alone 2* of toys that had simultaneously been developed as licensed products. Hughes and executives from 20th Century Fox "worked very closely" with the Illinois-based company Tiger Electronics to create several toys that could be showcased in *Home Alone 2*.[62] A *Los Angeles Times* subhead suggested that through the integration of product placement and merchandising strategies, "*Home Alone 2* May Redefine Merchandising."[63]

The development of the Talkboy cassette recorder for *Home Alone 2* was a remarkably coordinated collaboration between a major Hollywood studio and a toy manufacturer. Consistent with long-standing strategies for selling tie-in toys, Tiger's promotional materials claimed its products could help children extend their enjoyment of the movie. This strategy reflected the American entertainment industry's growing interest in products that, suggests Carolyn Jess-Cook, "are designed to recycle a film's narrative and repeat the spectatorial experience as far as possible."[64] One flyer (fig. 7.2) proclaimed, "Create your very own *Home Alone 2* adventure with these new toys from Tiger!," as well as revealing that the product range included "working replicas of the actual toys Kevin uses in the movie."[65] A basic version of the Talkboy sold moderately well following *Home Alone 2*'s cinematic release, leading to the development of the Talkboy Deluxe, which was closer in appearance and functionality to

Figure 7.2. Your *Home Alone 2* adventure: flyer for Tiger Toys' tie-ins.

the movie prop. The Talkboy Deluxe's box featured a photograph of Kevin McAllister using the toy and included a cassette tape "with real voices from *Home Alone 2*." Although the creators of the Talkboy clearly targeted children, its $34.95 price tag meant that adults had to see some value in the purchase beyond merely satisfying their children's desires. As a portable cassette recorder with an integrated speaker, it had practical features that helped justify its cost. By reflecting on consumer habits, Hughes, Fox, and Tiger had created a highly appealing product that harnessed the popularity of the *Home Alone* films.

The close relationship between Hughes Entertainment, 20th Century Fox, and Tiger Electronics generated significant debate in the American press. As the *Los Angeles Times* reported, the studio faced serious criticism from parents: "At issue is how far some companies will go to cash in on their movies. . . . Some critics view it as product placement at its ugliest."[66] For example, Jeff Chester, the codirector of the Center for Media Education, a Washington-based consumer group, remarked, "With Christmas just around the corner, this is a very, very slick and cynical move on the part of the filmmaker."[67] In response to the negative publicity, Al Ovadia, 20th Century Fox's licensing and merchandising president, asserted that the toys were a fundamental part of the creative vision for *Home Alone 2*. He maintained, "We didn't put them in the movie to sell toys. We put them in the movie because they were necessary elements for the film."[68] Parents' groups and industry commentators remained unconvinced. The controversy surrounding *Home Alone 2*'s promotion of the Talkboy cassette recorder thus demonstrated how overt attempts to market products to children through movies could unleash a barrage of criticism.

Despite the controversy that accompanied its inception, the Talkboy Deluxe became a best-selling toy. Tiger Electronics and 20th Century Fox timed the release of the Talkboy Deluxe to coincide with the video release of *Home Alone 2* in order to facilitate cross-promotion. Tiger "tagged" the video's release in its television commercials, and images and logos from the movie were featured prominently on the toy's packaging.[69] FoxVideo included a flyer for Tiger's *Home Alone* product range inside the videocassette's packaging.[70] In spite of *Home Alone 2*'s popularity, retailers failed to anticipate the popularity of the Talkboy Deluxe, and in the lead-up to Christmas 1993, demand significantly outstripped supply. After receiving orders for millions of units, Tiger Electronics was forced to increase production in Hong Kong, and it stopped airing commercials for the toy.[71] The only stores that continued to receive deliveries were the major chains Toys "R" Us, Walmart, and Kmart, which became the major beneficiaries of the toy's success.[72] To the surprise of retailers, demand for the Talkboy Deluxe continued for several years after the movie's theatrical release.[73] The toy, which was another profitable enterprise for Fox, confirmed Hughes's willingness to explore new avenues for the commercial exploitation and extension of his family films.

Baby's Day Out: A Box-Office Flop

After the success of the *Home Alone* franchise, 20th Century Fox had high expectations for *Baby's Day Out*, Hughes's next project for the studio. Hughes acted as creative producer and screenwriter and appointed Patrick Read Johnson as director. Johnson had previously directed just one movie—the critically panned but moderately profitable low-budget sci-fi parody *Spaced Invaders* (1990), which he also cowrote. Hughes had originally hired Johnson to direct *Dennis the Menace* at Warner Bros. but fired him over creative differences. Despite this apparent rift, a year later Hughes asked Johnson to direct *Baby's Day Out* on a "pay-or-play deal," which entitled him to payment even if he was released from the contract.[74] After the box-office success of *Home Alone 2*, Fox remained confident of Hughes's instincts, approving a blockbuster-level production budget of $50 million for the project, despite Johnson's inexperience and the film's lack of major stars.[75] The money was spent on "one of the biggest sets ever built" and "the most visual effects and stunts ever utilized on a Hughes movie," including computer-generated imagery and "eleven different mechanical dolls."[76] The sizable budget showed that Fox was willing to gamble on Hughes's ability to create another box-office hit of the same magnitude as *Home Alone*, despite the increased competition for family audiences.

Whereas Fox was able to capitalize on *Home Alone 2*'s status as a sequel to the highest-grossing comedy of all time, *Baby's Day Out* was based on an original concept. By emphasizing the movie's special effects and high production values, Fox aimed to differentiate it from the growing number of low- to mid-budget family and child-oriented comedies that recycled *Home Alone*'s pratfalls. In publicity materials, Hughes described the film as "the culmination of all our technological know-how, our stunt skill and our comic talents."[77] The trade press seemed to share Fox's belief in Hughes's ability to create a hit, with *Variety* suggesting that *Baby's Day Out* was one of "the strongest box office contenders" on Fox's production slate.[78] Released on 1 July 1994, *Baby's Day Out* grossed less than $6 million in its opening week in US theaters.[79] *Variety* noted that the movie's weak opening came as a surprise, because "John Hughes's films are usually surefire formulas for printing money."[80] A major disappointment for both Hughes and Fox, *Baby's Day Out* grossed less than $17 million during its domestic theatrical release.[81] By the end of the summer, *Variety* claimed that the movie had lost Fox millions of dollars, noting that box-office revenues "won't even cover marketing expenses."[82]

After the movie's dire box-office performance in theaters, *Baby's Day Out*'s video release in January 1995 became a crucial opportunity for Fox to recoup some of its investment. In remarks to a reporter in December 1994, Hughes predicted, "When it hits tape, it'll be fine—there's some great stuff in it."[83] FoxVideo, which did not share his confidence, initially priced the movie at around $100, as a rental title.[84] Although a growing number of family-film video releases were being priced for sell-through, Fox clearly remained doubtful that *Baby's Day Out* had sufficient mass appeal to sell in large quantities. Despite limited competition, the video failed to make a significant impression in the rental market. It dropped out of the *Billboard* Top 40 chart after just ten weeks and ranked eighty-ninth on *Billboard*'s rental chart for the year.[85] FoxVideo rereleased the video in April 1995, this time priced at $14.98. The distributor also included the video in a promotion that *Billboard* described as "using corporate synergy to create sales" for another expensive family-movie flop, *The Pagemaster* (Joe Johnston and Pixote Hunt, 1994), which offered a $5 rebate to consumers who bought both videos.[86] The sell-through release of *Baby's Day Out* generated enough sales that it peaked at number 11 on the *Billboard* sales chart, although the video lasted only five weeks in the top 40.[87] Video sales helped offset some of Fox's losses on *Baby's Day Out*, but its mediocre performance as both a rental and a sell-through title demonstrated how a movie's theatrical release had a significant impact on its value and success in ancillary markets.

In contrast to *Home Alone 2*, which provided a master class in creating lucrative merchandise, *Baby's Day Out* highlighted how vulnerable toy manufacturers were to box-office failures. Before the film's theatrical release, Fox sold licenses for a *Baby's Day Out* video game to Hi Tech Entertainment, which intended to produce games for the Super Nintendo, Game Boy, and Sega Genesis consoles. Emphasizing its cross-generational credentials, Hi Tech described itself as "a leading worldwide publisher of high quality, interactive software for the entire family."[88] In fact, the company was extremely opportunistic and focused on creating games that used licensed characters or properties. These games were often poorly designed and relied heavily on associations with popular brands to generate sales. Hi Tech originally planned to release the *Baby's Day Out* game during the film's theatrical run, but delayed until the film's video release.[89] In October 1994, the game seemed poised for release; *Entertainment Weekly* reviewed the game, but felt the kidnapping of the baby was "unsettling."[90] Although a trailer for the game appeared on the *Baby's Day Out* video in early 1995, it never went on sale. Hi Tech never disclosed the reason for the game's cancellation, but the movie's weak box-office performance and the prospect of further negative reviews undoubtedly hindered its commercial potential. The withdrawn game acted as final confirmation that *Baby's Day Out* was an expensive failure for both Hughes and Fox.

Remaking a Christmas Classic

While *Baby's Day Out* was in production, 20th Century Fox announced that Hughes would write and produce a remake of *Miracle on 34th Street* (George Seaton, 1947). To ensure that the film had production values befitting of a prestigious release, the studio allocated Hughes a substantial budget of $28 million.[91] Again, Hughes produced the film and wrote the script, which was adapted from George Seaton's screenplay, and Les Mayfield directed. Much like Patrick Read Johnson, Mayfield was a promising but inexperienced director. He too had directed only one feature film, the moderately successful high-school caveman comedy *Encino Man* (1992). Mayfield was an unusual choice for the traditional, festive movie, but again Fox deferred to Hughes's judgment. To generate some early buzz for the movie, Hughes held open auditions to find a young girl or boy to play the central child. An advertisement in the *New York Times* stated, "John Hughes and Twentieth Century Fox are looking for the next child star in New York City" and invited parents to bring children six to eight years old to the casting session.[92] Despite the claim that no previous acting experience was necessary to win the part, from the approximately one thousand girls who auditioned, Hughes and his associates cast an experienced child actor, Mara Wilson.[93] This was the first step in an expensive and highly orchestrated publicity campaign, paid for by Fox, which started in preproduction and continued after the movie's release.

Hughes encountered significant difficulties when Macy's refused to participate in the remake of *Miracle on 34th Street*. The department store was integral to the narrative of the 1947 film, and the press claimed that the store's refusal to appear in the movie was a significant blow to the production, because it would reduce the remake's fidelity to the original. A spokesperson for Macy's declared, "We feel the original stands on its own and could not be improved upon."[94] Hughes observed that Macy's decision was unusual because companies were often keen to appear in mainstream Hollywood movies.[95] Newspapers speculated that the retailer's refusal to participate might have been due to the company's debt of almost $6 billion.[96] Macy's absence increased production costs because it forced Hughes Entertainment to stage and shoot its own Thanksgiving Day parade, closing down a whole block in Manhattan. To help counter the potentially negative publicity created by the setback, Hughes Entertainment released a number of stories that detailed how smoothly the production was going. One such article focused on a deaf girl, Sami Krieger, who featured in a scene in which Santa converses with a child in sign language. Tinged with heartwarming sentiment, the piece described how Hughes Entertainment had "treated Sami like royalty," and promoted the remake's "holiday themes of faith and charity."[97]

To downplay any accusations that the remake was cynically motivated, Fox and Hughes were careful to frame their interest in the project in emotional terms, evoking nostalgia for traditional family Christmases and building on the original movie's status as a "classic." The movie's executive producer, Bill Ryan, reinforced Hughes's suitability for the project and focused on the personal reasons for his involvement in the remake. Shortly before the film's release, Ryan stated, "The film's themes are very dear to John. Faith; believing in people; and the meaning of Christmas, when people go out of their way to help each other."[98] Fox and Hughes also worked to position *Miracle on 34th Street* within a time-honored tradition of festive, family-oriented entertainment by staging the premiere at the 6,000-seat Radio City Music Hall in Manhattan, which members of the public could attend for $25 a ticket.[99] Adopting a format that harked back to the venue's musical hall origins, the event included a thirty-minute live show "featuring favorite scenes from The Radio City Christmas Spectacular" performed by the Radio City Rockettes.[100] Fox hired carolers to greet members of the press at the West Coast premiere, held at the Mann National Theater in Westwood.[101] The press drew attention to the novelty of such publicity strategies and helped reinforce the studio's message by tingeing their reports with nostalgia and pointing to the original *Miracle on 34th Street*'s status as a "Christmas Classic."[102]

Although 20th Century Fox and Hughes Entertainment's extensive prerelease publicity campaign for *Miracle on 34th Street* projected an aura of confidence, the studio was evidently concerned about the film's commercial prospects. The movie's narrower appeal and the weak box-office performance of *Baby's Day Out* led the studio to adopt a cautious theatrical-release strategy. Faced with significant competition for the family audience during the holiday season, Fox opened *Miracle on 34th Street* on only 1,190 screens. The film grossed roughly $4.3 million in its opening week, coming in seventh on the weekly chart.[103] In response to that weak box-office debut, Fox resorted to an "unusual and unprecedented marketing ploy."[104] During the Thanksgiving holiday weekend, the studio guaranteed that customers "not delighted by the film" could receive a full refund.[105] Bill Mechanic, head of the studio, explained, "There are a lot of choices in the marketplace. . . . What we're saying is

'Try it. If you don't like it, you're not out anything.'"[106] National publications printed articles about the promotion, and Fox included the offer in its print advertisements, including full-page spreads in major national newspapers.[107] Although the offer cost the studio tens of thousands of dollars, this sum was meager in comparison with the costs of producing and promoting the movie. Moreover, the stunt generated considerable free publicity for the struggling film.[108]

In spite of a publicity campaign spanning more than six months and 20th Century Fox's ticket promotion, *Miracle on 34th Street* did not become the major hit that Hughes and the studio had anticipated, grossing little more than $17 million during its domestic release.[109] The film fared somewhat better in international markets, where it grossed over $28 million.[110] It proved especially popular in the United Kingdom, where it topped the box office for two weeks in December 1994.[111] The movie's selection as the Royal Film Performance in November 1994, extensive publicity surrounding Richard Attenborough's central role, and the lack of a British release for Disney's *The Santa Clause* (John Pasquin, 1994), which was the movie's main competition in the United States, all contributed to the success of the British theatrical release. A $46 million worldwide gross was not disastrous, but *Miracle on 34th Street* failed to return Hughes to hit-maker status, especially after the costly failure of *Baby's Day Out*.

Despite the film's unremarkable box-office performance, FoxVideo adopted a much bolder strategy for *Miracle on 34th Street*'s video release than it had for *Baby's Day Out*. The distributor tried to stimulate sales of the tape by giving *Miracle on 34th Street* a suggested retail price of $14.95, which some retailers discounted to less than $10.[112] This approach undercut the prices on competing family-oriented releases, including *Batman Forever* (Joel Schumacher, 1995), *The Santa Clause*, and *Little Women* (Gillian Armstrong, 1994), which were priced at around $20.[113] Based on projected sales of eight million cassettes, *Variety* noted that *Miracle on 34th Street*'s home-video profits "could be four or five times" those of the box office.[114] Luckily for FoxVideo, the low-price, high-volume strategy worked. In the absence of other major box-office hits, *Miracle on 34th Street* became Fox's most successful 1995 video release. The distributor sold an estimated seven million copies, and it was the sixth-highest-selling video during the 1995 holiday season.[115] Not only did FoxVideo's aggressive pricing strategy help stimulate sales, according to *Billboard*, but the video also benefited from a "marketing campaign that was better attuned to the VCR crowd than the studio was to theatergoers."[116] The video sold particularly well in the United Kingdom, building on the film's theatrical success in the country.[117] *Miracle on 34th Street* thus became a rare example of a movie that was more profitable on video than at the cinema. Hughes remained, however, under pressure to create another major box-office hit for Fox.

Diminishing Returns: *Home Alone 3*

Home Alone 3 was the last film Hughes released through 20th Century Fox, and it reflected the growing challenges that he and Fox faced in pursuit of the family audience. By the mid-1990s, the filmmaker was struggling to maintain his prolific output, and his efforts were spread among Fox, Warner Bros., and Disney. When Hughes finally did get another movie into preproduction at 20th Century Fox, it was a new installment in his most successful franchise. In 1996, four years after the release of *Home Alone 2*, 20th Century Fox announced that Hughes would write and produce a third *Home Alone* film. Since Macaulay Culkin was sixteen years old and retired from acting, it came as little surprise when the studio confirmed that *Home Alone 3* would feature a new cast and new characters. To stir up interest in the rebooted franchise, Hughes Entertainment and Fox held open casting calls for a "talented, intelligent, and likable youngster" in several major cities, stating, "No experience is required."[118] As was the case with *Miracle on 34th Street*, instead of taking a risk on an unknown child, Hughes cast a professional child actor, Alex D. Linz, in the film's central role. Seven-year-old Linz had recently completed filming on another Fox production, the romantic comedy *One Fine Day* (Michael Hoffman, 1996), and already had numerous television and film credits. Media outlets immediately hailed Linz as "the next Macaulay Culkin," and the film received a publicity boost from numerous profiles of, and interviews with, the child star in newspapers and magazines and on television. It nevertheless remained unclear whether *Home Alone 3* would be able to duplicate the appeal of the earlier *Home Alone* movies.

Fox released *Home Alone 3* during the 1997 holiday season, a time of year that had produced excellent earnings for the first two *Home Alone* films. Despite the absence of major adult stars, the studio showed confidence in the appeal of the *Home Alone* brand by giving the movie a fairly wide domestic release, opening it on 2,147 screens.[119] The studio supported the film's release with a major marketing campaign, including television, radio, and print advertising. Publicity materials featured the same logo used in the first two *Home Alone* movies, reinforcing the film's connection with its successful precursors. The film's main poster carried two taglines, "There's a new kid on the block" and "Ready for more. Much more," which highlighted the new star and suggested that the sequel would surpass the original films. Seizing the opportunity for cross-promotion, 20th Century Fox Home Entertainment (FoxVideo's successor) also rereleased videos of the first two *Home Alone* films late in 1997. Priced at $14.98, the video releases were supported by television advertisements and other publicity materials as well as a $3 rebate offer for customers who purchased both cassettes.[120] The videos not only increased the visibility of the *Home Alone* franchise, but also reminded audiences of the appeal and pleasure of the original movies. Although *Home Alone 3* lacked the anticipation that surrounded the first sequel, Fox clearly remained confident that association with the *Home Alone* brand would help attract sizable audiences.

Although Fox invested in publicity for *Home Alone 3*, it faced considerable competition for the family audience. By 1997, the Hollywood studios' dogged pursuit of those viewers had saturated the market and spawned a large number of *Home Alone* imitators, which eroded *Home Alone 3*'s commercial prospects. One of its main competitors was another movie written and coproduced by Hughes, *Flubber* (Les Mayfield, 1997). The Robin Williams comedy was a big-budget production, supported by Disney's marketing and merchandising machine. The movie's other direct rivals were the live-action comedies *Mr. Magoo* (Stanley Tong, 1997), starring Leslie Nielsen, and *Mouse Hunt* (Gore Verbinski, 1997), starring Nathan Lane, both of which had production budgets similar to *Home Alone 3*'s and featured the same kinds of broad humor and slapstick gags. *Mouse Hunt* had considerable legs: Dreamworks kept the movie in theaters until June 1998, and the film took in over $61 million domestically.[121] In contrast, Disney pulled *Mr. Magoo* after a couple of weeks, and the film grossed just over $21 million.[122] *Home Alone 3* sat somewhere in between the two, grossing over $30 million during its short domestic run.[123]

Twentieth Century Fox Home Entertainment embarked on a major promotional push for *Home Alone 3*'s video release in the lead-up to the 1998 summer vacation period. The increased competition for family audiences at the box office created corresponding pressure on the home-video market, which forced Fox to invest heavily in marketing and pursue numerous corporate partnerships. Some of these promotional activities, such as rebate vouchers for Robotix motorized construction sets and Mega Bloks toys (made by Fisher-Price), replicated the strategies that had proved successful earlier in the decade.[124] Although the video release was not able to attract major partners like Pepsi or Coca-Cola, another soda brand, Sunkist, participated in a tie-in promotion, thereby increasing the video's visibility in supermarkets and convenience stores.[125] Using synergistic cross-promotion, Fox marketed *Home Alone 3* alongside the girl-oriented animated film *Anastasia*, supplying retailers and cable television channels with promotional materials for both videos as well as numerous prizes.[126] Offering a glimpse of the future of family-entertainment marketing, Fox Online Marketing created a dedicated *Home Alone 3* website, which featured a virtual house filled with games associated with the film's narrative. Fox secured numerous promotional prizes to support competitions on the website, including $150,000 toward a new house, Honda dirt bikes, Packard Bell computers, and a variety of toys.[127]

Despite Fox's investment in a variety of marketing methods, the commercial performance of *Home Alone 3* on video was as unremarkable as the movie's box-office returns. The video, priced at $19.98, spent eight weeks on *Billboard*'s Top 40 sales chart, peaking at number 5, and had a modest ten-week stint on the Top 40 rentals chart.[128] While this was by no means a disastrous result for Fox, it was a long way from the chart-topping performances of the first two *Home Alone* films. Clearly, the franchise was generating diminishing returns. Likewise, Hughes's partnership with Fox seemed to have lost momentum, although the home-entertainment distribution rights to his older films remained an asset for the studio. The emerging technology of DVDs presented another opportunity for Fox and the other Hollywood distributors to profit from family films old and new. Reinforcing the continued centrality of family films to Fox's home-entertainment offerings, *Home Alone 3* was one of the first eight movies that Fox released on DVD, in November 1998.[129] Hughes's older movies were also reissued extensively on DVD in the years that followed, but the filmmaker did not play a major role in driving forward family entertainment in the digital age. *Home Alone 3* was Hughes's last Hollywood family film.

Through the extraordinary box-office success of *Home Alone,* Hughes secured his position as one of the most powerful filmmakers in Hollywood. His major 1991 deal with 20th Century Fox was the culmination of a highly successful decade when, through a combination of strategy and serendipity, he consolidated his industrial influence and built a reputation as one of the industry's leading creators of family entertainment. The budgets of Hughes's family films for Fox were significantly larger than those of the movies he had released through Universal and Warner Bros. in the late 1980s and early 1990s, giving them noticeably higher production values than his other work, with the exception of 1994's *Dennis the Menace.* Hughes not only seized the opportunity to create prestigious family films, but also focused on developing marketable "concepts" that could capitalize on the economic and cultural factors behind the growth of family entertainment during the early 1990s. As he had done with his teen films in the mid-1980s, Hughes showed a high level of commercial awareness and developed movies that could be profitable to the studios on video and in other ancillary markets.

Hughes also benefited from 20th Century Fox's global ambitions during the 1990s. With the exception of the first two *Home Alone* films, Hughes's family films were not major box-office hits in the United States. Fox nonetheless invested in relatively wide foreign releases for these movies, spending significantly on marketing campaigns and prints. This outlay offered a clear indication that the studio, in step with wider industry trends, saw family films as a readily exportable and potentially lucrative commodity. As Noel Brown observes, "Hollywood family entertainment has undoubtedly become the material manifestation of a broader universalistic agenda, of which conglomeration, expansion, and synergy are corporate equivalents."[130] The popularity of Hughes's family films in overseas markets helped reinforce the major studios' belief in the commercial viability of family-oriented products. Foreign markets accounted for a significant proportion of the box-office revenues from Hughes' 20th Century Fox movies, as well as his Universal and Warner Bros. family films. These international successes confirmed that Hughes's signature blend of broad slapstick humor, populist sentiment, and nostalgic Americana could attract sizable audiences outside the United States.

Hughes's 20th Century Fox movies proved to be popular on home video. His family films were a good fit for the "values" of chains such as Blockbuster and Walmart, which built their public images around broader notions of family and entertainment. Hughes's movies not only suited this retail environment, but also benefited from FoxVideo's increasingly sophisticated promotional strategies for its North American video releases. Fox's global distribution network ensured that the movies generated substantial revenues in international video markets. Although for most of Hughes's films with Fox, he had minimal involvement in the studio's activities in the video and licensed-product markets, his close collaboration with Fox and Tiger Electronics on the Talkboy's integration into *Home Alone 2* demonstrated his willingness to comply with corporate agendas. The returns from ancillary markets were subject to time delays, however, and gradually accumulated in the years after the films' theatrical releases.[131] While 20th Century Fox may have profited from Hughes's family films eventually, it certainly preferred the rapid injections of cash provided by major box-office hits such as *Home Alone* and *Home Alone 2* to the slower returns from *Baby's Day Out*, *Miracle on 34th Street*, and *Home Alone 3*.

Hughes's reputation was incredibly resilient during the 1990s despite an incredibly mixed box-office record at 20th Century Fox. Although *Miracle on 34th Street* and *Baby's Day Out* were expensive flops, the film industry remained confident in his ability to create major hits. In the summer of 1995, *Variety* asserted, "The Hughes family entertainment machine is capable of hitting warp speed again at any time."[132] While Fox's continued investment in Hughes's projects seemed like a gamble, it was in fact a calculated risk based on the films' value in ancillary markets as well as on their box-office potential. During the early 1990s, the Hollywood studios saw family entertainment as a way to unlock synergies and create partnerships with major corporations. Through the success of the first two *Home Alone* films in particular, Hughes played a crucial role in fueling this production trend. His impact on the film industry at the time went beyond the success of his own movies. Major studios and smaller companies alike released a variety of films aimed at a cross-generational audience, many of which owed a significant creative debt to Hughes's work. In the next chapter, I explore the key textual features of Hughes's 20th Century Fox family films, which not only consolidated Hughes Entertainment's status as a family-oriented brand but also provided a template for many live-action family movies of the early 1990s.

CHAPTER 8

SLAPSTICK, SENTIMENTALITY, AND THE AMERICAN FAMILY

The surprise box-office success of *Home Alone* was a career-defining moment for John Hughes. Thanks to his newfound status as a major industry player, he was able to write and produce big-budget family movies with a relatively high level of autonomy from 20th Century Fox. His contractual obligations to Fox and other studios required him to deliver a large number of films during the early 1990s, and Hughes repeated and reused textual elements as a way to create movies quickly. Such recycling also aided the marketing of him films, providing imagery and themes that could be easily replicated. This tactic was by no means unique to Hughes or specific to 1990s Hollywood. Cinema has always relied on the repetition of elements from earlier texts in order to, as Amanda Ann Klein and R. Barton Palmer suggest, "streamline the production process and capitalize on and exploit viewer interest in previously successful or sensational story properties."[1] The frequency of Hughes's movie releases also helped him react to audience demand.[2] His 20th Century Fox family films introduced a certain degree of textual novelty while retaining elements that Hughes and his collaborators felt had been successful in his earlier work and his projects at other studios. Consequently, the *Home Alone* movies,

Baby's Day Out, and *Miracle on 34th Street* are a relatively cohesive collection of films.

Besides being crucial to Hughes's career trajectory, *Home Alone* provided the template for his subsequent family films. The movie follows the exploits of nine-year-old Kevin McCallister (Macaulay Culkin), whose family accidentally leaves him at home when they go on a Christmas vacation to Paris. The first half of the movie depicts Kevin's enjoyment of his newfound freedom. The second half shows the boy's efforts to prevent two burglars, Harry (Joe Pesci) and Marv (Daniel Stern), known as the Wet Bandits, from infiltrating his house. All the while, Kevin's mother, Kate (Catherine O'Hara), tries desperately to return home. At regular intervals, the film cuts away to scenes of Kevin's family in Paris and Kate's long journey back to Chicago. As well as offering periodic breaks from the rising action of the main narrative, *Home Alone*'s parallel narrative structure allows adults in the audience to identify with the on-screen adults, particularly Kevin's mother. A subplot concerning Kevin's relationship with his elderly neighbor Mr. Marley (Roberts Blossom) provides an additional layer of sentiment as well as adding further adult interest. The film's conclusion shows Kevin reunited with his family and Marley's reunion with his son and granddaughter. This narrative formula proved to be a major source of inspiration for Hughes's future movies. To varying extents, all the family films he wrote and produced during the early 1990s borrow elements from *Home Alone*.

Home Alone 2 is a highly self-aware sequel that deliberately plays with audiences' knowledge of the original film.[3] Set one year after the original, *Home Alone 2* depicts Kevin McCallister's adventures in New York after he accidentally boards the wrong plane at a busy airport shortly before Christmas. After the Wet Bandits and Kevin cross paths again, the focus of the plot becomes Kevin's efforts to foil their attempts to steal charity donations from a toy store. *Home Alone 3*, in contrast, features a different set of characters and has no narrative connection with the earlier *Home Alone* movies. The film focuses on eight-year-old Alex Pruitt (Alex D. Linz), who finds himself in possession of a missile-cloaking chip worth $10 million; he has to defend himself against four international criminals hired by North Korean terrorists. Alex rigs his house with booby traps to repel a possible invasion by the thieves, unleashing slapstick mayhem. Borrowing heavily from the *Home Alone* formula, *Baby's Day Out* follows the events that unfold after three hapless criminals abduct a baby in order to extract a ransom from his millionaire parents. Bennington Austin Cotwell IV, known as Baby Bink, soon evades his captors and goes on a day out in the big city. In their pursuit of the baby, the kidnappers—Eddie (Joe Mantegna), Veeko (Brian Haley), and Norby (Joe Pantoliano)—suffer a variety of physical traumas. All three movies deploy the same basic framework—a child's encounter with incompetent crooks that culminates in a slapstick finale—and conclude with family reunions and the villains heading to jail.

Although *Miracle on 34th Street* was a departure from Hughes's slapstick comedies, it explores themes of family unity, childhood innocence, festive cheer, community, and faith. The film also gives prominence to the feel-good elements of fantasy and sentimentality that were key ingredients in his family comedies. As a remake of the 1947 Christmas classic, it also relies on the logic of repetition. Like the original, the movie combines elements of the family film with melodrama, romantic comedy, and courtroom drama. *Miracle on 34th Street* focuses on six-year-old Susan (Mara Wilson) and her mother, Dorey (Elizabeth Perkins), as they journey toward a belief in Santa Claus after the arrival of Kris Kringle (Richard Attenborough) at Cole's department store. The movie concludes with Susan, Dorey, and Bryan (Dylan McDermott), a lawyer, forming a traditional nuclear family in a large suburban house filled with expensive furnishings, Christmas decorations, and toys. The film's ending not only restores Susan's innocence and belief in Santa Claus but also positions the upper-middle-class nuclear family as an aspirational American ideal, regardless of the realities of American society in the mid-1990s.

Much like Hughes's movies released through Universal and Warner Bros., his Fox family films acknowledge certain changes to the family and childhood. But the movies try to resolve issues arising from these transformations through a combination of slapstick and sentiment. Unusually, these movies harness the power of slapstick to shore up traditional institutions rather than to undermine them. Much like his Warner Bros. family films, Hughes's Fox movies rely heavily on emotion and always conclude with a seemingly heartwarming message about family. The use of sentiment helps offset the slapstick violence while reinforcing the narratives' moral messages. This approach is fairly typical of the family film genre, which uses these kinds of textual strategies to offer straightforward stories that reinforce dominant social discourses and values.[4] In this chapter, I explore how narrative framing and particular elements of film style are used to stimulate emotions and promote childhood innocence, family unity, the sanctity of suburbia, and Christian values in the family movies Hughes released through Fox.

Childhood Innocence and Slapstick Violence

The slapstick violence in Hughes's 20th Century Fox family films is linked closely with their complex and at times contradictory attitudes toward childhood. In *Home Alone,* which served as a model for Hughes's later movies, much of the humor stems from the child's ability to make a fool of adults, inverting real-life expectations of the scenarios presented on-screen. As Robert R. Shandley observes in relation to violence in Looney Tunes cartoons, "The humor derives from the inversion of the relationship in which the would-be predator becomes the prey."[5] The narrative climax of *Home Alone* shows the Wet Bandits falling foul of the booby traps that Kevin has rigged up to defend his large suburban home. Laying the foundations for the comic mayhem to follow, a montage sequence shows the boy gathering items such as glass Christmas decorations, paint cans, an iron, and Micro Machines in order to turn his house into a fortress. Slapstick violence can, as Peter Krämer notes, "realize the destructive potential of the everyday world," revealing "the hidden power of objects as well as the latent aggressions of people" and emphasizing "the vulnerability of the human body and the fragility of the social order."[6] Kevin's ability to weaponize his home in order to repel the Wet Bandits reflects the ambiguity through which *Home Alone* plays with the child's knowingness and innocence.

Home Alone's Kevin is not simply an "innocent" preteen child battling two adult men; he is a precocious, wealthy white boy brutalizing two working-class men who appear to be of Italian and Jewish descent. *Home Alone*'s slapstick finale therefore offers mixed ideological messages. Steven Shaviro argues that "like all forms of the Bakhtinian carnivalesque, slapstick is deeply ambiguous: it is potentially subversive, but at the same time easily recuperable by power."[7] *Home Alone* relies on a simple opposition between good and evil, as Louise Peacock has compellingly argued, and the slapstick climax is executed in such a way as to discourage reflection on Kevin's motivations and the morality of his actions.[8] The film also relies on the assumption that Kevin is justified in using violence to defend his home. American law has long enshrined citizens' rights to defend themselves in their own homes (the "castle doctrine"), and during the 1990s, many states enacted "stand your ground" and other "no duty to retreat" laws. As Richard Maxwell Brown argues, "The notion of no duty to retreat is an expression of American values," and as such, it rests heavily on "concepts of individualism, individual self-determination and the desire to dominate situations."[9] Kevin's actions thus echo long-standing attitudes to self-defense in the United States, and are bolstered by his white upper-middle-class masculinity. His status as a minor, however, has the potential to cause unease because it highlights the incursion of violence into the lives of American children.

While some parents and commentators criticized the comic violence in *Home Alone,* features of the film's climax prevent the movie from becoming, as Marsha Kinder describes it, "a second-grader's version of *Straw Dogs*."[10] Before the burglars' siege commences, Kevin pumps his BB rifle and says to the camera, "This is it. Don't get scared now." This moment reinforces

Kevin's omnipotence and attempts to allay the fears of children in the audience through direct address. The extended slapstick sequence that follows is a tightly choreographed series of sight gags and stunts, clearly designed to elicit laughter. "As long as the viewer is laughing at the burglars' pain," argues Louise Peacock, "then the moral message that Kevin is justified in the means he employs to defend his house is strengthened."[11] The reactions of Harry and Marv are crucial in establishing the cartoonlike tone of the sequence. They register their pain in comically excessive fashion, yelling and doubling up in agony, but then quickly recover. Certain sounds on the Foley track are amplified for comic effect, emphasizing some aspect of each stunt, particularly any moments of impact on the characters' bodies. John Williams's score creates a lighthearted tone, and the editing of the sequence helps pace the stunts so that the audience and, by implication, the burglars have moments of respite from the intense action. *Home Alone* thus relies on exaggeration and fantasy, as well as on a simple moral message, to generate laughter through slapstick comedy.

Although Hughes's later comedies followed the template for slapstick gags provided by *Home Alone*, variations in narrative framing affect the potential ideological significance of the films' comic violence. This is particularly evident in *Home Alone 2*. Rather than defending his home from invasion by the burglars, in the sequel Kevin lures Harry and Marv to a building that he has rigged with booby traps. In contrast to the warm, inviting family home of the first movie, the building is an empty brownstone. The subdued color palette of browns, grays, and blacks, along with the use of muted, low-key lighting, is more suggestive of a horror movie than a family film. Crucially, the new setup means that Kevin's actions no longer constitute self-defense and defense of property. The film's violence is therefore not supported by the same "moral frame" used in the original, which positioned the boy as a "vulnerable victim."[12] Instead, Kevin's vigilante actions are retribution for the burglars' theft of donations to charity and for making death threats against him. Although the slapstick climax of *Home*

Figure 8.1. Laughter and morality: Harry (Joe Pesci) on the receiving end of slapstick violence in *Home Alone*.

Alone 2 is comic in tone, and the gags are cartoonish in their execution, Kevin's sadistic enjoyment of the revenge he wreaks on the burglars highlights the aggression that underscores the action. He is also more directly involved in inflicting pain on the burglars. He throws four bricks at Marv's head from the top of the building; he turns on a generator to electrocute Marv; he sets a rope dipped in kerosene alight while the burglars are climbing down it. In all these instances, close-up shots record Kevin's gleeful satisfaction at having bested his adversaries. At one point he even asks, "Have you had enough pain?!"

Although Macaulay Culkin's blond hair, pouty lips, and wide-eyed expressions, as James R. Kincaid notes, evoke the image of the "adorable" child, Kevin's behavior contradicts this impression.[13] In its depiction of Kevin, *Home Alone* acknowledges that "although they are in some ways children, pre-teens do not fit the assumption of a vulnerable, unconditionally cooperative infant."[14] Despite Kevin's family's perception that he, as his sister puts it, is "little and helpless," he demonstrates that he has the skills needed to look after himself, the ability to outwit adults, and, through his advice to Mr. Marley, a certain degree of emotional sensitivity. Rather than offering a representation of childhood based primarily on adults' nostalgia for their own youth, *Home Alone* provides a more equivocal perspective on contemporary childhood. But the film's "cynicism" toward the blurred boundaries between childhood and adulthood, as Sandra Chang-Kredly argues, does not fundamentally challenge or undermine societal attitudes toward childhood.[15] *Home Alone* nevertheless reveals tensions around the independence and self-reliance of preteen children, particularly through Kevin's defense of property and his acts of consumption.

The climax of *Home Alone 3* aspires to be more fun and less mean than the concluding mayhem of the original films. Unlike Kevin, who immediately takes matters into his own hands, Alex in *Home Alone 3* adopts a more civic strategy by calling the police and the US Air Force to report the criminals. The adults' refusal to believe him forces him to defend himself by using sophisticated booby traps. But the devices' complexity means they are beyond the power of many children to plausibly create, a sophistication that sidesteps the kind of realistic ingenuity present in the original *Home Alone*. The physical gags are also less visceral and much more stylized, featuring special effects such as exaggerated "electricity" and slow motion. The villains' reactions, which are shown in numerous close-ups, suggest surprise rather than pain, and their injuries look much more comical. Moreover, despite their anger at being bested by an eight-year-old, the criminals never pose a serious physical threat to Alex. By relying on absurdity and excess to distance the action from the real dangers that children face, *Home Alone 3* fails to replicate the pleasure of seeing a child defeat adult adversaries and escape potentially life-threatening situations, as seen in *Home Alone* and *Home Alone 2*.

By separating children from their parents and forcing them to defend themselves, the *Home Alone* films provide male preteens with an opportunity to function as self-sufficient and independent people. Robert C. Allen argues that as a consequence, *Home Alone* offers an inconclusive vision of childhood and the family: "While the film appears to maintain that we all need and want families, it also shows us that Kevin does not need his."[16] This goes against prevalent cultural attitudes to children in America, which center on the belief that children should be innocent and dependent. As Henry Giroux argues, "Marked as innately pure and passive, children are afforded the right to protection but are denied a sense of agency and autonomy."[17] The *Home Alone* films play with this tension, attempting to retain aspects of Kevin's and Alex's innocence while giving them a certain amount of freedom. They are not idealized children; they have flaws as well as specific talents and endearing qualities. That said, both benefit from their conventionally cute looks and status as white middle-class boys.

In *Baby's Day Out*, Hughes avoided the issue of the erosion of innocence and the child's intentions by placing a baby in the central role. The film relies on the assumption that Bink is innately pure and blissfully unaware of the jeopardy he encounters or the havoc he accidentally unleashes. Through special effects, including puppetry and computer-generated imagery, the film inserts the baby into numerous scenarios that would be incredibly dangerous (and most likely fatal) in real life. Suspense is a major source of humor, particularly in the extended slapstick sequence on the construction site, which shows Bink eluding his would-be captors through "baby luck." The absurdity of seeing a baby crawling across a busy road or climbing along an iron construction girder is clearly intended to evoke delight and laughter. Unlike much of the violence in the *Home Alone* films, which is perpetrated by the children, many of the physical gags in *Baby's Day Out* stem from coincidence or the criminals' stupidity. So while the bad guys receive their comeuppance, it is not at the hands of a child and remains distant from the kind of real-life retribution perpetrated by real people. The majority of the stunts involving the kidnappers rely on slapstick's characteristic use of "absurdity, lack of reality and excess" in order to create a comic tone and encourage laughter.[18] As the film progresses, the stunts become so spectacular and the physical trauma inflicted on Eddie, Veeko, and Norby becomes so extreme that it turns into a live-action cartoon,

Figure 8.2. Absurdity and spectacle: Baby Bink visits a construction site in *Baby's Day Out*.

clearly divorced from reality. Baby Bink has little awareness of the events unfolding around him and, instead, gurgles and laughs his way through this fantasy world.

The exaggerated, childlike world of *Baby's Day Out* is supported by the movie's overall visual style, which takes its cues from Bink's favorite picture book. Doug Kraner, the production designer on *Baby's Day Out* and *Miracle on 34th Street*, had previously worked with Hughes on *Uncle Buck* and *Curly Sue*. His production design for *Baby's Day Out* mixes styles and signifiers from a range of periods, including the 1890s, 1920s, and 1940s. Consequently, most of the film has a retro aesthetic that, as in Hughes's *Dennis the Menace* and *Miracle on 34th Street*, obscures the period when the film is set. This is in contrast to *Home Alone*, which aspires to visual timelessness without a reliance on mimicry and retains a contemporary edge through its characters and social concerns. By setting *Baby's Day Out* in some "indefinable nostalgic past" that is "beyond history," Hughes and the film's director, Patrick Read Johnson, divorce the film's action from any realistic social or cultural context.[19] As a consequence, *Baby's Day Out* offers relatively limited commentary on contemporary American childhood or the family, in comparison with Hughes's other Fox family movies.

Maternal Responsibility and Guilt

Hughes's 20th Century Fox family films suggest a preoccupation with motherhood, which also permeates *Curly Sue, Beethoven,* and *Dennis the Menace*. To be reunited with Kevin in *Home Alone,* Kate McCallister embarks on a lengthy multistage journey from Paris to Chicago that recalls the trip homeward in *Planes, Trains & Automobiles*. She is aided by the family's wealth, and barters when she needs to by using $500 cash, her Rolex, and her diamond ring. She alone bears the guilt and responsibility for leaving their son at home. The mother's journey acts as a display of maternal penitence and corroborates Molly Haskell's observation that Hollywood narratives emphasize the sacrifices that women make for their offspring, driven by subconscious feelings of guilt about not wanting children.[20] Following her long odyssey, Kate apologizes to Kevin for accidentally abandoning him. Her travails turn out to have been unnecessary, since the family pile in through the front door moments after she arrives. Once his family reappears, Kevin is transformed back into the young dependent child seen at the start of the movie. He has worked through his rebellious urges and released the anger he felt toward his family, and is now willing to reassume his role as his devoted mother's youngest child.

The theme of maternal guilt and martyrdom endures through both *Home Alone 2* and *Home Alone 3*. In *Home Alone 2,* Kate McCallister again shoulders the blame for Kevin's separation from the family. She walks the streets of New York at night, looking for her son and ignoring both her husband's and the Plaza concierge's pleas to remain at the hotel. When Kate and Kevin are finally reunited, in front of the Rockefeller Plaza Christmas tree, he is the first to apologize. Although Kevin has proved yet again that he can look after himself, he still needs to feel cherished and emotionally supported by his mother. The mother-son relationship is also at the core of *Home Alone 3,* with Alex's siblings and father relatively marginal to the narrative. Karen Pruitt (Haviland Morris) is an attentive and caring mother who has a good relationship with her son. Even when Alex gets in trouble with the police, her frustration is relatively mild. As *Variety*'s Joe Leydon mused in his 1997 review, "In recent years, the term 'Home Alone' has been used as a kind of journalistic shorthand for highly publicized cases of child neglect. Perhaps mindful of this, Hughes goes out of his way to justify the convenient absences of Alex's working parents."[21] Karen attempts to stand up to her demanding boss and talks quite candidly with her son about her work situation, provoking his sympathy in spite of his sadness at being left alone. After the film's climax, Alex and his mother are almost immediately reunited, reinforcing both her physical proximity and emotional closeness to her son. In both *Home Alone 2* and *Home Alone 3*, the boys' relationships with their mothers secure their continued emotional dependence on adults.

Whereas children are the protagonists in Hughes's other family films released between 1990 and 1994, Susan is not the lead in *Miracle on 34th Street*. The narrative is focalized primarily through Susan's mother, Dorey. Instead of being introduced as a mother, Dorey is first shown in a professional context, overseeing the Thanksgiving Day parade in her role as Cole's director of special projects. Her status as a working mother is not a problem per se, but the film does not always present her efforts as a lone mother in a particularly sympathetic light. Specifically, Dorey is responsible for exposing her daughter to certain aspects of the adult world, such as the reality of commerce. To restore Susan's childhood innocence, *Miracle on 34th Street* has to first "redeem" her mother. After Dorey rejects Bryan's first marriage proposal, he tells Kris, "She's filled with these bitter thoughts. The worst part is she's dragging Susan into this with her." It transpires that Dorey's husband, whom she married in college, was an alcoholic who abandoned the family after the birth of his daughter. Despite Dorey's resistance to settling into a long-term relationship, *Miracle on 34th Street* maintains her "need for the right man to complete the family ideal" and thus fits within a wider trend in Hollywood comedy, which frames women's career achievements "in traditional family terms."[22] Kris Kringle not only restores Dorey's faith but also contrives for her to marry Bryan, thereby asserting the link between heterosexual marriage, family, and child rearing.

Through its representation of Susan, *Miracle on 34th Street* illustrates how childhood innocence is closely entwined with social status and the idealization of motherhood.[23] Susan, who is largely presented from an adult's perspective, is depicted as an "object of adoration."[24] Much of the light humor in the movie centers on her wry observations, which are not the words or thoughts of a typical six-year-old, as when she discusses the department store's financial situation with Bryan. Clearly, these kinds of jokes would not appeal to children. In American culture, white middle-class childhood represents the epitome of innocence, but at the same time, affluent children are inheritors of their parents' wealth and status. The knowledge that Susan displays suggests that she is being primed to follow in her mother's footsteps. But Susan's precocity sometimes lapses into cynicism, most obviously when she tells Bryan, who is both her babysitter and her mother's boyfriend, that she does not believe in Santa Claus. This loss of belief, which represents the erosion of childhood innocence, is attributed to Dorey's parenting style. Although Susan has adopted certain adult traits, much like Sue does in *Curly Sue*, she also harbors an apparently innate desire for a conventional nuclear family. She tells Kris that she would believe in Santa Claus if she received "a house, a brother, and a dad" for Christmas.

Wealth and Privilege

The suburban family was always at the core of Hughes's films. His signature product was strongly identified with the middle-class inhabitants of Chicago's North Shore or, as one critic succinctly put it, "white suburbia."[25] While this approach enabled Hughes to introduce and develop characters efficiently, it also limited his films' engagement with a wider set of social issues. Criticism of this limited worldview intensified once his movies began to attract larger audiences. In 1994, concerned by Hughes's lack of progress in this area, the Associated Press's Dolores Barclay argued, "John Hughes has an extremely narrow view of America. To Hughes, the only people who exist in this country are white, Christian and privileged, and there's no room for anyone else."[26] Hughes acknowledged these critiques but attempted to justify the absence of nonwhite characters from his films on the grounds that he did not "know the black experience."[27] In fact, he narrowed the focus of his 20th Century Fox family films even further, concentrating exclusively on white upper-class families. *Home Alone* marked a clear shift in Hughes's body of work toward extremely affluent protagonists. The characters' wealthy, often extravagant lifestyles are presented as aspirational, as emblems of the American Dream. This bourgeois world also fit with a hope that the movies would be recognized as "classic" and "quality" family films.

When making *Home Alone*, Chris Columbus (the director) and a carefully selected team of collaborators set out to create a "timeless" look. The McCallisters' large family home in Winnetka, the wealthiest of Chicago's North Shore suburbs, has an elegant, imposing exterior and a lavishly furnished interior. To create a festive atmosphere, John Muto's production design uses a color palette of reds, greens, and golds. The sets are nonetheless sophisticated, and while there are some nods to late-1980s fashions, the overall aesthetic harks back to an earlier era. In capturing these settings, the cinematographer, Julio Macat, deployed fairly classical approaches to composition. His efforts to shoot much of the film "from the perspective of a little kid," by using low and wide shots to create a sense of scale, further accentuated this sense of grandeur.[28] While the pace of editing is rapid at times, particularly in the comedic scenes, the editor, Raja Gosnell, refrained from using any gimmicky transitions or jarring cuts. John Williams's score plays an invaluable role in tying the different elements of the film together. As well as adding to the overall impression of timelessness and festivity, the nondiegetic music helps accentuate both the comedy and the sentiment in the movie. These elements of style attempted to give *Home Alone* a warm and timeless feel while also inviting the audience to indulge in the fantasy of family life more lavish in scale than any seen in Hughes's previous movies.

Home Alone's major themes of family, self-reliance, and consumption fit comfortably within conservative visions of American suburban life in the Reagan-Bush era. These ideas are complemented by a more explicit emphasis on faith and religion, specifically Christianity, than that found in any of Hughes's earlier movies. Somewhat downcast after his meeting with "Santa," Kevin visits his local church. This warm and contemplative scene contrasts with Kevin's awkwardly transactional encounter with Santa in the street outside a gaudy Christmas grotto. As Kevin walks down the central aisle, the camera moves slowly to capture the statues, stained-glass windows, and crucifixes that fill the imposing Gothic-style building. The boy's face captures his sense of awe and thoughtful mood. As the choir performs traditional hymns, Kevin reflects on his behavior and his relationship with his family and discusses his conflicted feelings with his kindly neighbor Mr. Marley. In this way, *Home Alone* suggests the importance of Christianity as a force for uniting communities and encouraging personal improvement. Kevin's faith is revisited shortly before the film's climax when he says grace over dinner before the burglars arrive. The juxtaposition of this quiet religious act with scenes of extreme comic violence quietly suggests the uneasy relationship between Christianity, power, and violence in American society. Despite tensions of this kind, *Home Alone* manages to hold together its core themes of family, self-reliance, consumption, and faith, concepts also underpinning Hughes's other 20th Century Fox family films, particularly *Miracle on 34th Street*.

Privilege and consumption are a crucial part of the narrative logic of *Home Alone 2*. Kevin is able to act out his fantasies of independence and to evade adult detection because of the cultural and economic capital he enjoys. Finding himself in possession of his father's credit card and a large quantity of cash, he sets about enjoying his own vacation in New York City and visits several major tourist attractions, including Radio City Music Hall and the World Trade Center. He is able to commit credit card fraud because he uses his understanding of the adult world to manipulate the hotel staff. Although *Home Alone 2* emphasizes the excessive nature of Kevin's self-indulgence, his adventures still tap into children's fantasies. When Kevin checks into a suite at the Plaza Hotel, after using his Talkboy cassette player to make a reservation over the telephone, his responses to the room mimic adult observations, but he is most excited by the candy-stocked closet and large television. During his stay at the hotel, he practices cannonballs in the hotel pool, has a waiter serve ice cream to him in bed, and hires a stretch limousine. While cruising around Manhattan, he watches television, eats pizza, and drinks Coca-Cola out of a champagne glass. Kevin's choices are shaped by his wealthy background and awareness of the cultural capital associated with certain goods, services, and leisure activities.

In *Home Alone*, Kevin's trip to the supermarket to buy typical household products demonstrates his acceptance of adult responsibility. In the sequel, Kevin's consumption is more extravagant and framed by his class status. He flaunts his wealth and compensates for his excessive consumption by making ostensibly philanthropic gestures. During his spending spree, Kevin visits Duncan's Toy Chest, a toy store owned by Mr. Duncan (Eddie Bracken), a kindly old man whose "loving smiles," asserts Joe Kincheloe, "prove that capitalism cares and the status quo is just."[29] While paying for Monster Sap soap (available in real life through Tiger Toys), a map, and a Swiss Army knife, Kevin donates twenty dollars to Mr. Duncan's charity appeal. He explains, "I'll probably spend it on stuff that'll rot my teeth or my mind." Mr. Duncan rewards Kevin's kindness with an ornament from the Christmas tree. While the film celebrates Kevin's apparently generous nature, he is still spending his father's money, illustrating how, as Francie Ostrower observes, "philanthropy is . . . a mark of privilege and high social status."[30] Kevin's belief in the importance of philanthropy also provides the justification for his vigilante actions against the Wet Bandits after they attempt to steal charity donations destined for the children's hospital. The retribution that the boy seeks is inseparable from the social dynamics that allow him to navigate the big city and aspects of the adult world with relative ease.

Consistent with the movie's general excess and its attempts

to outdo the *Home Alone* films, the parents at the center of *Baby's Day Out* are millionaires. As in *Home Alone*, the opening scenes of *Baby's Day Out*, which feature a stately mansion staffed by an English nanny and butler, signal the extent of the Cotwells' wealth. Whereas in *Home Alone* the McCallister family's affluence is primarily suggested visually, and only explicitly discussed by the burglars, the opening scenes of *Baby's Day Out* show that Laraine (Lara Flynn Boyle) and Bennington Cotwell (Matthew Glave) are overly preoccupied with wealth and their status within the ranks of the city's elite. In an exchange with Nanny Gilbertine (Cynthia Nixon), Bink's mother dismisses the nanny's clothing suggestions because "Baby Bink is not a regular baby." Her desperation to get the baby's picture in the newspaper is what provides the kidnappers with an opportunity to abduct her son. Following a $5 million ransom demand for Bink's return, multiple police squad cars, a forensics team, detectives, and an FBI agent descend on the Cotwell mansion. While this use of comic exaggeration fits with the film's efforts to appeal to younger children, the massive police response further attests to the family's status and privilege and confirms that, as Bink's mother states, "rich babies" are "important babies."

In *Miracle on 34th Street*, the characters' lifestyles and rituals reflect a particular vision of whiteness that is closely interlinked with class privilege as well as a nostalgia for an imagined American past. Dorey and Bryan each inhabit an affluent professional world, and their high-powered careers enable them to live in an upscale apartment building overlooking Central Park and to enjoy sophisticated lifestyles. When they eat Thanksgiving dinner together, their WASP status is emphasized through reference to Norman Rockwell's famous painting *Freedom from Want*. Bryan sits at the head of the table, assuming the role of patriarch, and Dorey and Susan sit either side of the large turkey dinner. Like Rockwell's work, *Miracle on 34th Street* celebrates a fairly conservative vision of American culture, one centered on home and the white middle-class family. As Dorey and Susan start to eat, Bryan asks, "Do we give blessings in this house?" and then proceeds to say grace while they all bow their heads over the heavily laden table. The characters' performative

Figure 8.3. The American Dream: the privileged white family (Mara Wilson, Dylan McDermott, and Elizabeth Perkins) in *Miracle on 34th Street.*

whiteness is thus presented as inherently American. Moreover, *Miracle on 34th Street* noticeably avoids representing identities that might call into question the characters' power and privilege. There is not a single nonwhite speaking character in the film, and even crowd scenes contain very few faces that are not white. The ostensible alibi for this lack of diversity is the film's evocation of the mid-1940s—a time when more than 90 percent of New York's population was white.[31] This imposition of a vision of whiteness allows the film to celebrate Dorey and Bryan's racial and class privilege while ignoring the inequalities in American society.

Miracle on 34th Street relies on a conspicuously nostalgic aesthetic to reinforce the narrative's articulation of themes of faith and family togetherness. It is a blatant example of what Fredric Jameson calls the "nostalgia film," which, "by reinventing the feel and shape of characteristic art objects of an older period," attempts to "reawaken a sense of the past associated with those objects."[32] In addition to festive reds and greens, browns and cream tones dominate the film's color palette. Although the characters' hairstyles reflect 1990s fashions, the costumes suggest the late 1940s. Children wear structured clothes, such as fitted wool or felt coats, smart dresses, berets, and flat caps. Most noticeably, policemen wear uniforms that are almost identical to the New York City Police Department's uniforms of the 1940s. In certain instances, the costume design directly refers to the original film, as with Kris Kringle's tweed three-piece suit and Susan's red coat. Julio Macat's cinematography likewise alludes to Hollywood cinema of the 1940s, using fewer close-ups and more mid-shot compositions and medium wide shots. Much like *Baby's Day Out*, *Miracle on 34th Street* uses style to obscure the time period of the film, which allows for a more sentimental vision of upper-class New York life.

Miracle on 34th Street challenges aspects of American capitalism through its critique of the domination of American retail by heartless corporate chains. A feud between Cole's, a traditional department store, and Shopper's Express, a modern discount store, is central to the movie's narrative. In the original *Miracle on 34th Street*, Kris ends the hostilities between two competing store owners. In Hughes's 1994 remake, however, the ruthless CEO of Shopper's Express, Victor Landberg (Joss Ackland), is the antagonist. He is a stereotypical "evil" corporate executive who tries to put Cole's out of business, initially through aggressive pricing policies and later by setting up Kris's arrest. During the trial, he bribes the prosecutor and tells the judge that he will fund his reelection campaign. But Landberg's highly unethical actions are presented as examples of his villainy rather than as failings of the American economic and political system. In this way, the film offers "a highly contained and tightly regulated critique" of capitalism that, observes Mark Connelly, is typical of movies featuring Santa Claus.[33] Although *Miracle on 34th Street* condemns corporate greed and corruption, it does not challenge Americans' freedom to consume or the concept of free enterprise, nor does the film acknowledge the class and racial inequalities that capitalism perpetuates.

Instead of putting American society or its systems on trial, *Miracle on 34th Street* uses its climactic court case to present a message about faith and religious belief. Although these are central themes in the 1947 version, they are not explicitly linked with religion, nor do they figure in the court case. In the original, the outcome of the case is based on a rational, secular argument. The lawyer wins by reasoning that if the US Postal Service recognizes Santa Claus as a real person, then the US government must do so, too. The 1994 movie takes a much less subtle approach: just before the judge gives his ruling, Susan approaches his bench with a Christmas card that contains a one-dollar bill, on which the words "In God We Trust" are circled. The judge concludes that if the US Treasury can believe in God, then the people of New York can believe in Santa Claus. In fact, *Miracle on 34th Street* repeatedly emphasizes Santa Claus's mythic, quasi-religious significance. At one point, Kris explains to Dorey what he represents: "I'm a symbol of the human ability to suppress the selfish and hateful tendencies that rule the major part of our lives. If you can't believe, if you can't accept anything on faith, then you're doomed to a life dominated by doubt." In Hughes's *Miracle on 34th Street*, belief is what brings disparate communities in New York together and provides Dorey with her route to "redemption" as a mother.

Hughes was seemingly aware that his early-1990s movies presented an idealized vision of family life, distant from the reality of most audiences. In a 1996 interview, he remarked, "The first *Home Alone* was the dream life of the '80s—a family with a big house, beautifully decorated. A family who vacationed in France over the holidays."[34] Explaining that *Home Alone 3* would adopt a different outlook, he stated, "We'll be dealing with the reality of the American family of today—people who live in a modest house that needs renovation, the parents worrying about coping with the needs of the kids, about their jobs, child care."[35] The "American family of today," in Hughes's eyes, was still solidly middle class and white and still comprised two parents and their children. Although Alex has to shovel snow to earn money, and numerous references are made to the family's financial situation, the Pruitt family lives in a large house in a pleasant neighborhood, and each of the children has a bedroom filled with toys and gadgets. This more mundane setting removes some of the aspirational elements that were fundamental to the original films' appeal, a point underscored by the ending of the film. Conveniently, the family's financial security is confirmed when the company that made the stolen computer chip offers Alex a six-figure reward for recovering it. *Home Alone 3* thus confirms that upper-middle-class status is still the American Dream.

The combination of slapstick humor and sentiment at the core of *Home Alone* built on Hughes's widespread use of comedy in his earlier movies, including his 1980s teen movies, to offset overt sentimentality. While it has roots in his earlier work, *Home Alone* manages to blend broad slapstick gags and heartwarming moments in a new way, which proved incredibly popular with audiences of all ages. All of Hughes's later family films owe a major debt to *Home Alone*. Reusing features of his most commercially successful movie in an attempt to re-create its box-office appeal was a logical tactic. That said, although the later films take their cues from *Home Alone*, Hughes's 20th Century Fox family films combine varying quantities of knockabout comedy and sentiment. *Home Alone 2*, *Home Alone 3*, and *Baby's Day Out* emphasize comedy but still try to include a hearty dose of emotion. *Miracle on 34th Street* has some lighter moments of comic relief, but it is a much more sentimental tale. Hughes's family films use emotion to reinforce their messages of family unity and "traditional" values, but in a way that does not completely negate the movies' references to wider social problems affecting children and American families in the 1990s.

Through their depictions of children dealing with abandonment and danger, the *Home Alone* films are fantasies of child autonomy and omnipotence. By giving Kevin and Alex agency, the *Home Alone* films suggest that children can exist without the presence of their families. Despite efforts to create narratives and moral frameworks that justify Kevin's and Alex's actions, the slapstick brutality that they perpetrate hints at children's latent capacity for violence. At the same time, the movies suggest that the nuclear family is where children belong. This contradiction, created in part by the film's efforts to appeal to both children's and adult's fantasies, is not particularly unusual for the genre. Robert C. Allen argues that "moral and, by extension, ideological ambivalence is a defining feature of the family film."[36] The primary way in which the films try to work through, or at least mitigate, the issue of children's autonomy and innocence is through the mother-child relationship, which ultimately positions the preteen child as dependent on the mother for emotional comfort and support. Consequently, the mothers in Hughes's 20th Century Fox films bear much more responsibility and guilt than the fathers for the problems facing the family and for any errant behavior by their children. That said, in contrast to *Curly Sue*, *Beethoven*, and *Dennis the Menace*, these films avoid directly criticizing mothers, including working mothers. They nonetheless reinforce certain social expectations around motherhood and, particularly overtly in *Miracle on 34th Street*, suggest that the mother functions best as part of a traditional nuclear family.

While the box-office underperformance of *Baby's Day Out*, *Miracle on 34th Street*, and *Home Alone 3* seemed to suggest that Hughes's particular brand of heartwarming family film lacked long-term appeal, the situation was more complicated than it might appear. The family comedies that Hughes released through Disney later in the 1990s—*101 Dalmatians* (Stephen Herek, 1996) and *Flubber* (Les Mayfield, 1997)—both performed incredibly well at the box office. Although their success was undoubtedly aided by Disney's marketing prowess and the star performances of Glenn Close and Robin Williams, respectively, the films combined slapstick and sentiment and explored themes around the family and relationships in ways typical of Hughes's family films. Both films were remakes of earlier hits, suggesting that repetition was not an inherent barrier to commercial success, despite the skepticism it engendered in the press. Perhaps of greater importance is the fact that numerous other family films of the mid-1990s used *Home Alone* as a source of inspiration, reworking its textual features and introducing a variety of novel components in an effort to grab cross-generational audiences' interest.[37] In fact, *Home Alone* remains one of the seminal family films of the New Hollywood era.

CONCLUSION

Mainstream Maverick?

> Through luck, skill, timing, and tenacity, John Hughes has become a genuine anomaly in the film industry: He's his own studio. Not since the glory days of Sam Goldwyn and David Selznick has a mainstream maverick made such a name for himself. True, those two old icons were masters of the prestige release; Hughes, with his Chicago-based Hughes Entertainment company, is more like a Midwestern factory boss overseeing the mass production of jujubes.
>
> Ty Burr, *Entertainment Weekly*

In his 1992 review of the video release of *Curly Sue*, Ty Burr, *Entertainment Weekly*'s film critic, summed up the image that Hughes had managed to develop in the trade and mainstream presses. From the mid-1980s through the mid-1990s, Hughes was one of the most powerful filmmakers in Hollywood, despite apparently harboring "a marked antipathy toward official Hollywood."[1] He was clearly not a maverick in the conventional sense, however. Popular criticism has often celebrated "maverick" or "rebel" filmmakers whose work is somehow "antimainstream" or who allegedly refuse to yield to corporate pressure during the creative process.[2] Hughes's immense success as a creator of popular entertainment challenged the critical and industry voices that had used discourses of individualistic rebellion and nonconformity to promote the artistry and cultural significance of New Hollywood cinema. By calling Hughes a "mainstream maverick," Burr was acknowledging the seemingly contradictory way in which Hughes used his creative control and industrial clout to create unashamedly populist entertainment. The highly commercial nature of his movies meant that his alleged disagreements with studios did not fit with the romantic image of the defiant auteur, fighting to retain artistic credibility. To no small extent, the awkward way in which Hughes's reputation chafed against established auteurist discourses sheds some light on critics' and scholars' struggles to engage with his career.

Through his focus on teen films and family films, Hughes carved a niche for himself within mainstream American cinema, albeit one that relied on a highly standardized approach to filmmaking. Burr's comparison of Hughes to a "Midwestern factory boss" creating sweet treats was therefore somewhat justified. Hughes's films are a prime example of "what is most central to popular media production: repetition, continuation, profit."[3] Critics' references to the "John Hughes method," "Hughes's standard procedure," and the "John Hughes factory" signaled the formulaic nature of his movies.[4] Filmmakers with more "elite" aspirations, as Amanda Ann Klein observes, "avoid making films that simply repeat the plots, characters, and themes of previously successful films, or that appear to pander to the audience's every whim."[5] Hughes seemingly had few qualms about continuing to create highly commercial movies for specific target markets of suburban teenagers and families. Moreover, the films' ability to deliver a predictable set of pleasures was a major factor in their success. His formulaic approach also suited industry agendas; by combining presold elements likely to appeal to audiences, it presumably reduced risk. Although the mixed commercial results that the "John Hughes method" yielded demonstrate that in Hollywood, mastery and control are often illusory.

By focusing primarily on teen movies and the family films, Hughes developed ways of deploying genre conventions in order to establish quickly the characteristics of his stories, shaping audience expectations from the opening sequence of every film. The highly regulated narratives he scripted take his audiences on largely predictable, but nonetheless pleasurable emotional journeys. Moreover, the mixture of comedy and fantasy in his movies encourages a range of responses, from laughter to tears. Much of the comedy lightly satirizes "typical" suburban American life through observational humor directed at characters, settings, and rituals familiar from that milieu. The filmic fantasies connect with the hopes, wishes, and ambitions of the characters, frivolous and short-lived as these may be. Hughes and his team of collaborators also ensured that the narrative pleasures of his films were accentuated through an appealing use of visual styles and music. His 1980s teen movies increasingly adhered to high-concept filmmaking's emphasis on presenting characters, and the stars portraying them, through their taste in clothing, accessories, and music. Throughout Hughes's career, one of the hallmarks of his approach to filmmaking was the use of popular music to both convey character information and to heighten the emotional impact of a scene. Thus, through a variety of tried-and-tested Hollywood techniques combined with elements of novelty, Hughes and his collaborators developed his signature product, which could be branded and commodified in line with specific studios' agendas.

Virtually all of Hughes's movies use suburbia as a backdrop, relying on this location's familiarity, its apparent ability to represent Middle America, and its wider cultural connotations. This setting, most strongly embodied by the fictional town of Shermer, Illinois, helps provide a seemingly realistic milieu for a film's action and grounding its more fantastical elements. Suburbia, proposes Delores Hayden, is not only "the dominant American cultural landscape" in a literal sense, but also "the site of promises, dreams, and fantasies" and, thus, "a landscape of the imagination."[6] Departures from the mundane reality of suburban life signal the existence of new possibilities and alternative scenarios. These fantasies are nevertheless closely linked with the social contexts in which Hughes's films were produced. For example, the ambitions of his teenage characters suggest an anxiety around the generation gap and concerns about their generation's future; characters' life trajectories are already strongly linked with their social class. While these themes have been at the core of the teen film since at least the 1950s, the divide between members of Generation X and their parents is informed by a particular set of social circumstances, and those concerns were interrogated in a number of 1980s teen movies.[7] Similarly, in Hughes's family films, childhood is an ambiguous state, with his preteen characters often proving that they can exist independently of adults. The representations of Kevin in *Home Alone* and Sue in *Curly Sue*, in particular, suggest that social and economic changes in American society shaped childhood in the 1990s. Moreover, the movies' exaggerated, often whimsical portrayals of real social issues often expose contradictions in political discourses of the time. The films are never entirely subversive, however, and any challenges to the status quo are largely contained by Hughes's use of genre conventions and his steadfast commitment to the happy ending.

Hughes was criticized throughout his career for his limited focus on white, predominantly middle-class protagonists, but these complaints had little impact on his reputation within the film industry or among his fans. His films are deliberately mainstream in their politics, often erring on the side of conservatism, reflecting wider trends in Hollywood cinema of the 1980s and early 1990s. This tendency toward "traditional" values is particularly overt in the movies' engagement with gender and sexual politics, which are noticeably tied to prevalent discourses in America during this period. The teen girls in his films, most notably Samantha in *Sixteen Candles* and Andie in *Pretty in Pink*, both played by Molly Ringwald, tend to conform to gender norms and aspire to highly conventional heterosexual romances centered on the fantasy of "the one." Even the tomboy Watts in *Some Kind of Wonderful* believes wholeheartedly in a long-term monogamous relationship with a man. Compared with their male peers, they lack agency beyond their romantic encounters and personal style. The teenage boys in Hughes's movies are restricted in different ways, by being expected to conform to masculine ideals of aggression and virility.

The maintenance of the gender binary and traditional gender roles is also overt in Hughes's family films. Fatherhood is rooted in a man's acceptance of the role of provider and patriarch. Motherhood, in contrast, is fraught with contradictions. While Hughes's films increasingly acknowledged the dilemmas faced by working mothers, they nonetheless implied that mothers shoulder the majority of child care responsibilities and suggested that most mothers would be happier at home. More broadly, Hughes's films advocated for the traditional nuclear family, even while acknowledging familial dysfunctionality. Although typical of the family film, this insistence on family unity takes on a unique resonance in the context of the "family values" debates of the late 1980s and early 1990s. By grappling with these issues, in often troubled and contradictory ways, Hughes's movies demonstrated the ways in which mainstream New Hollywood movies had to negotiate the complex terrain of identity politics.

Hughes's most successful films managed to strike a chord with audiences not just in America, but also worldwide, generating substantial box-office grosses. While his formulaic approach to developing and producing projects led to mixed results, the lingering sense that he could create another hit like *Home Alone* kept studios willing to invest in his work. Costly mistakes like *Baby's Day Out* and *Miracle on 34th Street* did little to tarnish his reputation, given his overall success in both theatrical and ancillary markets during the years 1984–1994. Moreover, as studios rapidly came to terms with new technologies and an increasingly globalized marketplace, Hughes's willingness to be reactive and to fit his work within studio agendas, as well as his ability to deliver projects quickly, made him an appealing partner. Thanks to these favorable conditions, Hughes Entertainment had the potential to become a major independent production company—although with the exception of *Only the Lonely* (Chris Columbus, 1991), the firm had only produced Hughes's own movies. Despite the pressure to maintain his prolific output and the challenges presented by the possible expansion of his operations, Hughes had significant ambitions to build on the successes of his movies of the mid-1980s to mid-1990s.

Disney, Great Oaks, and Indie Ambitions

After several years of negotiations, Hughes signed a six-picture deal with Disney in January 1995.[8] The pact was linked with the development of his new production company, Great Oaks Entertainment. Founded in February 1995, Great Oaks was a partnership between Hughes and the producer Ricardo Mestres, whom he knew from his time on a development deal at Paramount in the early 1980s.[9] Hughes told *Variety* that he had been struggling to balance the different aspects of running Hughes Entertainment: "I decided to find someone who could maximize all my creative abilities. It's difficult for me to manage a creative career and a business career. I think that I could do more than I had in the past if I had a partner who is pulling the same sort of weight that I can pull."[10] Outlining their ambitions, Mestres stated, "The goal for Great Oaks is to be a broadly based, popular entertainment company."[11] Significantly, the announcement came against a backdrop of speculation concerning Disney's corporate strategy. After a decade of immense financial success, the corporation found itself at a turning point after the sudden death of the company's president, Frank G. Wells. Working closely with Michael Eisner, Wells had turned Disney into a highly streamlined and genuinely synergistic operation and had helped increase the corporation's annual revenues from $1.5 billion to $8.5 billion over the course of a decade.[12] Under the leadership of the studio's chairman, Joe Roth, with whom Hughes had worked at 20th Century Fox in the early 1990s, Walt Disney Studios was seeking to reorient its live-action films toward a family audience. Hughes was a logical partner, thanks to his extensive experience of creating live-action family films, proven ability to generate both box-office and home-video revenues, and understanding of marketability.

In March 1995, Disney announced that Hughes would write the script for a live-action version of *101 Dalmatians* (1961). The studio placed *101 Dalmatians* (Stephen Kerek, 1996) at the forefront of its attempts to expand its live-action label during the mid-1990s. The *Los Angeles Times*, paraphrasing Roth, described *101 Dalmatians* as "the first test of whether the entire Disney company, from the film division through its theme parks and consumer products, can promote a Disney live-action picture as if it were an animated film."[13] The fact that Roth and his team were willing to stake their reputations on a production developed in liaison with Hughes was a testament to the filmmaker's status as one of the most successful live-action family-film creators of all time. From Hughes's perspective, the movie benefited from Disney's extensive production resources and marketing expertise. The production budget—rumored to be in excess of $60 million—dwarfed that of the filmmaker's earlier productions.[14] Great Oaks and Disney were able to secure a high-profile cast, including Glenn Close, who had recently completed a two-year, Tony Award–winning stint as Norma Desmond in *Sunset Boulevard* on Broadway. In line with wider industry trends, the studio also invested heavily in cutting-edge animatronics and computer-generated imagery. The overall package for *101 Dalmatians* was therefore extremely promising, combining a mixture of new and familiar elements in an attempt to attract a cross-generational audience.

The marketing campaign for *101 Dalmatians* started 101 days before the movie's theatrical release. The well-orchestrated and highly consistent branding strategy made judicious use of divisions of the Disney corporation, for example, by promoting the film heavily in Disney theme parks and by airing a half-hour prime-time behind-the-scenes special, *101 Dalmatians. A Canine's Tale*, on ABC.[15] Disney also secured cross-promotional deals with major corporations, such as McDonald's, and placed a *101 Dalmatians* float in the Macy's Thanksgiving Day parade.[16] The studio clearly branded the film "A Walt Disney Picture," relying on the brand associations that this invited, rather than "A John Hughes Film." Disney's sustained, high-profile promotional efforts reaped immediate rewards. During its first three days of release, *101 Dalmatians* grossed roughly $33.5 million, which was the highest Thanksgiving-weekend gross of all time in unadjusted dollars. The movie was the sixth-highest-grossing movie of 1996, taking in $136 million at the domestic box office and over $184 million internationally.[17] The theatrical release of *101 Dalmatians* was accompanied by a "Christmas Merchandising blitz of Santa-shaking proportions."[18] Disney contracted over 130 companies to create merchandise for the movie, which included plush toys, electronic games, Giga Pets, a Barbie doll, a cassette player, a PC game, pet products, and designer accessories.[19] The combination of revenues from those licensed products and home video generated significant additional income for Disney, matching the cross-promotional successes of its animation films. Unlike Hughes's earlier successes, which the press and studios typically attributed to his input as a screenwriter and producer, *101 Dalmatians* was portrayed primarily as a victory for Disney.

The other live-action comedy that Hughes wrote and produced under his deal with Disney was *Flubber* (Les Mayfield, 1997), based on *The Absent-Minded Professor* (Robert Stevenson, 1961). Disney secured Robin Williams, who had proved his wide-ranging appeal in family movies, including *Aladdin* (1992), *Mrs. Doubtfire* (Chris Columbus, 1993), and *Jumanji* (Joe Johnston, 1995), to play the film's central role. *Flubber*'s broad physical comedy and zany humor was a good match for Williams's on-screen persona. Again, the studio awarded the film a substantial budget, investing heavily in the special effects crucial to bringing *Flubber* to life. Despite *Variety*'s suggestion that the film was "funny and frenetic family entertainment," with "possibly greater cross-generational appeal" than *101 Dalmatians*, it was not a hit of the same magnitude.[20] Unlike *101 Dalmatians*, the animated version of which had been a major hit as a theatrical rerelease and on home video, *Flubber* lacked brand recognition among children. Consequently, Disney struggled to develop a distinctive marketing campaign based around a specific visual identity, and also found it difficult to sell licenses for tie-in products. By no means a failure, *Flubber* grossed just shy of $93 million at the domestic box office and an estimated $85 million internationally.[21] The movie nonetheless highlighted to

Disney the risks involved in live-action family-film production, particularly in an increasingly crowded market.

Although the partnership with Disney had been highly lucrative, Great Oaks lasted only two and a half years before Hughes and Mestres went their separate ways, in November 1997. The split followed what the *Hollywood Reporter* called "an often uneasy alliance" between the two producers.[22] Consequently, Hughes and Mestres never fulfilled their ambitions to "pursue projects in all areas of entertainment, including motion pictures, television, publishing and interactive media."[23] Projects that did not come to fruition included a thirteen-episode sitcom for NBC, "a darker, more disturbing" live-action adaptation of *Peter Pan* for Disney and TriStar, and a special-effects comedy called *The Bee*.[24] Great Oaks' international ambitions also ended after the split. During 1995, the company had opened an office in London in order to find successful comedy writers and performers from the UK and Europe to collaborate with, a strategy that Hughes had been pursuing since the early 1990s without much success.[25] The only project that emerged from Hughes's efforts at European expansion was an English-language remake of a popular French comedy, *Les Visiteurs* (Jean-Marie Poiré, 1993), for TriStar. Hughes instigated the project, secured the central cast, and collaborated with the original screenwriter, Christian Clavier, on the script for the remake.[26] After Hughes withdrew from the project, Disney was reluctant to agree to a distribution deal.[27] Despite their reservations, the studio eventually released the remake, *Just Visiting* (Jean-Marie Poiré, 2001). The movie, which cost at least $50 million, grossed less than $5 million in the United States, making it a major box-office flop.[28]

Toward the end of the 1990s, Hughes took a step back from big-budget Hollywood productions. His next project was a low-budget coming-of-age film, *Reach the Rock* (William Ryan, 1998), that he wrote and produced. The movie was something of a homecoming for Hughes, since it was shot in Illinois and set in the town of Shermer, home of his 1980s teen films. In many respects, *Reach the Rock* was the antithesis of the hyped, big-budget movies that he had focused on for the past decade. The R-rated movie did not feature any well-known actors and lacked any kind of commercial hook beyond Hughes's name. Released in just a handful of cinemas during October 1998, *Reach the Rock* generated only a few thousand dollars at the US box office.[29] *Variety*'s Lael Lowenstein described the film as perhaps "Hughes's darkest film yet," and the *New York Times*' Anita Gates suggested it was "like the dark side" of his 1980s teen films.[30] Another project that signaled Hughes's turn away from mainstream projects was *New Port South* (Kyle Cooper, 2001), a high school drama written by his son, James Hughes, who was just twenty-one years old. Hughes Sr. acted as executive producer of the movie through Hughes Entertainment, securing a production budget of $9 million from Disney.[31] In many respects, the film was a reaction to the slew of late-1990s Hughes-inspired teen movies, such as *She's All That* (Robert Iscove, 1999), *10 Things I Hate About You* (Gil Junger, 1999), and *Never Been Kissed* (Raja Gosnell, 1999), which were reinvigorating romantic fantasies of suburban high school life. In a publicity interview, the film's director, Kyle Cooper, announced that the movie "doesn't conveniently fall into the John Hughes genre" and suggested that it "technically and stylistically doesn't pander to a youthful audience."[32] Deciding that the film's appeal was too narrow, Disney gave *New Port South* a very limited theatrical release through Touchstone in September 2001.[33] Hughes may have fulfilled his ambitions to challenge himself creatively and to work outside the Hollywood mainstream, but the resulting films failed to engage with even niche audiences.

The "Myth" of John Hughes

Despite rumors that Hughes would return to directing, he never worked on a movie again. His departure from Hollywood, after over a decade of commercial success, helped elevate him to almost mythical status. Occasional articles in the mainstream press or film publications developed an aura of mystery around Hughes during the late 2000s. The most overt example of this myth-building process was a seven-page feature in the

September 2008 edition of the British movie magazine *Empire*, which asked, "What on Earth Ever Happened to John Hughes?" Highlighting Hughes's credentials as "one of the biggest players in Hollywood" and a "brand," the article presented his sudden departure from the film industry as a "tantalizing Hollywood mystery."[34] Published after Hughes's death, David Kamp's March 2010 *Vanity Fair* article "Sweet Bard of Youth" sought to dispel some of the rumors that had surrounded Hughes after he left Hollywood. Kamp had managed to secure interviews with Hughes's sons, John III and James, during the autumn of 2009, and gained access to a treasure trove of artifacts, notebooks, and other items that Hughes had kept. Kamp argued against the perception that Hughes had suddenly disappeared from Hollywood to become a recluse. While John Candy's death of a heart attack in 1994 seemed to affect the filmmaker deeply, his withdrawal from the film industry had, in fact, been a gradual one.[35] Ultimately, Hughes preferred rural family life in the Midwest to a life of celebrity in Los Angeles. As Kamp explained, Hughes spent the last ten to fifteen years of his life with his family, pursuing his two main interests, writing and listening to music.[36] The apparent tension between the myths that had developed around Hughes and the reality of his life illustrates how the "biographical legend" of the auteur is not the same as the biography of the filmmaker as an individual.

Proponents of a mythologized, nostalgia-tinged vision of Hughes's work include the large number of Generation X comedy actors and filmmakers who are self-confessed fans of Hughes's work, particularly his teen movies. One of the major figures in early-1990s "slacker cinema," Kevin Smith, has been the most outspoken of Hughes's acolytes from this generation of filmmakers.[37] Smith's films frequently make reference to aspects of Hughes's 1980s movies, including the mythical town of Shermer. Paul Feig, one of Hollywood's leading comedy filmmakers of the 2010s, has also cited Hughes's work as an inspiration, particularly for his feature film debut, *Unaccompanied Minors* (2006).[38] Like Hughes, Feig makes movies that are unashamedly mainstream, and also adopts a similar directorial approach, amassing hours of footage and then shaping his movies carefully in the editing room. Judd Apatow, one of Hollywood's most prolific comedy producers of the 2000s and 2010s, has argued that the concepts he has developed contain elements that were "all there first in John Hughes films."[39] Besides specializing in comedies focused on outsider characters, Apatow is also a highly prolific creative producer, known for his ability to create popular movie formulas and for his high level of influence within Hollywood. Of course, the list of filmmakers crediting Hughes's work as providing inspiration for their own movies extends beyond the likes of Smith, Feig, and Apatow. In a 2008 *Los Angeles Times* article, the apparently widespread allegiance to the filmmaker prompted Kenneth Turan to proclaim, somewhat hyperbolically, "It's hard to find a thirty- or forty-something writer or filmmaker who doesn't credit Hughes as a seminal figure in their movie education."[40]

Hughes's work has not simply inspired individual filmmakers. His movies have also had a major impact on the teen movie and, to a lesser extent, the family film. Roz Kaveney's assertion that developments in the teen film genre in the 1990s and early 2000s were often "a creative response to the 1980s John Hughes films" and other movies from that time has a certain validity.[41] Many filmmakers who created mainstream teen and youth movies during the 1990s and 2000s have explicitly acknowledged that Hughes's films influenced their work. Kirsten Smith, cowriter of *10 Things I Hate About You* and *Legally Blonde* (Robert Luketic, 2001), for example, has stated, "My movie worldview was shaped by the Shakespeare of Teen Cinema, John Hughes."[42] Even the creators of edgier teen films, such as Daniel Waters and Michael Lehmann, the writer and director of *Heathers* (Michael Lehmann, 1988), have frequently claimed that the teen-suicide satire is a reaction to Hughes's work.[43] Of course, interpretation of films is not simply the product of their creators' intentions. Through a mixture of critical appraisals, studio publicity, and audience responses, Hughes's mid-1980s movies have been elevated to the rank of prime exemplars of the New Hollywood teen film. As Rick Altman argues, "Rhetorically, the most effective method of redefining a genre is not to do so overtly, but rather to promote a subset of the genre to a representative position."[44] While filmmakers may not always deliberately intend to pay tribute or allude to Hughes, his movies are a major part of the discourse on post-1980s teen films. Consequently, when critics and audiences discuss other teen movies, they often link their interpretations to Hughes's work.

Hughes's impact on the family film was more immediate and, arguably, shorter in duration. *Home Alone* played a crucial role in fueling a cycle of live-action family films. It seems unlikely that Hollywood studios would have invested heavily in films such as *3 Ninjas* (Jon Turtletaub, 1992), *Monkey Trouble* (Franco Amurri, 1994), *The Little Rascals* (Penelope Spheeris, 1994), *Richie Rich* (Donald Petrie, 1994), *Blank Check* (Rupert Wainwright, 1994), *Getting Even with Dad* (Howard Deutch, 1994), *Casper* (Brad Siberling, 1995), *Man of the House* (James Orr, 1995), *Matilda* (Danny DeVito, 1996), and *Mouse Hunt* (Gore Verbinski, 1997) had *Home Alone* not proved the commercial viability of live-action family entertainment. While their creators may not have deliberately set out to mimic Hughes's work, these films nonetheless share the same narrative tropes and themes with *Home Alone*. Specifically, many of these movies feature quick-witted children outsmarting adults and combine broad, slapstick comedy with a hearty dose of sentiment designed to accentuate an overriding message about the importance of family or friendship. But Hughes's impact on the Hollywood family film was short-lived because of wider transformations in the genre. The more modest live-action family film fell out of favor when big-budget cross-generational entertainment became the overriding logic in Hollywood blockbuster production, as studios began focusing instead on PG-13-rated transmedia franchises.[45] That said, Hughes's movies and other family films of the early 1990s continue to be consumed widely, on a variety of platforms, which suggests that there is a continued appetite for these kinds of movies.

The emotional associations that Hughes's movies created

for their original audiences are, undoubtedly, a major factor in their prolonged consumption. For people who were teenagers in the 1980s, notes Stephen Prince, his teen movies "defined the quintessential look and sound for an affluent suburban youth culture" of that period.[46] The films' "availability to nostalgia" is at the core of their commercial afterlives, as well as being a major factor in their continued use as cinematic reference points.[47] Audiences' memories and feelings about Hughes's movies also helped fuel a second wave of merchandising in the late 2000s and 2010s. Myriad products, ranging from *Sixteen Candles* T-shirts to *Ferris Bueller's Day Off* Hot Wheels cars, have been released during the past decade or so in an effort to cash in on fans' nostalgia. Companies have created merchandise for Hughes's family films too, targeted primarily at the Millennials who consumed the movies as children. *Home Alone*, in particular, has proved to be a highly durable brand. Since the late 2000s, 20th Century Fox has issued licenses for numerous products linked with the movie, including clothing, action figures, bobblehead toys, a board game, a "Classic Illustrated Storybook," an "Official Coloring Book," and other branded products bearing logos, images, and catchphrases from the film. This commercial strategy is part of a wider trend within the entertainment industry, which has seen the major studios devise further ways to profit from their back catalogues, in a period when the value of the films themselves has declined. Advertisements such as "Matthew's Day Off" for the Honda CR-V (2012), starring Matthew Broderick, and "Home Alone Again with the Google Assistant" (2018), starring Macaulay Culkin, were designed to tap into audiences' memories of Hughes's movies and the fantasies they portrayed, in order to sell other consumer products. Evidently, so long as audiences feel nostalgia for Hughes's films, they will continue to have commercial value as both texts and paratexts.

Several best-selling print books have also tapped into the lucrative market for 1980s-movie nostalgia by focusing on the impact that Hughes's work had on the authors' childhood or adolescence as well as their generation. These texts include the edited volume *Don't You Forget About Me: Contemporary Writers on the Films of John Hughes* (2007) and several books published in 2016: Hadley Freeman's *Life Moves Pretty Fast: The Lessons We Learned from Eighties Movies (and Why We Don't Learn Them from Movies Any More)*, Jason Diamond's *Searching for John Hughes: Or, Everything I Thought I Needed to Know about Life I Learned from Watching '80s Movies*, Kevin Smokler's *Brat Pack America: A Love Letter to '80s Teen Movies*, and James King's *Fast Times and Excellent Adventures: The Surprising History of the '80s Teen Movie*. These books are part of a wider trend of reevaluating Hughes's work that has grown in force since his death and has been fueled primarily by audiences rather than film critics. The filmmaker's fans and detractors have documented their perspectives on his films in numerous online and print articles, blog entries, and social media posts. The myriad perspectives that audiences have offered on his work demonstrate that his movies are capable of generating a variety of interpretations, as well as confirming his films' prominence in the canon of American popular culture.

Hughes's Continued Influence

In spite of ongoing debates about their aesthetic worth and political values, Hughes's movies continued to exert a significant influence on mainstream teen films and youth-oriented television during the 2010s. Recent films that refer to Hughes's work range from teen comedy-romances such as *Easy A* (Will Gluck, 2010) and *The Duff* (Ari Sandel, 2015) to the action blockbuster *Spider-Man: Homecoming* (Jon Watts, 2017). A similarly diverse range of teen-oriented television shows have drawn on the characters, themes, and tropes associated with Hughes's work, including *Gossip Girl* (CBS, 2007–2012), *Glee* (Fox, 2009–2015), *Awkward* (MTV, 2011–2016), *13 Reasons Why* (Netflix, 2017–), and *Stranger Things* (Netflix, 2016–). Tapping into the adolescent audiences' seemingly voracious appetite for high school dramas, Netflix launched a cycle of overtly Hughes-inspired straight-to-streaming teen films during 2018, including *The Kissing Booth* (Vince Marcello, 2018), *Candy Jar* (Ben Shelton,

2018), *Alex Strangelove* (Craig Johnson, 2018), *To All The Boys I've Loved Before* (Susan Johnson, 2018), and *Sierra Burgess Is a Loser* (Ian Samuels, 2018). The company's sudden commitment to young adult movies led the *New York Times* to announce, "A specter is haunting Netflix: The specter of late director John Hughes."[48] Canonical films that are "reworked, alluded to, satirized," argues Janet Staiger, "become privileged points of reference, pulled out from the rest of cinema's predecessors."[49] Given the status now afforded to Hughes's teen films, it would be an extremely difficult undertaking to create an American coming-of-age story set after 1980 and *not* allude to Hughes's work in some way.

Contemporary movies and television shows often take a more "revisionist" approach to the teen genre, displaying a greater "understanding of their generic heritage."[50] Their creators draw on the storytelling techniques and conventions of Hughes's work, and of teen movies from earlier decades, while updating the text's aesthetics and politics to appeal to a new generation of teenagers. References to his movies are sometimes combined with other, seemingly incongruous popular-culture allusions. The teen fantasy-drama *Riverdale* (CW, 2017–), for example, combines homage to Hughes's movies with references to darker texts, including *Carrie* (Brian De Palma, 1976), *River's Edge* (Tim Hunter, 1986), *Heathers*, and *Twin Peaks* (ABC, 1990–1991). While these productions celebrate Hughes's work, often in retro and nostalgic terms, they also increasingly acknowledge the films' weaknesses as well as their strengths. In a speech lamenting the fact that "John Hughes did not direct my life," *Easy A*'s Olive (Emma Stone) highlights the gulf between the fantasy romances of '80s movies and her own situation, which is more reflective of the complexities of teenage sexual politics. In *To All the Boys I've Loved Before*, the Asian American lead, Lara Jean (Lana Condor), describes *Sixteen Candles* as "a classic," but she also confidently states that Long Duk Dong is "extremely racist." The awareness shown by the characters in these movies and their ability to articulate a complex understanding of their situations are typical of the teen genre's growing sophistication.

Hughes's teen films also provided inspiration for less overtly mainstream movies during the 2010s. Part of the wider "Indiewood" trend, these films are generally marketed as quirky coming-of-age films rather than as teen movies. Diablo Cody, who won an Oscar for penning the screenplay of the teen comedy-drama *Juno* (Jason Reitman, 2007), has cited Hughes's work as a major influence. Greta Gerwig, another critically lauded female filmmaker, has consistently affirmed her "love" for Hughes's movies, particularly *Pretty in Pink*. While acknowledging a creative debt to his work, Gerwig has suggested that her work attempts to offer more complex insights into teenagers' emotions. Her screenplays for *Lady Bird* (Greta Gerwig, 2017) and *Frances Ha* (Noah Baumbach, 2012) focus on outsider teenagers and young adults struggling to find themselves, but deliberately challenge the traditional romantic ideal that Hughes portrayed in his films.[51] Other indie filmmakers of the 2010s who explicitly acknowledged the influence of Hughes's teen movies on their work include Kelly Fremon Craig, writer-director of *The Edge of Seventeen* (2016), and Wes Anderson.[52] Intriguingly, certain filmmakers working outside the white suburban milieu typical of many contemporary coming-of-age films still credit Hughes as an influence on their work. For example, in its portrayal of early-1990s black teenage nerds, Rick Famuyiwa's *Dope* (2015) pays homage to Hughes's awkward but endearing outsider characters while challenging stereotypes concerning urban youth.[53] Film critics often find these stories about young adults more palatable than their highly commercial counterparts, and some of these films have received Academy Awards and other critical accolades. It is notable, then, that the filmmakers are willing to acknowledge the debt their work owes to Hughes's 1980s movies.

John Hughes was undoubtedly a major figure in 1980s and 1990s Hollywood. He engaged strategically with numerous industry trends, showing an instinctive understanding of what would appeal to Middle American audiences. Consequently, the major Hollywood studios showed considerable confidence in his abilities as a screenwriter, producer, and, to a lesser extent, director. His work was often dismissed by critics, even when it was embraced by his fans. In the years following his death, it became clear that his movies had become part of the fabric of American popular culture, referred to not just in teen and family movies, but also in all manner of media, including cartoons, advertisements, and music videos. Through the films' repetition and wide intertextual circulation, they have become familiar sources of imagery and sounds evocative of a shared past. The fact that the makers of films and television shows of all types continue to find inspiration in his work confirms that Hughes's creative influence endures. His reputation is not static, however, and will no doubt be subject to further revision as attitudes change and certain discourses gain prominence. The battles to reconcile nostalgia for his movies with a greater awareness of their ideological complexities need not, however, erase the significant contribution that Hughes made to New Hollywood cinema.

NOTES

Introduction

1. Andrew Wallenstein, Associated Press, "82nd Annual Academy Awards—TV review," *Hollywood Reporter*, 7 March 2010, https://www.hollywoodreporter.com/review/82nd-annual-academy-awards-tv-29376; Vadim Rizo, "The Strangeness of that John Hughes Tribute," IFC.com, 8 March 2010, https://www.ifc.com/2010/03/hughes.

2. Roger Ebert, "No Pain for *Hurt Locker* Bigelow," RogerEbert.com, 7 March 2010, https://www.rogerebert.com/festivals-and-awards/no-pain-for-hurt-locker-bigelow.

3. "John Hughes, Bard of Teen Angst, Dead at 59," E! Online, 6 August 2009; Tom Peck, "John Hughes, Leader of the Brat Pack, Dies from Heart Attack at 59," *Independent* (UK; online), 7 August 2009; "Fallece en Nueva York John Hughes, padre de *Solo en casa*," *El País* (online), 7 August 2009.

4. Lindsay Goldwer, "Director John Hughes Dies at 59," ABC News (online), 6 August 2009; "Director John Hughes Dead at 59," FoxNews.com, 6 August 2009.

5. "Film Director John Hughes Dies, Aged 59," *Guardian*, 7 August 2009

6. Barbara Klinger, *Melodrama and Meaning: History, Culture, and the Films of Douglas Sirk* (Bloomington: Indiana University Press, 1994), xiii.

7. Joli Jensen, "On Fandom, Celebrity, and Mediation: Posthumous Possibilities," in *Afterlife as Afterimage: Understanding Posthumous Fame*, ed. Steve Jones and Joli Jensen (New York: Peter Lang, 2005), xviii.

8. A. O. Scott, "The '80s Auteur of Teenage Angst," *New York Times*, 8 August 2009, C1.

9. John Caughie, introduction to *Theories of Authorship: A Reader*, ed. John Caughie (London: Routledge, 1981), 15.

10. Terri Minsky, "Dr. Jekyll and Mr. Hughes," *Premiere*, July 1988, 55.

11. Warren Buckland, *Directed by Stephen Spielberg: The Poetics of the Contemporary Blockbuster* (London: Continuum, 2006), 223.

12. Jonathan Gray and Derek Johnson, "Introduction: The Problem of Media Authorship," in *A Companion to Media Authorship*, ed. Jonathan Gray and Derek Johnson (Malden, MA: Wiley-Blackwell), 6.

13. Berys Gaut, "Film Authorship and Collaboration," in *Film Theory and Philosophy*, ed. Richard Allen and Murray Smith (Oxford: Oxford University Press, 1997), 166.

14. Rita Kempley, "Same Kind of Wonderful," *Washington Post*, 27 February 1987, N29.

15. John Hughes, "Americans Seeking Screen Satisfaction, Escape from Reality," interview by Bob Thomas, Associated Press, 15 August 1985, Lexis-Nexis Academic.

16. Gray and Johnson, "Introduction," 3.

17. Timothy Corrigan, "The Commerce of Auteurism: A Voice without Authority," *New German Critique* 49 (Winter 1990): 46.

18. Steven Cohan, *Hollywood by Hollywood: The Backstudio Picture and the Mystique of Making Movies* (New York: Oxford University Press), 7.

19. Jerome Christensen, *America's Corporate Art: The Studio Authorship of Hollywood Motion Pictures* (Stanford, CA: Stanford University Press).

20. James Chapman, Mark Glancy, and Sue Harper, introduction to *The New Film History: Sources, Methods, Approaches*, ed. James Chapman, Mark Glancy, and Sue Harper (Basingstoke, UK: Palgrave, 2007), 1.

21. Richard Maltby, "New Cinema Histories," in *Explorations of New Cinema History: Approaches and Case Studies*, ed. Richard Maltby, Daniel Biltereyst, and Philippe Meers (Malden, MA: Wiley-Blackwell, 2011), 3.

22. Eric Smoodin, "The History of Film History," in *Looking Past the Screen: Case Studies in American Film History and Method*, ed. Jon Lewis and Eric Smoodin (Durham, NC: Duke University Press, 2007), 3.

23. Charles Musser, "Historiographic Method and the Study of Early Cinema," *Cinema Journal* 44, no. 1 (Autumn 2004): 105.

24. Stephen Prince, *A New Pot of Gold: Hollywood under the Electronic Rainbow, 1980–1989* (Berkeley: University of California Press, 2002), 211.

25. Geoff King, *New Hollywood Cinema: An Introduction* (London: Tauris, 2002), 84.

26. Steve Neale, "'The Last Good Time We Ever Had?': Revising the Hollywood Renaissance," in *Contemporary American Cinema*, ed. Linda Ruth Williams and Michael Hammond (Maidenhead, UK: Open University Press, 2005), 91.

27. See, for example, Richard Nowell, *Blood Money: A History of the First Teen Slasher Cycle* (New York: Continuum, 2011); Richard Nowell, "'For Girls': Hollywood, the Date-Movie Market, and Early-1980s Teen Sex Comedies," *Post Script: Essays in Film and the Humanities* 33, no. 1 (Fall 2014): 16–32.

28. Robert C. Allen, "Home Alone Together: Hollywood and the 'Family Film,'" in *Identifying Hollywood's Audiences*, ed. Richard Maltby and Melvyn Stokes (London: BFI, 1999), 109–134; Peter Krämer, "'The Best Disney Film Disney Never Made': Children's Films and the Family Audience in American Cinema Since the 1960s," in *Genre and Contemporary Hollywood*, ed. Steve Neale (London: BFI, 2002), 185–200; Krämer, "Would You Take Your Child To See This Film? The Cultural and Social Work of the Family-Adventure Movie," in *Contemporary Hollywood Cinema*, ed. Steve Neale and Murray Smith (London: Routledge, 1998), 294–311.

29. Noel Brown, *The Hollywood Family Film: A History from Shirley Temple to Harry Potter* (London: Tauris, 2012), 145–190.

30. John Hughes, discussion and Q&A with AFI fellows, AFI Harold Lloyd Master Seminars, 1 May 1985.

31. Richard Natale, "WB Pic Proves There's Life after First Week," *Variety*, 18 November 1991, 3.

32. Robert C. Allen and Douglas Gomery, *Film History: Theory and Practice* (New York: McGraw-Hill, 1985), 90.

33. Thomas Austin, *Hollywood, Hype and Audiences* (Manchester: Manchester University Press, 2002), 133.

34. Molly Ringwald, "What about *The Breakfast Club*? Revisiting the Movies of My Youth in the Age of #MeToo," *New Yorker*, 6 April 2018, https://www.newyorker.com/culture/personal-history/what-about-the-breakfast-club-molly-ringwald-metoo-john-hughes-pretty-in-pink.

35. Ibid.

36. Andy Medhurst, *A National Joke: Popular Comedies and English National Identity* (Abingdon, UK: Routledge, 2007), 38.

37. See, for example, Timothy Shary, *Generation Multiplex: The Image of Youth in Contemporary American Cinema* (Austin: University of Texas Press, 2002); Christina Lee, *Screening Generation X: The Politics and Popular Memory of Youth in Contemporary Cinema* (Farnham, UK: Ashgate, 2010); Catherine Driscoll, *Teen Film: A Critical Introduction* (Oxford: Berg, 2011); Barbara Jane Brickman, *New American Teenagers: The Lost Generation of Youth in 1970s Film* (New York: Bloomsbury, 2012); Frances Smith, *Rethinking the Hollywood Teen Movie: Gender, Genre, and Identity* (Edinburgh: Edinburgh University Press, 2017).

38. See, for example, Brown, *The Hollywood Family Film*; Noel Brown and Bruce Babbington, eds., *Family Films in Global Cinema: The World beyond Disney* (London: Tauris, 2015).

39. Andrew Britton, "Blissing Out: The Politics of Reaganite Entertainment (1986)," in *Britton on Film: The Complete Film Criticism of Andrew Britton*, ed. Barry Keith Grant (Detroit: Wayne State University Press, 2009), 97.

40. Robin Wood, "80s Hollywood: Dominant Tendencies," *CineAction!* 1 (Spring 1985): 2.

41. Ibid., 5.

42. Chris Jordan, *Movies and the Reagan Presidency: Success and Ethics* (Westport, CT: Praeger, 2003); Leger Grindon, "Movies and Fissures in Reagan's America," in *American Cinema of the 1980s: Themes and Variations*, ed. Stephen Prince (New Brunswick, NJ: Rutgers University Press, 2007), 148–151.

43. Janet Staiger, "The Future of the Past," *Cinema Journal* 44, no. 1 (Autumn 2004): 128.

44. John Gibbs and Douglas Pye, *Style and Meaning: Studies in the Detailed Analysis of Film* (Manchester: Manchester University Press, 2005), 4.

Chapter 1: Building a Brand

1. Roger Ebert, "John Hughes: When You're 16, You're More Serious than You'll Ever Be Again," *Chicago Sun-Times*, 29 April 1984, available at Roger Ebert's Journal, https://www.rogerebert.com/rogers-journal/john-hughes-when-youre-16-youre-more-serious-than-youll-ever-be-again.

2. "*National Lampoon's Vacation*: Box Office Summary," Box Office Mojo, https://www.boxofficemojo.com/movies/?id=nationallampoonsvacation.htm.

3. "*Mr. Mom*: Box Office Summary," Box Office Mojo, https://www.boxofficemojo.com/movies/?id=mrmom.htm.

4. Sean M. Smith, "Teen Days That Shook The World," *Premiere*, December 1999. Elsewhere, Hughes said the figure was in the region of $750,000; see John Hughes, discussion and Q&A with AFI fellows, AFI Harold Lloyd Masters Seminars, 1 May 1985.

5. S. Smith, "Teen Days That Shook The World."

6. Hughes, discussion and Q&A.

7. David A. Cook, *Lost Illusions: American Cinema in the Shadow of Watergate and Vietnam* (Berkeley: University of California Press, 2002), 313.

8. Hughes, discussion and Q&A.

9. Joshua Greenberg, "Universal Signs Hughes to 3-Year Pact," *Variety*, 2 May 1984, 19.

10. David Waterman, *Hollywood's Road to Riches* (Cambridge, MA: Harvard University Press, 2005), 290.

11. Ibid., 290–291.

12. Stephen Prince, *A New Pot of Gold: Hollywood under the Electronic Rainbow, 1980–1989* (Berkeley: University of California Press, 2002), 1–2.

13. Harold Vogel, *Entertainment Industry Economics: A Guide for Financial Analysis*, 8th ed. (New York: Cambridge University Press, 2001), 97–98.

14. Jennifer Holt, *Empires of Entertainment: Media Industries and the Politics of Deregulation, 1980–1996* (New Brunswick, NJ: Rutgers University Press, 2011), 3.

15. Jon Lewis, "Hollywood in the Corporate Era," in *The New American Cinema*, ed. Jon Lewis (Durham, NC: Duke University Press, 1998), 97.

16. Aljean Harmetz, "After *E.T.* They're 'Chosen People' at Universal," *New York Times*, 25 August 1982, C17.

17. Ibid.

18. Ibid.

19. Cook, *Lost Illusions*, 312.

20. Gene Siskel, "John Hughes Wakes Up to Needs of Teens with *Breakfast Club*," *Chicago Tribune*, 17 February 1985, http://articles.chicagotribune.com/1985-02-17/entertainment/8501090893_1_sixteen-candles-writer-director-john-hughes-film.

21. Sharon Lloyd Spence, "Chicago Screenwriter Makes His Directorial Debut," *Back Stage*, 12 August 1983, 54; Jack Barth, "John Hughes: On Geeks Bearing Gifts," *Film Comment*, June 1984.

22. "Hughes to Direct on *The Breakfast Club*," PR Newswire, Universal City, CA, 28 March 1984, LexisNexis Academic; Hughes, discussion and Q&A. Many online sources inaccurately state that the final movie was made for $1 million.

23. "Illinois Film Office Enjoys Banner Year in '84," *Back Stage*, 8 March 1985, 43; June Sawyers, "Famous Faces Who Call Chicago Home," *Back Stage*, 24 May 1985, 10B.

24. "Illinois Film Office Enjoys Banner Year," 43.

25. "Hot Chicago Film Scene Lures John Hughes Back Home," *Back Stage*, 16 August 1985, 48.

26. S. Smith, "Teen Days That Shook The World."

27. Hughes, discussion and Q&A; S. Smith, "Teen Days That Shook The World."

28. S. Smith, "Teen Days That Shook The World"; Aljean Harmetz, "Frank Price Named to Head MCA's Universal Studio," *New York Times*, 12 November 1983, 28.

29. Hughes, discussion and Q&A; S. Smith, "Teen Days That Shook The World."

30. S. Smith, "Teen Days That Shook The World."
31. John Ellis, *Visible Fictions: Cinema, Television, Video* (New York: Routledge, 1982), 30.
32. Steve Neale, *Genre and Hollywood* (London: Routledge, 2000), 36.
33. S. Smith, "Teen Days That Shook The World."
34. Ibid.
35. Ibid.
36. Siskel, "John Hughes Wakes Up."
37. "*Sixteen Candles*: Box Office Summary," Box Office Mojo, http://boxofficemojo.com/movies/?id=sixteencandles.htm; "*The Breakfast Club*: Box Office Summary," Box Office Mojo, http://boxofficemojo.com/movies/?id=breakfastclub.htm; "*Weird Science*: Box Office Summary," Box Office Mojo, http://boxofficemojo.com/movies/?id=weirdscience.htm.
38. Jim Hillier, *The New Hollywood* (London: Studio Vista, 1993), 14.
39. Lisa Scharoun, *America at the Mall: The Cultural Role of a Retail Utopia* (Jefferson, NC: McFarland, 2012), 70.
40. Josh Stenger, "Consuming the Planet: Planet Hollywood, Stars and the Global Consumer Culture," in *Hollywood: Critical Concepts in Media and Cultural Studies*, ed. Thomas Schatz (London: Routledge, 2004), 351.
41. Prince, *New Pot of Gold*, 11.
42. Jean Williams, "MCA Adds Three Labels in Accelerated Drive," *Billboard*, 21 July 1979, 3.
43. Jeff Smith, *The Sounds of Commerce: Marketing Popular Music* (New York: Columbia University Press, 1998), 189.
44. "MCA Inc Hits Financial High," *Billboard*, 20 November 1982, 4.
45. Jack Banks, *Monopoly Television: MTV's Quest to Control the Music* (Oxford: Westview, 1996), 42.
46. R. Serge Denisoff, *Inside MTV* (New Brunswick, NJ: Transaction, 1988), 182.
47. Ibid., 100.
48. Banks, *Monopoly Television*, 32.
49. Ibid., 38.
50. Denisoff, *Inside MTV*, 247.
51. J. Smith, *Sounds of Commerce*, 200.
52. Ibid., 198.
53. Denisoff, *Inside MTV*, 84.
54. For example, when the idea of "pay for play" was mooted, MCA was cautious about any changes to the status quo because executives were concerned that MTV would prioritize major artists over new acts (ibid., 145).
55. Admittedly, the cassette version of the album signals the inclusion of "Don't You" and "Fire in the Twilight."
56. Virgin Records handled the release of "Don't You" outside the United States.
57. "*The Breakfast Club: Original Motion Picture Soundtrack*," advertisement, *Billboard*, 23 February 1985, 7.
58. Ibid.
59. Banks, *Monopoly Television*, 42.
60. Denisoff, *Inside MTV*, 128.

61. "MTV Programming as of January 26, 1985," *Billboard*, 26 January 1985, 29. MTV's playlist categories during the period were Power Rotation, Heavy Rotation, Active Rotation, Medium Rotation, Breakout Rotation, Light Rotation, and New.

62. "MTV Programming: As of May 8, 1985," *Billboard*, 18 May 1985, 32; "MTV Programming as of April 17, 1985," *Billboard*, 27 April 1985, 36.

63. "Top Pop Albums," *Billboard*, 18 May 1985, 72; "Top Pop Albums," *Billboard*, 25 May 1985, 80; "Top Pop Album: Soundtracks / Original Cast," *Billboard*, 28 December 1985, T-22.

64. "Simple Minds: Chart History," Billboard.com, https://www.billboard.com/music/simple-minds/chart-history/hot-100.

65. "Hits of the World," *Billboard*, 25 May 1985, 73; "Hits of the World," *Billboard*, 25 May 1985, 65.

66. "MTV Programming as of April 17, 1985," *Billboard*, 27 April 1985, 36; "MTV Programming as of May 15, 1985," *Billboard*, 25 May 1985, 34.

67. "Newsmakers," *Billboard*, 13 April 1985, 8.

68. "Breakfast Reception," *Billboard*, 22 June 1985, 76.

69. Ethlie Ann Vare, "Simple Minds Tours for Human Rights," *Billboard*, 12 April 1986, 26.

70. Timothy Corrigan, *A Cinema without Walls: Movies and Culture after Vietnam* (London: Routledge. 1991), 108.

71. "John Hughes Musical Legacy," MTV.com, 6 August 2009 [1986], mtv.com/video-clips/7pgfrb/john-hughes-musical-legacy.

72. Robert Christgau, "Consumer Guide," *Village Voice*, 25 June 1985, http://www.robertchristgau.com/xg/cg/cgv6-85.php.

73. Andrew Goodwin, *Dancing in the Distraction Factory* (Minneapolis: University of Minnesota Press, 1992), 7.

74. Ibid., 8.

75. Ibid., 28.

76. Simon Frith, "Frankie Said: But What Did They Mean?," in *Consumption, Identity and Style: Marketing, Meanings and the Packaging of Pleasure*, ed. Alan Tomlinson (London: Routledge, 1990), 123.

77. "Audio Track: Los Angeles," *Billboard*, 20 July 1985, 24; "Audio Track: Los Angeles," *Billboard*, 3 August 1985, 41; "Audio Track: Los Angeles," *Billboard*, 24 August 1985, 38.

78. Ethlie Ann Vare, "Oingo Boingo Aims for the Center: Eclectic Troupe Moves to MCA," *Billboard*, 10 August 1985, 36.

79. Ibid.

80. Ethlie Ann Vare, "Beyond Video: Media Flips for Clips," *Billboard*, 28 September 1985, NT10.

81. "MTV Programming: As of August 21, 1985," *Billboard*, 31 August 1985, 52.

82. "MTV Programming: As of August 28, 1985," *Billboard*, 7 September 1985, 33.

83. "Hot 100 Singles," *Billboard*, 19 October 1985, 86; "Hot 100 Singles," *Billboard*, 16 November 1985, 64.

84. "*Weird Science: Motion Picture Soundtrack*: Awards," Allmusic, http://

www.allmusic.com / album / weird-science-mw0000320764 / awards; "Top Pop Albums," *Billboard*, 16 November 1985, 73.

85. Steve Gett, "Soundtrack Craze: Mixed Reviews," *Billboard*, 23 August 1986, 4.

86. "MTV Programming: For Week Ending October 26, 1985," *Billboard*, 26 October 1985, 41; "MTV Programming: As of October 23," *Billboard*, 2 November 1985, 46.

87. John Hughes, "The Sound of Money: Soundtracks Thrived in the Summer of '85," interview by Rob Tanenbaum, *Rolling Stone*, 21 November 1985, 17.

88. Ibid.

89. Vare, "Oingo Boingo Aims for the Center," 36.

90. Prince, *New Pot of Gold*, 97.

91. Tony Seidman, "Newsline," *Billboard*, 20 July 1985, 32.

92. Bill Carter, "Him Alone," *New York Times*, 4 August 1991, 34, 44.

93. "Everyone's Watching MCA," advertisement, *Billboard*, 31 August 1985, VSDA-51.

94. Ibid.

95. "Breakfast is Really Ready," advertisement, *Billboard*, 16 November 1985, 27.

96. Earl Paige, "Distributor Ignites *Sixteen Candles*," *Billboard*, 22 December 1984, 41.

97. Ibid.

98. Fred Goodman, "How One Michigan Dealer Does His Best to Stand Out: Wagenaar's Aggressive Promotions," *Billboard*, 31 August 1985, 35.

99. Ibid.

100. Joshua M. Greenberg, *From Betamax to Blockbuster: Video Stores and the Invention of Movies on Video* (Cambridge, MA: MIT Press, 2008), 14.

101. Moira McCormick, "VTR Plans More Seminars: Distributor Meeting with Dealers," *Billboard*, 21 September 1985, 34.

102. Greenberg, *From Betamax to Blockbuster*, 7.

103. Tony Seidman, "Newsline," *Billboard*, 18 January 1986, 30.

104. Ibid.

105. "Top Videocassettes Rentals," *Billboard*, 20 October 1984; "Top Videocassettes Sales," *Billboard*, 12 October 1985, 34; "New Releases: Home Video," *Billboard*, 8 February 1986, 26.

106. MCA priced *Sixteen Candles* at $29.98, *The Breakfast Club* at $34 95, and *Weird Science* at $34.98. "Top Videodisks," *Billboard*, 24 November 1984, 27; "Top Videodisks," *Billboard*, 2 November 1985, 33; "Top Videodisks," *Billboard*, 19 April 1986, 61.

107. During this period, *Billboard* had to base its weekly charts on sample rentals and sales data, and therefore computed notional rankings, because it was not possible to collect reliable nationwide data. Although the trade journal normally indicates when videos exceeded certain revenue and sales targets, figures on actual sales and rental transactions are difficult to establish. Ultimately, the data presented in *Billboard* suggests a video's perceived success in the market, relative to other titles.

108. Frederick Wasser, *Veni, Vidi, Video: The Hollywood Empire and the VCR* (Austin: University of Texas Press, 2001), 101.

109. "Top Videocassettes Rentals," *Billboard*, 20 April 1985, 34, and 27 April 1985, 29.

110. "Top Videocassettes Rentals," *Billboard*, 26 October 1985, 27, and 23 November 1985, 28.

111. "Top Videocassettes Rentals," *Billboard*, 10 May 1986, 60, and 17 May 1986, 48.

112. "Top Videocassettes Rentals," *Billboard*, 19 July 1986, 42, and 26 July 1986, 42.

113. "Top Videocassettes Rentals," *Billboard*, 9 March 1985, 36, and 26 October 1985, 27; Tony Seidman, "Lennon Live is the First Music Title to Ship Gold," *Billboard*, 22 March 1986, 39.

114. Tony Seidman, "Newsline," *Billboard*, 20 July 1985, 32.

115. Barbara Klinger, "Digressions at the Cinema: Reception and Mass Culture," *Cinema Journal* 28, no. 4 (Summer 1989): 10.

116. Jon Lewis "The Perfect Money Machine(s): George Lucas, Steven Spielberg, and Auteurism in the New Hollywood," in *Looking Past the Screen: Case Studies in Film History and Method*, ed. Jon Lewis and Eric Smoodin (Durham, NC: Duke University Press, 2007), 68.

Chapter 2: Realities and Fantasies of Suburban Adolescence

1. Janet Staiger, "Hybrid or Inbred: The Purity Hypothesis and Hollywood Genre History," in *Film Genre Reader IV*, ed. Barry Keith Grant (Austin: University of Texas Press), 207.

2. Catherine Driscoll, *Teen Film: A Critical Introduction* (Oxford: Berg, 2011), 3.

3. Rick Altman, "A Semantic/Syntactic Approach to Genre," *Cinema Journal* 23, no. 3 (Spring 1984): 11.

4. "Bobbie Wygant Interviews John Hughes for *Sixteen Candles*," NBC5 Entertainment, KXAS-TV (Dallas–Fort Worth), 1984, posted by EC Films, http://vimeo.com/15462712.

5. Richard Maltby, *Hollywood Cinema*, 2nd ed. (Oxford: Blackwell, 2003), 14–16.

6. David Bordwell, *The Way Hollywood Tells It: Story and Style in Modern Movies* (Berkeley: University of California Press, 2006), 42.

7. "Wygant Interviews Hughes."

8. Skip Sheffield, "*Breakfast Club* Best Film Yet on Teens," *Boca Raton News*, 19 February 1985, 1B.

9. Jack Barth, "John Hughes: On Geeks Bearing Gifts," *Film Comment*, June 1984, 46.

10. Roger Ebert, "John Hughes: When You're 16, You're More Serious than You'll Ever Be Again," *Chicago Sun Times*, 29 April 1984, available at Roger Ebert's Journal, https://www.rogerebert.com/rogers-journal/john-hughes-when-youre-16-youre-more-serious-than-youll-ever-be-again.

11. Sean M. Smith, "Teen Days That Shook The World," *Premiere*, December 1999.

12. John Ellis, *Visible Fictions: Cinema, Television, Video* (New York: Routledge, 1982), 73.

13. Ibid.

14. Hannah Lack, "Marilyn Vance on Dressing the Brat Pack," *Dazed*, 19 October 2012, dazeddigital.com/fashion/article/14917/1/marilyn-vance-on-dressing-the-brat-pack.

15. Kirk Honeycutt, *John Hughes: A Life in Film* (New York: Race Point, 2015), 16.

16. Charles Affron and Mirella Affron, *Sets in Motion* (New Brunswick, NJ: Rutgers University Press, 1995), 158.

17. Kari Kallioniemi, "'The Sound of Thatcherism on Vinyl': New Pop, Early Neo-Right Aspirations and Spandau Ballet," *Journal of European Culture* 8, no. 2 (October 2017): 125–138.

18. John Hughes, "Molly Ringwald Interviews John Hughes," *Seventeen*, March 1986, transcript available at https://web.archive.org/web/20090809144057/http://www.riverblue.com/hughes/articles/molly17.html.

19. Amy Maria Kenyon, *Dreaming Suburbia: Detroit and the Production of Postwar Space and Culture* (Detroit: Wayne State University Press, 2004), 1.

20. Bennett M. Berger, *Working-Class Suburb: A Study of Auto Workers in Suburbia* (Berkeley: University of California Press, 1960), 1–14.

21. "Sixteen Candles," *Variety*, 2 May 1984, 16.

22. Rupa Huq, *Making Sense of Suburbia through Popular Culture* (London: Bloomsbury, 2013), 193.

23. Corey Brunish, "John Hughes #1: Eye on the Movies," c. 1985, YouTube, 27 September 2010, https://youtu.be/eLEETkxai2k.

24. Pauline Kael, "*Sixteen Candles*," *New Yorker*, 28 May 1984, reprinted in Pauline Kael, *State of the Art: Film Writings, 1983–1985* (New York: Dutton), 173.

25. Richard Corliss, "Is There Life after Teenpix?," *Time*, 18 February 1985, 90.

26. Sharon Lloyd Spence, "Chicago Screenwriter Makes His Directorial Debut," *Back Stage*, 12 August 1983, 54.

27. "Wygant Interviews Hughes."

28. Robert B. Ray, *A Certain Tendency of the Hollywood Cinema, 1930–1980* (Princeton, NJ: Princeton University Press, 1985), 38.

29. Tim Appelo, "The Truth about John Hughes and Dede Allen," IndieWire, 28 April 2010, https://www.indiewire.com/2010/04/the-truth-about-john-hughes-and-dede-allen-238766.

30. Janet Maslin, "John Hughes's *Breakfast Club*," *New York Times*, 15 February 1985, C18.

31. John Hughes, *Sixteen Candles*, final draft screenplay, June 22, 1983, 5, available at The Script Savant, https://thescriptsavant.com/pdf/Sixteen_Candles.pdf.

32. Stephanie J. Ventura, Selma M. Taffel, and William D. Mosher, "Estimates of Pregnancies and Pregnancy Rates for the United States, 1976–85," *American Journal of Public Health* 78, no. 5 (May 1988): 507.

33. Hughes, "Ringwald Interviews Hughes."

34. Driscoll, *Teen Film*, 71.

35. Steve Neale, "Melodrama and Tears," *Screen* 27, no. 6 (1986): 7.

36. Ibid.

37. John Hughes, discussion and Q&A with AFI Fellows, AFI Harold Lloyd Masters Seminars, 1 May 1985.

38. Curran Nault, "The Cinematic Quiet Girl from *The Breakfast Club* to *Badlands*," *Feminist Media Studies* 13, no. 2 (2013): 308.

39. Maryn Wilkinson, "The Makeover and the Malleable Body in 1980s American Teen Film," *International Journal of Cultural Studies* 18, no. 3 (May 2015): 390.

40. Anthony C. Bleach, "Postfeminist Cliques: Class, Postfeminism, and the Molly Ringwald–John Hughes Films," *Cinema Journal* 49, no. 3 (Spring 2010): 39.

41. Nault, "Cinematic Quiet Girl," 309.

42. Wilkinson, "Makeover and the Malleable Body," 387.

43. R. W. Connel and James W. Messerschmidt, "Hegemonic Masculinity: Rethinking the Concept," *Gender and Society* 19, no. 6 (2005): 848.

44. Susan Jeffords, *Hard Bodies: Hollywood Masculinity in the Reagan Era* (New Brunswick, NJ: Rutgers University Press, 1993).

45. C. J. Pascoe, *Dude, You're a Fag: Masculinity and Sexuality in High School* (Berkeley: University of California Press, 2007), 5.

46. Bleach, "Postfeminist Cliques," 37.

47. Timothy Shary, *Generation Multiplex: The Image of Youth in Contemporary American Cinema* (Austin: University of Texas Press, 2002), 194.

48. Lesley Speed, "Loose Cannons: White Masculinity and the Vulgar Teen Comedy Film," *Journal of Popular Culture* 43, no. 4 (August 2010): 831.

49. Shirley R. Steinberg and Joe L. Kincheloe, "Privileged and Getting Away with It: The Cultural Studies of White, Middle-Class Youth," *Studies in the Literary Imagination* 31, no. 1 (Spring 1998): 110.

50. Shary, *Generation Multiplex*, 40.

51. Cordula Quint, "Boys Won't Be Boys: Cross-Gender Masquerade and Queer Agency in *Ma Vie En Rose*," in *Where the Boys Are: Cinemas of Masculinity and Youth*, ed. Murray Pomerance and Frances Gateward (Detroit: Wayne State University Press, 2005), 41.

52. Steinberg and Kincheloe, "Privileged and Getting Away with It," 112.

53. Driscoll, *Teen Film*, 49.

54. Pascoe, *Dude, You're a Fag*, 5.

55. Steinberg and Kincheloe, "Privileged and Getting Away with It," 112.

56. Helen K. Lee, *Between Foreign and Family* (New Brunswick, NJ: Rutgers University Press, 2018), 71.

57. Kent A. Ono and Vincent Pham, *Asian Americans and the Media* (Cambridge: Polity, 2008), 71.

58. Jim Moorhead, "Even Anthony Michael Hall Can't Save This," *St. Petersburg (FL) Evening Independent*, 6 August 1985, 9B.

59. Sheila Benson, "*Science* Fulfils Teenage Dreams," *Los Angeles Times*, 2 August 1985, http://articles.latimes.com/1985-08-02/entertainment/ca-5793_1_movie-review.

60. Steve Bailey and James Hay, "Cinema and the Premises of Youth," in *Genre and Contemporary Hollywood*, ed. Steve Neale (London: BFI, 2002), 221.

61. Bleach, "Postfeminist Cliques," 35.

62. Driscoll, *Teen Film*, 77.

63. Robert C. Bulman, *Hollywood Goes to High School* (New York: Worth, 2005), 10.

64. John Taylor, "'Society Stinks': Suburban Alienation and Violence in the Early Films of Penelope Spheeris," in *Filmurbia: Screening the Suburbs*, ed. David Forrest, Graeme Harper, and Jonathan Rayner (London: Palgrave, 2017), 18.

65. Barbara Jane Brickman, *New American Teenagers: The Lost Generation of Youth in 1970s Film* (New York: Bloomsbury, 2012), 216.

66. Richard Nowell, *Blood Money: A History of the First Teen Slasher Cycle* (New York: Continuum, 2011); Nowell, "'For Girls': Hollywood, the Date-Movie Market, and Early-1980s Teen Sex Comedies, *Post Script: Essays in Film and the Humanities* 33, no. 1 (Fall 2014): 16–32.

67. Driscoll, *Teen Film*, 45.

68. Catherine Driscoll, *Girls: Feminine Adolescence in Popular Culture and Cultural Theory* (New York: Columbia University Press, 2002), 217.

69. Hughes, discussion and Q&A; Andrew M, "John Hughes: I Didn't Plan My Career," c. 1996, YouTube, posted 28 March 2017, https://youtu.be/hCBlPiGY320.

70. Jimmy Summers, "*Sixteen Candles*," *Boxoffice*, July 1984, R-84.

71. Henry Jenkins, "Historical Poetics," in *Approaches to Popular Film*, ed. Joanne Hollows and Mark Jancovich (Manchester: Manchester University Press, 1995), 115.

72. Hughes, discussion and Q&A.

73. Richard Dyer, "Entertainment and Utopia," in *Only Entertainment*, 2nd ed. (London: Routledge, 2002), 20.

Chapter 3: The Creative Producer

1. "Hughes in Deal with Paramount," *Screen International*, 30 March 1985, 4; "Hughes Signs to Paramount," PR Newswire, New York, 21 March 1985, LexisNexis Academic.

2. Aljean Harmetz, "Tanen to Head Paramount Film Unit," *New York Times*, 9 October 1984, C14.

3. "Hughes Signs to Paramount."

4. "Chinich Switches to Hughes Ent," *Screen International*, 19 October 1985, 41B.

5. Janet Staiger, "The Package-Unit System: Unit Management after 1955," in *The Classical Hollywood Cinema: Film Style and Mode of Production to 1960*, ed. David Bordwell, Kristin Thompson, and Janet Staiger (New York: Columbia University Press, 1985), 332; Richard Maltby, "Nobody Knows Anything: Post-classical Historiography and Consolidated Entertainment," in *Contemporary Hollywood Cinema*, ed. Steve Neale and Murray Smith (London: Routledge, 1998), 31.

6. Paul Grainge, *Brand Hollywood: Selling Entertainment in a Global Media Age* (London: Routledge, 2008), 83.

7. Robert Lindsey, "The New Tycoons of Hollywood," *New York Times*, 7 August 1977, SM4.

8. Justin Wyatt, *High Concept: Movies and Marketing in Hollywood* (Austin: University of Texas Press, 1994), 104.

9. Sandra Salmans, "Barry Diller's Latest Starring Role," *New York Times*, 28 August 1983, F9.

10. Ibid.

11. Frederick Wasser, *Veni, Vidi, Video: The Hollywood Empire and the VCR* (Austin: University of Texas Press, 2005), 132–133.

12. Salmans, "Barry Diller's Latest Starring Role," F1.

13. Ibid., F9.

14. Adam Leaver, "A Different Take: Hollywood's Unresolved Business Model," *Review of International Political Economy* 17, no. 3 (August 2010): 463.

15. Andrew L. Yarrow, "The Studio's Move on Theaters," *New York Times*, 25 December 1987, D1, D10.

16. Stephen Prince, *A New Pot of Gold: Hollywood under the Electronic Rainbow, 1980–1989* (Berkeley: University of California Press, 2002), 84.

17. Jennifer Holt, "In Deregulation We Trust: The Synergy of Politics and Industry in Reagan-Era Hollywood," *Film Quarterly* 55, no. 2 (Winter 2001): 22.

18. Tony Schwartz, "Hollywood's Hottest Stars," *New York*, 30 July 1984, 27–33.

19. Tony Schwartz, "Son of Hollywood's Hottest Stars," *New York*, 8 October 1984, 43.

20. Martin Davis, quoted in ibid., 44.

21. Aljean Harmetz, "Frank Mancuso Named Chairman of Paramount," *New York Times*, 13 September 1984, C17.

22. Bernard K. Dick, *Engulfed: The Death of Paramount Pictures and the Birth of Corporate Hollywood* (Lexington: University Press of Kentucky, 2001), 176–178.

23. Charles Champlin, "On the Lot with Frank Mancuso, New Age Mogul," *Los Angeles Times*, 10 September 1989, http://articles.latimes.com/1989-09-10/entertainment/ca-2671_1_frank-mancuso.

24. Wyatt, *High Concept*, 83.

25. Tony Schwartz, "Hollywood's Hottest Stars," *New York*, 30 July 1984, 27. Both mainstream and academic accounts have credited Barry Diller and Michael Eisner with transferring the principles of high concept from television to movies and developing high concept as a guiding principle at Paramount during the 1980s. See, for example, Wyatt, *High Concept*, 8; Dick, *Engulfed*, 178.

26. Wyatt, *High Concept*, 8.

27. David Bordwell, *The Way Hollywood Tells It: Story and Style in Modern Movies* (Berkeley: University of California Press, 2006), 7.

28. David Ansen, "The Producer Is King Again," with Peter McAlevey, *Newsweek*, 20 May 1985, 84.

29. Ibid.

30. Quoted in ibid.

31. Staiger, "Package-Unit System," 330.

32. Philip Wuntch, "Director John Hughes: 'Pied Piper of the Brat Pack,'" Knight News Service, *Charleston (SC) Post and Courier*, 8 March 1986, 35.

33. John Hughes, "Molly Ringwald Interviews John Hughes," *Seventeen*, Spring 1986; "MTV Feature Presentation: *Pretty in Pink* Premiere Party," MTV, 27 February 1986.

34. John Hughes, discussion and Q&A with AFI Fellows, AFI Harold Lloyd Masters Seminars, 1 May 1985.

35. Ibid.; see also Hughes, "Ringwald Interviews Hughes."

36. Hughes, discussion and Q&A; see also Hughes, "Ringwald Interviews Hughes."

37. "Hughes Opts for L.A.," *Back Stage*, 24 May 1985, 39B; "Hot Chicago Film Scene Lures John Hughes Back Home," *Back Stage*, 16 August 1985, 48.

38. "Midwest Feature Films Blossom," *Back Stage*, 27 April 1984, 48.

39. Peggy Herbst, "Chicago-Based Film Offices Battle Neighborhood Burn-Out," *Back Stage*, 22 August 1986, 47.

40. "Hot Chicago Film Scene," 48.

41. Paul Grein, "Chart Beat," *Billboard*, 10 May 1986, 6.

42. Sam Sutherland, "A&M Gives Green Light to *Pink* Campaign," *Billboard*, 15 February 1986, 4.

43. Grein, "Chart Beat," 6.

44. Chin, "Dance Trax," *Billboard*, 1 March 1986, 57.

45. "*Pretty in Pink: Original Motion Picture Soundtrack*," *Billboard*, 15 February 1986, 70.

46. Sutherland, "A&M Gives Green Light," 4.

47. Ibid.

48. Ibid.; Brian Chin, "Dance Trax," *Billboard*, 22 February 1986, 57.

49. "They're All Pretty in Pink," advertisement, *Billboard*, 15 February 1985, 2.

50. "MTV Feature Presentation: *Pretty in Pink*"; Chris McGowan, "Bright Connection for New Artists, New Music," *Billboard*, 21 June 1986, S-4.

51. "MTV Feature Presentation: *Pretty in Pink*."

52. Ibid.

53. Ibid.

54. Ibid.

55. "Video Track," *Billboard*, 22 February 1986, 28.

56. "MTV Feature Presentation: *Pretty in Pink*."

57. "MTV Programming as of January 29 1986," *Billboard*, 8 February 1986, 52; "MTV Programming as of February 26 1986," *Billboard*, 8 March 1986, 45.

58. "*Pretty in Pink*—Trailer," posted by YouTubeMovies, 29 May 2012, http://youtu.be/y-X5ixDLuhM.

59. *Pretty in Pink* (1986), TV trailer, posted to YouTube by XippVid, 3 September 2007, http://youtu.be/tcSMDqXT52s.

60. *Pretty in Pink*, print advertisement, *New York Times*, 9 March 1986, H15; *Pretty in Pink*, print advertisement, *New York Times*, 7 March 1986, C9.

61. David Hutchings, "Molly Ringwald Goes to the Head of the Teen Class with *Pretty in Pink*, but She'd Rather Play Grown-Up," *People*, 24 March 1986, 87.

62. Molly Ringwald, interview by Steve Pond, *Elle*, October 1985, 74.

63. Hutchings, "Molly Ringwald Goes," 87.

64. Ibid.

65. Jamie Portman, "The Very Bankable Molly Ringwald," Southam News Syndicate (Hollywood), *Ottawa Citizen*, 21 February 1986, F6.

66. "*Pretty in Pink*: Weekly Box Office," Box Office Mojo, http://boxofficemojo.com/movies/?page=weekly&id=prettyinpink.htm.

67. "*Pretty in Pink*: Box Office Summary," Box Office Mojo, http://boxofficemojo.com/movies/?page=main&id=prettyinpink.htm; Louise Farr, "The Teeny Tales of Director John Hughes," *Palm Beach Daily News*, 3 October 1986, 6.

68. "Top Pop Albums," *Billboard*, 1 March 1986, 75; Paul Grein, "April Brings Certifications Shower," *Billboard*, 10 May 1986, 91; "Top Pop Albums," *Billboard*, 3 May 1986, 72.

69. "Top Pop Albums: Soundtrack / Original Cast," *Billboard*, 27 December 1986, Y-22; "Top Pop Albums," *Billboard*, 27 December 1986, Y-19.

70. "Hot 100: Sales," *Billboard*, 7 June 1986, 89.

71. "Hot 100: Sales & Airplay," *Billboard*, 31 May 1986, 65.

72. "John Hughes' Musical Legacy," MTV.com, 6 August 2009 [1986], mtv.com/video-clips/7pgfrb/john-hughes-musical-legacy.

73. "MTV Feature Presentation: *Pretty in Pink* Premiere Party."

74. Paul Grein, "Chart Beat," *Billboard*, 10 May 1986, 6.

75. Stephen Holden, "Movie Music Spices a Variety of Scenarios," *New York Times*, 6 April 1986, H6.

76. Ibid., H26.

77. J. D. Considine, "Short Rock Takes: Original Soundtrack: *Pretty in Pink*," *Musician*, April 1986, 92.

78. "Top Videocassettes Sales," *Billboard*, 25 October 1986, 52.

79. Wasser, *Veni, Vidi, Video*, 133.

80. "*Pretty in Pink*: The Videocassette Event," print advertisement, *Billboard*, 6 September 1986, 50.

81. "Top Videocassettes Rentals," *Billboard*, 25 October 1986, 44.

82. "Top Videocassettes Rentals," *Billboard*, 26 December 1987, Y-40.

83. "*Ferris Bueller's Day Off*," *Variety*, 4 June 1986, 16.

84. "*Ferris Bueller's Day Off*," print advertisement, *New York Times*, 29 June 1986, H10.

85. "*Ferris Bueller's Day Off*," print advertisement, *New York Times*, 29 June 1986, H10.

86. Steve Gett, "Music, Movies Prove to be a Perfect Summer Pair," *Billboard*, 20 September 1986, 86.

87. William Ham, "Straight Outta Sherman [*sic*]," Lollipop.com, 2003, http://www.lollipop.com/issue47/47-02-03.html.

88. Ibid.

89. Ibid.

90. Steve Gett, "On the Beat: Short Takes I," *Billboard*, 9 August 1986, 31.

91. "Top Pop Albums," *Billboard*, August 23, 1986, 91.

92. Grainge, *Brand Hollywood*, 85.

93. "*Top Gun* & *Ferris Bueller* 1986 Trailer," posted to YouTube by robatsea2009, 11 August 2010, http://youtu.be/HvYMZUBOMLY.

94. "*Ferris Bueller's Day Off*: Box Office Summary," Box Office Mojo, http://boxofficemojo.com/movies/?id=ferrisbuellersdayoff.htm.

95. Aljean Harmetz, "How Summer's Films Ranked at the Box Office," *New York Times*, 8 September 1986, C17.

96. Richard Harrington, "On the Right Sound Track," *Washington Post*, 25 February 1987, B7.

97. Patrick Goldstein, "John Hughes in the Pink at MCA," *Los Angeles Times*, 1 March 1987, http://articles.latimes.com/1987-03-01/entertainment/ca-6707_1_john-hughes.

98. Ibid.

99. Ibid.

100. "Sire Shutters London Office: Ups A&R Role," *Billboard*, 18 July 1981, 71.

101. P. Goldstein, "John Hughes in the Pink."

102. Frederic Sibler, "Some Kind of Wonderful," *Fanfare* 10, no. 5 (1987): 256.

103. "Top Pop Albums," *Billboard*, 18 April 1987, 78, and 9 April 1988, 92.

104. Jeff Smith, *The Sounds of Commerce: Marketing Popular Music* (New York: Columbia University Press, 1998), 204.

105. Norma Coates, "Teenyboppers, Groupies, and Other Grotesques: Girls and Women and Rock Culture in the 1960s and early 1970s," *Popular Music Studies* 15, no. 1 (2003): 71.

106. Doyle Greene, *Teens, TV, and Tunes: The Manufacturing of American Adolescent Culture* (Jefferson, NC: McFarland, 2012), 32.

107. Quoted in Ted Mico, "Power Discord," *Spin*, December 1989, 16.

108. A. D. Murphy, "North American Theatrical Film Rental Market Shares: 1970–1990," *Variety*, 14 January 1991, 12.

109. Geraldine Fabrikant, "Paramount's Surprise Streak," *New York Times*, 22 December 1986, D1.

110. Ibid.

111. Simon Frith, "The Industrialisation of Popular Music," in *Taking Popular Music Seriously: Selected Essays* (Aldershot, UK: Ashgate, 2007), 117.

112. Patrick Goldstein, "Big Deals," *Los Angeles Times*, 17 January 1988, http://articles.latimes.com/1988-01-17/entertainment/ca-36447_1_hughes-music.

113. Farr, "Teeny Tales of John Hughes," 6.

114. Richard Corliss, "Well, Hello Molly!," *Time*, May 26, 1986, 71.

115. Farr, "Teeny Tales of John Hughes."

116. Ibid.

117. Bob Thomas, "Star Watch: Learning How to Give a Good Interview," Associated Press, 13 March 1987.

118. Nina Darnton, "A Youth's Day Off," *New York Times*, 11 June 1986, C24.

119. Timothy Shary, *Generation Multiplex: The Image of Youth in Contemporary American Cinema* (Austin: University of Texas Press, 2002), 29.

Chapter 4: Gender, Generation, and Coming-of-Age in 1980s America

1. Janet Maslin, "Marching toward Maturity," *New York Times*, 15 March 1987, 90.

2. Jimmy Summers, "*Pretty in Pink*," *Boxoffice*, April 1986, R-37.

3. "*Ferris Bueller's Day Off*," *Variety*, 4 June 1986, 16; Ina Warren, "Jones's Academic Klutz Is as Memorable as Ferris," *Calgary Herald*, 12 July 1986, C8.

4. Timothy Shary, "Buying Me Love: 1980s Class-Clash Teen Romances," *Journal of Popular Culture* 44, no. 3 (2011): 564, 566.

5. Shary, "Buying Me Love," 575.

6. Paramount Pictures Corporation, *Some Kind of Wonderful: Handbook of Production Information* (1987), 5.

7. Jane Feuer, "Melodrama, Serial Form and Television Today," *Screen* 25, no. 1 (1984): 10.

8. Sharon Barrett, "Hughes Takes Time Off from Teen Films," *Chicago Sun-Times*, 15 June 1986.

9. John Hughes, "Director's Commentary," *Ferris Bueller's Day Off*, DVD, region 2 (2000).

10. Declan McGrath, *Editing and Post-Production* (Boston: Focal Press, 2001), 79.

11. Ibid.

12. Gabriella Oldham, *First Cut: Conversations with Film Editors* (Berkeley: University of California Press, 1992), 192.

13. David Bordwell, *Narration in the Fiction Film* (Madison: University of Wisconsin Press, 1985), 204.

14. Justin Wyatt, *High Concept: Movies and Marketing in Hollywood* (Austin: University of Texas Press, 1994), 104.

15. Emma Griffiths, "Music Supervisor Tarquin Gotch on Working with John Hughes," *Synchblog*, 13 September 2016, https://www.synchtank.com/blog/music-supervisor-tarquin-gotch-on-working-with-john-hughes-managing-acdcs-brian-johnson-more.

16. Kathryn Kalinak, "The Classical Hollywood Film Score," in *The Classical Hollywood Reader*, ed. Steve Neale (Abingdon: Routledge, 2012), 268.

17. Jillian Capewell, "The Costume Designer for *Pretty in Pink* Finally Explains That Prom Dress," *Huffington Post*, 25 February 2016, huffingtonpost.com/entry/pretty-in-pink-prom-dress-marilyn-vance_us_56cdfcaee4b041136f192cfd.

18. Kay Dickinson, "Pop, Speed, Teenagers and the 'MTV Aesthetic,'" in *Movie Music: The Film Reader*, ed. Kay Dickinson (London: Routledge, 2003), 146.

19. Joe Berkowitz, "John Hughes's Costume Designer on *Pretty in Pink*, His Most Fashion-Conscious Film," Fast Company, 1 March 2016, https://www.fastcompany.com/3057056/john-hughes-costume-designer-on-pretty-in-pink-his-most-fashion-conscious-film.

20. Amanda Ann Klein, *American Film Cycles: Reframing Genres, Screening Social Problems, and Defining Subcultures* (Austin: University of Texas Press, 2011), 137.

21. Janet Maslin, "John Hughes's *Pretty in Pink*," *New York Times*, 28 February 1986, C8.

22. Richard Corliss, "Growing Pains: *Pretty in Pink*," *Time*, 3 March 1986, 3.

23. John Hughes, *Some Kind of Wonderful*, screenplay, 1 July 1986, 6, available at somekindofwonderful.org/pdf/skowscript.pdf.

24. Elizabeth G. Traube, *Dreaming Identities: Class, Gender, and Generation in 1980s Hollywood Movies* (Boulder, CO: Westview, 1992), 76.

25. Christina Lee, "Going Nowhere? The Politics of Remembering (and Forgetting) Molly Ringwald," *Cultural Studies Review* 13, no. 1 (March 2007): 101.

26. Shirley R. Steinberg and Joe L. Kincheloe, "Privileged and Getting Away with It: The Cultural Studies of White, Middle-Class Youth," *Studies in the Literary Imagination* 31, no. 1 (Spring 1998): 114.

27. Maslin, "John Hughes's *Pretty in Pink*," C8.

28. Christina Lee, *Screening Generation X: The Politics and Popular Memory of Youth in Contemporary Cinema* (Farnham, UK: Ashgate, 2010), 55.

29. John Hughes, *Pretty in Pink*, 5th draft, 9 May 1985, 117, available at Cinema Bandit, https://cinemabandit.files.wordpress.com/2018/07/pretty-in-pink-john-hughes-05-09-85-scan.pdf.

30. Richard Dyer, "Entertainment and Utopia," in *Only Entertainment*, 2nd ed. (London: Routledge, 2002), 28.

31. Susannah Gora, *You Couldn't Ignore Me If You Tried: The Brat Pack, John Hughes, and Their Impact on a Generation* (New York: Crown, 2010), 149.

32. Catherine Driscoll, *Teen Film: A Critical Introduction* (Oxford: Berg, 2011), 48.

33. Shary, "Buying Me Love," 573.

34. Hilary Radner, "Pretty Is as Pretty Does: Free Enterprise and the Marriage Plot," in *Film Theory Goes to the Movies*, ed. Jim Collins, Hilary Radner, and Ava Preacher Collins (New York: Routledge, 1999), 59.

35. Shary, "Buying Me Love," 574.

36. Michael D. Dwyer, *Back to the Fifties: Nostalgia, Hollywood Film, and Popular Music of the Seventies and Eighties* (Oxford: Oxford University Press, 2015), 94.

37. Ibid., 93.

38. Paramount, *Some Kind of Wonderful:* Handbook, 5.

39. Lee, *Screening Generation X*, 53.

40. Chris Jordan, *Movies and the Reagan Presidency: Success and Ethics* (Westport, CT: Praeger, 2003), 139.

41. Driscoll, *Teen Film*, 5.

42. R. L. Rutsky and Justin Wyatt, "Serious Pleasures: Cinematic Pleasure and the Notion of Fun," *Cinema Journal* 30, no. 1 (Autumn 1990): 14.

43. Michael Moffat, "Do We Really Need 'Postmodernism' to Understand *Ferris Bueller's Day Off*?," *Cultural Anthropology* 5, no. 4 (November 1990): 368.

44. William J. Palmer, *The Films of the Eighties: A Social History* (Carbondale: Southern Illinois University Press, 1993), 297.

45. See, for example, Leger Grindon, "Movies and Fissures in Reagan's America," in *American Cinema of the 1980s: Themes and Variations*, ed. Stephen Prince (New Brunswick, NJ: Rutgers University Press, 2007), 159; Traube, *Dreaming Identities*, 78.

46. Grindon, "Movies and Fissures in Reagan's America," 159.

47. Jordan, *Movies and the Reagan Presidency*, 128.

48. Moffat, "Do We Really Need 'Postmodernism,'" 369.

49. Dwyer, *Back to the Fifties*, 97.

50. Thomas Doherty, *Teenagers and Teenpics: The Juvenalization of American Movies in the 1950s* (Boston: Unwin Hyman, 1988), 237.

51. Grindon, "Movies and Fissures," 158.

52. Noel King, "Lost in the Funhouse," *Cinema Journal* 31, no. 3 (Spring 1992): 60.

53. Vicky LeBeau, "Daddy's Cinema: Femininity and Mass Spectatorship," *Screen* 33, no. 3 (1992): 256.

54. Janet Staiger, *Perverse Spectators: The Practices of Film Reception* (New York: New York University Press, 2000), 121.

55. Wyatt, *High Concept*, 61.

56. Ibid., 17.

57. Barbara Jane Brickman, *New American Teenagers: The Lost Generation of Youth in 1970s Film* (New York: Bloomsbury, 2012), 213.

58. Steve Neale, "The Big Romance or Something Wild? Romantic Comedy Today," *Screen* 33, no. 3 (1992): 298.

59. Pauline Kael, "Mars," reprinted in *Hooked: Film Writings, 1985–88* (London: Boyars, 1990), 134.

60. Driscoll, *Teen Film*, 46–47.

61. Janet Maslin, "*Some Kind of Wonderful*," *New York Times*, 27 February 1987, C17.

62. Bob Strauss, "Steve Martin and John Hughes: Director Graduates to the Adult World." *Chicago Sun-Times*, 22 November 1987.

63. "*Ferris Bueller's Day Off*," *Variety*, 4 June 1986, 16.

64. Kris Turnquist, "*Some Kind of Wonderful*," *Boxoffice*, May 1987, R-43.

65. Klein, *Film Cycles*, 97.

Chapter 5: Solid Family Fare

1. Bob Strauss, "Steve Martin and John Hughes: Director Graduates to the Adult World," *Chicago Sun-Times*, 22 November 1987.

2. Geoff King, *New Hollywood Cinema: An Introduction* (London: Tauris, 2002), 93.

3. Terri Minsky, "Dr. Jekyll and Mr. Hughes," *Premiere*, July 1988, 56.

4. "*Planes, Trains and Automobiles*: Weekly Box Office," Box Office Mojo, http://boxofficemojo.com/movies/?page=weekly&id=planestrainsandautomobiles.htm.

5. *Planes, Trains and Automobiles*: Box Office Summary," Box Office Mojo, http://boxofficemojo.com/movies/?page=main&id=planestrainsandautomobiles.htm.

6. Michael Cieply, "Creative Tension: Sources See Changes at Paramount," *Los Angeles Times*, 31 July 1987, http://articles.latimes.com/1987-07-31/entertainment/ca-287_1_paramount-spokeswoman.

7. Ibid.

8. Ibid.

9. "Hughes Inks Prod. Deal With Universal; Off Paramount Lot," *Variety*, 27 April 1988, 6.

10. Deborah Caulfield, "Movies: Morning Report," *Los Angeles Times*, 21 April 1988, http://articles.latimes.com/1988-04-21/entertainment/ca-2210_1_hughes-associates.

11. Lawrence Cohn, "'87 Pics Made to Beat Strike Flooding Mart," *Variety*, 23 March 1988, 36.

12. Bill Carter, "Him Alone," *New York Times*, 4 August 1991, SM51.

13. A. D. Murphy, "North American Theatrical Film Rental Market Shares: 1970–1989," *Variety*, 17 January 1990, 15.

14. "John Hughes Returns to Universal Pictures," PR Newswire, April 20, 1988, LexisNexis Academic.

15. Ibid.

16. Minksy, "Dr. Jekyll and Mr. Hughes," 55.

17. "John Hughes: I Didn't Plan My Career," c. 1996, posted to YouTube by Andrew M, 28 March 2017, https://youtu.be/hCBlPiGY320.

18. Holly Chard, "'Give People What They Expect': John Hughes' Family Films and Seriality in 1990s Hollywood," *Film Studies* 17 (Autumn 2017), 123.

19. Jim Whalley, *Saturday Night Live, Hollywood Comedy, and American Culture* (London: Palgrave, 2010), 61.

20. Charles Acland, *Screen Traffic: Movies, Multiplexes, and Global Culture* (Durham, NC: Duke University Press, 2003), 92.

21. Robert J. Gibbs, *Principles of Urban Retail Planning and Development* (Hoboken, NJ: Wiley, 2012), 15.

22. Frederick Wasser, *Veni, Vidi, Video: The Hollywood Empire and the VCR* (Austin: University of Texas Press, 2005), 137.

23. Acland, *Screen Traffic*, 118.

24. A. D. Murphy, "Ticket Sales to Fall to a 15-Year Low," *Variety*, 15 December 1991, 5.

25. Charles Fleming, "Snackbar Slowdown Bitter Pill For Exhibs," *Variety*, 21 January 1991, 93; Richard Gold, "U.S. Overscreened? Not for Mega-hits," *Variety*, 28 January 1991, 60.

26. Fleming, "Snackbar Slowdown Bitter Pill," 3.

27. "VCR Penetration Climbs to 76.6%," *Variety*, 13 May 1991, 45.

28. Marc Berman, "Majors Snare Lions Share of Shrinking Wholesale Market," *Variety*, 19 August 1991, 28; Berman, "*Home Alone* Takes Fox to Vid Pinnacle," *Variety*, 7 October 1991, 36.

29. Paul Sweeting, "Spotlight: VSDA '90," *Billboard*, 11 August 1990, V-5.

30. Carter, "Him Alone," SM32.

31. Graeme Turner, "The Economy of Celebrity," in *Stardom and Celebrity: A Reader*, ed. Sean Redmond and Su Holmes (London: Sage, 2007), 195.

32. Andrew Wernick, *Promotional Culture: Advertising, Ideology and Symbolic Expression* (London: Sage, 1991), 92.

33. Peter Smith, "*Great Outdoors* Is Well . . . Outdoors," *St. Petersburg (FL) Times*, 17 June 1988, Weekend, 7.

34. "*The Great Outdoors*: Weekly Box Office," Box Office Mojo, http://www.boxofficemojo.com/movies/?page=weekly&id=greatoutdoors.htm.

35. Vernon Scott, "John Candy—A Box Office Sweetie," United Press

International, 18 January 1989; Marilyn Moss, "Delirious!," *Boxoffice*, March 1991, 10.

36. Moss, "Delirious!," 9.

37. "*Uncle Buck*," *Variety*, 16 August 1989, 21.

38. Vincent Canby, "Uncouth Uncle against the Suburban Grain," *New York Times*, 16 August 1989, C13.

39. Ibid.

40. Sam Friedman, *Comedy and Distinction: The Cultural Currency of a 'Good' Sense of Humour* (Abingdon, UK: Routledge, 2014), 138.

41. Mike Clarke, "Candy's *Buck* is a Victim of Comedy Devaluation," *USA Today*, 16 August 1989, 4D.

42. "Weekend Boxoffice Report," *Variety*, 23 August 1989, 8.

43. "*Uncle Buck*: Box Office Summary," Box Office Mojo, https://www.boxofficemojo.com/movies/?id=unclebuck.htm.

44. John Evan Frook, "Hughes to Make *Peanuts* for WB," *Variety*, 16 November 1992, 5.

45. Aljean Harmetz, "It's Fade-Out for the Cheap Film as Hollywood Budgets Soar," *New York Times*, 7 December 1989, C19.

46. Ben Kenber, "Jeremiah S. Chechik Looks Back at Making *National Lampoon's Christmas Vacation*," *The Ultimate Rabbit* (blog), 25 December 2016, https://theultimaterabbit.com/2016/12/25/jeremiah-s-chechik-looks-back-at-making-national-lampoons-christmas-vacation.

47. Stephen Prince, *A New Pot of Gold: Hollywood under the Electronic Rainbow, 1980–1989* (Berkeley: University of California Press, 2002), 20.

48. Matty Simmons, *"If You Don't Buy This Book, We'll Kill This Dog!": Life, Laughs, Love and Death at "National Lampoon"* (New York: Barricade, 1994), 302.

49. Janet Maslin, "On Vacation Once Again," *New York Times*, 1 December 1989, C12.

50. Patricia Hanson and Steve Hanson, "*National Lampoon's Christmas Vacation*," *Screen International*, 9 December 1989, 43.

51. "*Christmas Vacation*: Weekend Box Office," Box Office Mojo, http://www.boxofficemojo.com/movies/?page=weekend&id=christmasvacation.htm.

52. "*National Lampoon's Christmas Vacation*," *Variety*, 6 December 1989, 32.

53. Michael Fleming, "How Hughes Found a Home at Fox," *Variety*, 3 December 1990, 103.

54. Roger Watkins, "Time & Warner: Yank Heroes," *Variety*, 8 March 1989, 2.

55. Prince, *New Pot of Gold*, 65–68.

56. Tino Balio, *The American Film Industry*, rev. ed. (Madison: University of Wisconsin Press, 1985), 585.

57. Charles Fleming, "Daly Diet for Warners: Easy on the Fatty Deals," *Variety*, 28 January 1991, 1.

58. Ibid., 8.

59. Richard Natale, "WB Pic Proves There's Life after First Week," *Variety*, 18 November 1991, 3.

60. Ibid.

61. Ibid., 3, 5.

62. "*Curly Sue* Adopted by Audiences Nationwide," PR Newswire, 11 November 1991, LexisNexis Academic.

63. "*Curly Sue*: Weekly Box Office," Box Office Mojo, http://boxofficemojo.com/movies/?page=weekly&id=curlysue.htm.

64. "*Curly Sue*: Box Office Summary," Box Office Mojo, http://www.boxofficemojo.com/movies/?id=curlysue.htm.

65. Peter M. Nichols, "Home Video," *New York Times*, 2 April 1992, C22; "Boy Scout Tops Rental as Dalmatians Ships 11.4 million," *Video Week*, 27 April 1992, 3; Marc Berman, "Vid Wholesale Market Tops $1 Bil," *Daily Variety*, 24 July 1992, 1.

66. "Video Notes," *Video Week*, 20 January 1992, 7.

67. "Top Video Rentals," *Billboard*, 15 August 1992, 64; "Top Video Rentals," *Billboard*, 9 January 1993, V-13.

68. Amy Dawes, "Prolific U Plans 24 Films for '90," *Variety*, 10 May 1989, 34.

69. Carter, "Him Alone," SM44.

70. Susan Spillman, "Hughes at Home: Suburban Life Is Movie Material," *USA Today*, 19 November 1992, 1D.

71. Caryn James, "Bite vs. Bark or *Beethoven* vs. *Ferngully*," *New York Times*, 17 May 1992, H22.

72. "Principal Production Begins on Universal Pictures' *Beethoven*," PR Newswire, 2 May 1991, LexisNexis Academic.

73. King, *New Hollywood Cinema*, 58.

74. "*Beethoven*: Box Office Summary," Box Office Mojo, http://boxofficemojo.com/movies/?page=main&id=beethoven.htm.

75. Roger Ebert, "*Beethoven*," *Chicago Sun-Times*, 3 April 1992, available at RogerEbert.com, https://www.rogerebert.com/reviews/beethoven-1992.

76. James, "Bite vs. Bark," H22.

77. "1992 Worldwide Grosses," Box Office Mojo, http://www.boxofficemojo.com/yearly/chart/?view2=worldwide&yr=1992&p=.htm.

78. Kathleen O'Steen, "Fox in Family Film Hunt via Nickelodeon Pact," *Variety*, 17 May 1993, 5.

79. "MCA/UA Trots *Beethoven* to Sale," *Daily Variety*, July 8, 1992, 7

80. "MCA/Universal Will Unleash *Beethoven* for Sellthrough," *Video Week*, 13 July 1992, 2.

81. "MCA/UA Trots *Beethoven* to Sale," 7.

82. "MCA/Universal Will Unleash *Beethoven*," 2.

83. Marc Berman, "Rentals Reap Bulk of 1991 Vid Harvest," *Variety*, 6 January 1992, 22.

84. Wasser, *Veni, Vidi, Video*, 151.

85. "MCA/UA Trots *Beethoven* to Sale," 7.

86. "MCA/Universal Will Unleash *Beethoven*," 2.

87. Earl Page, "MCA/Universal Orchestrates *Beethoven* Sell-Thru Drive," *Billboard*, 18 July 1992, 52; MCA, "*Beethoven*: Your Best Friend This Sell-Through Season," advertisement, *Billboard*, August 1, 1992, 81.

88. MCA, "*Beethoven*: Your Best Friend," 81.

89. "MCA / Universal Will Unleash *Beethoven*," 2.

90. Page, "MCA / Universal Orchestrates *Beethoven*," 52.

91. MCA, "*Beethoven*: Your Best Friend," 81.

92. Craig Rosen and Earl Paige, "The Power of Home Video Increases," *Billboard*, 26 December 1992, 72.

93. Charles Fleming, "New Plan to Put Warners in Family Way," *Variety*, 9 December 1991, 1.

94. Christian Moerk, "Family Volume at WB," *Daily Variety*, 14 May 1993, 3.

95. Bernard Weintraub, "Hollywood Is Testing Family Values' Value," *New York Times*, 12 November 1992, C15.

96. Ibid.

97. "John Hughes to Produce Live-Action *Dennis the Menace* Feature for Warner Bros.," PR Newswire, July 18, 1991, LexisNexis Academic.

98. Claudia Eller, "Hughes Producing *Dennis* at WB," *Variety*, 22 July 1991, 22.

99. "Warner Bros. Announces Creation of Family Entertainment Label," PR Newswire, 13 May 1993, LexisNexis Academic.

100. Ibid.

101. Steve Aggergaard, "'Dennis The Menace' Search a Tale of 10 Towheads," *Chicago Tribune*, 1 July 1992, http: // articles.chicagotribune.com / 1992-07-01 / news / 9202270784_1_john-hughes-finalists-movie-star.

102. Ibid.

103. "Hollywood's Big Numbers Attributed to Marketing Efforts," CNN, news transcript, 7 December 1992, LexisNexis Academic.

104. Chard, "Give People What They Expect," 121–122.

105. "Promo Guide: Warner Bros.," *Boxoffice*, April 1993, 16.

106. Mari Florence, "*Dennis the Menace*," *Boxoffice*, September 1993, R-65.

107. Roger Ebert, "*Dennis the Menace*," *Chicago Sun-Times*, 25 June 1993, available at RogerEbert.com, https: // www.rogerebert.com / reviews / dennis-the-menace-1993.

108. Leonard Klady, "*Sleepless* Awakens to $17 Mil," *Daily Variety*, 28 June 1993, 1.

109. "*Dennis the Menace*: Box Office Summary," Box Office Mojo, https: // www.boxofficemojo.com / movies / ?id=dennisthemenace.htm.

110. "Warner Bros. Announces Creation of Label."

111. Trudi Miller Rosenblum, "Suppliers Aim Kid Vids at Parents," *Billboard*, 25 June 1994, 43.

112. Ibid.

113. "Warner Bros. Announces Creation of Label."

114. Paul Grainge, *Brand Hollywood: Selling Entertainment in a Global Media Age* (London: Routledge, 2008), 86.

115. Advertisement for Warner Bros. Family Entertainment, *Billboard*, 10 December 1994, 85.

116. Barbara Klinger, *Beyond the Multiplex: Cinema, New Technologies, and the Home* (Berkeley: University of California Press, 2006), 94.

117. Warner Bros., "Family Entertainment," flyer from *Thumbelina* UK video case, 1994.

118. "Warner Bros. Announces Creation of Label."

119. E. Scott Reckard, "Warner Creates Family Entertainment Umbrella for Wholesome Fare," Associated Press, 13 May 1993, LexisNexis Academic.

120. "Promo Guide: Warner Bros.," 16.

121. Ibid.

122. Ocean of America, *Dennis the Menace* Nintendo Game Boy instructions, 1993, 20–21.

123. "Work in Progress: *Dennis*," *SNES Force*, October 1993, 18–20; "Gambling on Success," *SNES Force*, October 1993, 22–23.

124. Paul McDonald, *Hollywood Stardom* (Malden, MA: Wiley-Blackwell, 2013), 18, 19.

125. Jim Kozak, "*Uncle Buck*," *Boxoffice*, October 1989, R-63–R-64.

126. Richard Gold, "Known Properties the Best Bet for Merchandising Spin Offs," *Variety*, 21 June 1989, 14.

127. Sheila Johnston, "What a Scream," *Independent*, 12 December 1992, 30.

128. Spillman, "Hughes at Home," 1D.

Chapter 6: Pressures of Parenthood and Fantasies of Childhood

1. Heather Addison, "Children's Film in the 1990s," in *Film Genre 2000: New Critical Essays*, ed. Wheeler Winston Dixon (Albany, NY: SUNY Press, 2000), 178.

2. Peter Krämer, "'The Best Disney Film Disney Never Made': Children's Films and the Family Audience in American Cinema since the 1960s," in *Genre and Contemporary Hollywood*, ed. Steve Neale (London: BFI, 2002), 186.

3. Noel Brown, *The Children's Film: Genre, Nation, and Narrative* (New York: Wallflower, 2017), 54.

4. Robert C. Allen, "Home Alone Together: Hollywood and the 'Family Film,'" in *Identifying Hollywood's Audiences*, ed. Richard Maltby and Melvyn Stokes (London: BFI, 1999), 114.

5. Bill Carter, "Him Alone," *New York Times*, 4 August 1991, SM30.

6. Addison, "Children's Film in the 1990s," 178.

7. Noel Brown, *The Hollywood Family Film: A History, from Shirley Temple to Harry Potter* (London: Tauris, 2012), 6.

8. Richard Dyer, "Entertainment and Utopia," in *Only Entertainment*, 2nd ed., ed. Richard Dyer (London: Routledge, 2002), 20.

9. Brown, *Hollywood Family Film*, 2.

10. Andrew Hartman, *A War for the Soul of America: A History of the Culture Wars* (Chicago: University of Chicago Press, 2015), 199.

11. Patrick Joseph Buchanan, "Culture War Speech: Address to the Republican National Convention," 17 August 1992, transcript available at Voices of Democracy: The U.S. Oratory Project, http://voicesofdemocracy.umd.edu/buchanan-culture-war-speech-speech-text.

12. Claire Cain Miller, "The Divorce Surge Is Over, but the Myth Lives On," *New York Times*, 2 December 2014, https://www.nytimes.com/2014/12/02/upshot/the-divorce-surge-is-over-but-the-myth-lives-on.html.

13. Rita Kempley, "John Candy's Sugar Pop," *Washington Post*, 16 August 1989, D1.

14. US Census Bureau, "Table 1337. Single-Parent Households: 1980 to 2009," *Statistical Abstract of the United States: 2012*, 840, https://www2.census.gov/library/publications/2011/compendia/statab/131ed/2012-statab.pdf.

15. Warner Bros., *"Curly Sue": Production Information*, 1991, 2; this booklet was included in the film's press kit.

16. Judith Havemann, "In Europe, It's Not an Issue," *Washington Post*, 29 October 1991, Z13.

17. Imelda Whelehan, "Aging Appropriately: Postfeminist Discourses of Aging in Contemporary Hollywood," in *Postfeminism and Contemporary Hollywood Cinema*, ed. Joel Gwynne and Nadine Muller (Basingstoke, UK: Palgrave Macmillan, 2013), 85.

18. Diane Negra, *What a Girl Wants: Fantasizing the Reclamation of Self in Postfeminism* (Abingdon, UK: Routledge, 2009), 21.

19. Elizabeth Palley and Corey S. Shadaimah, *In Our Hands: The Struggle for U.S. Childcare Policy* (New York: New York University Press, 2014), 9.

20. Jack Boozer, *Career Movies: American Business and the Success Mystique* (Austin: University of Texas Press, 2002), 56.

21. Henry Jenkins, "Childhood Innocence and Other Modern Myths," *The Children's Culture Reader*, ed. Henry Jenkins (New York: New York University Press, 1998), 3.

22. Ibid., 2.

23. Jacqueline Rose, *The Case of Peter Pan, or The Impossibility of Children's Fiction* (Philadelphia: University of Pennsylvania Press, 1984), 10.

24. Michelle Ann Abate, *Tomboys: A Literary and Cultural History* (Philadelphia: Temple University Press, 2008), 197.

25. Ibid., 221.

26. Ibid.

27. John Hughes, "A Conversation with John Hughes," on *Dennis the Menace: Special Edition*, DVD, Warner Home Video, 2005.

28. Filipa Antunes, "Attachment Anxiety: Parenting Culture, Adolescence, and the Family Film in the US," *Journal of Children and Media* 11, no. 2 (2017): 225.

29. Howard P. Chudacoff, *Children at Play: An American History* (New York: New York University Press, 2007), 181.

30. Henry Jenkins, "Dennis the Menace: The All-American Handful," in *The Revolution Wasn't Televised: Sixties Television and Social Conflict* (New York: Routledge, 1997), 133.

31. Hughes, "Conversation with John Hughes."

32. Leslie Fielder, *Love and Death in the American Novel* (1960; rept. ed., Champaign, Ill.: Dalkey Archive, 2003), 270.

33. Erica H. Seifert, *The Politics of Authenticity in Presidential Campaigns* (Jefferson, NC: McFarland, 2012), 97.

34. Ryan Poll, *Main Street and Empire: The Fictional Small Town in the Age of Globalization* (New Brunswick, NJ: Rutgers University Press, 2012), 13.

35. Army Archerd, "Just for Variety," *Daily Variety*, 10 September 1992, LexisNexis Academic.

36. Hughes, "A Conversation with John Hughes."

37. Mari Florence, "*Dennis The Menace*," *Boxoffice*, September 1993, R-65.

38. Warner Bros., "*Dennis the Menace*": *Production Information*, 1993, 5; this booklet came with the film's press kit.

39. Sarah Harwood, *Family Fictions: Representations of the Family in 1980s Hollywood Cinema* (New York: Palgrave Macmillan, 1997), 34.

40. Fredric Jameson, *Postmodernism; or, The Cultural Logic of Late Capitalism* (Durham, NC: Duke University Press, 1991), 20.

41. Poll, *Main Street and Empire*, 87.

42. Juliann Garey, "Doggy Downer," *Entertainment Weekly*, 3 April 1992.

43. Caryn James, "Bite vs. Bark, or *Beethoven* vs. *Ferngully*," *New York Times*, 17 May 1992, H22.

44. Ty Burr, "*Dennis the Menace*," *Entertainment Weekly*, 9 July 1993.

45. Hughes, "A Conversation with John Hughes."

46. Lynn Spigel, *Welcome to the Dreamhouse: Popular Media and Postwar Suburbs* (Durham, NC: Duke University Press, 2001), 241.

47. James Kincaid, *Erotic Innocence: The Culture of Child Molesting* (Durham, NC: Duke University Press, 1998), 121.

48. Rita Kempley, "*Dennis the Menace*: A Romp through the Age of Innocence," *Washington Post*, 25 June 1993, C1.

49. Florence, "*Dennis the Menace*," R-65.

50. James, "Bite vs. Bark," H22.

51. Harwood, *Family Fictions*, 68.

52. Peter Krämer, "Would You Take Your Child to See This Film? The Cultural and Social Work of the Family-Adventure Movie," in *Contemporary Hollywood Cinema*, ed. Steve Neale and Murray Smith (London: Routledge, 1998), 304.

Chapter 7: Family Film Franchises

1. Bill Carter, "Him Alone," *New York Times*, 4 August 4 1991, SM30.

2. "*Home Alone*: Weekly Box Office," Box Office Mojo, https://www.boxofficemojo.com/movies/?page=weekly&id=homealone.htm.

3. "*Home Alone*: Box Office Summary," Box Office Mojo, http://boxofficemojo.com/movies/?id=homealone.htm.

4. Peter Bart, "Can Hughes Lose?," *Variety*, 8 April 1991, 3.

5. Paul Gorman, "Hughes Links with Fox in Seven-Feature Slate," *Screen International*, 19 April 1991, 6; Michael Cieply, "Fox Says 'Big Deal' to New Hollywood Frugality," *Los Angeles Times*, 14 February 1991, http://articles latimes.com/1991-02-14/business/fi-1646_1_fox-film.

6. "*Home Alone*: Weekly Box Office."

7. Gorman, "Hughes Links with Fox," 6.

8. Cieply, "Fox Says 'Big Deal.'"

9. Gorman, "Hughes Links with Fox"; "Directors," *Screen International*, 11 December 1992, 22.

10. Cameron Stauth, "Masters of the Deal," *American Film*, 1 May 1991, 30.

11. Terry Ilott, "Wary Bankers Keep Murdoch Hanging," *Variety*, 14 January 1991, 131; Paul Noglows, "Bankers Bearing Down," *Variety*, 4 February 1991, 1.

12. Charles Fleming, "A-List Helmers Healthy despite Poor Year," *Variety*, 25 March 1991, 109.

13. Richard W. Stevenson, "Taming Hollywood's Spending Monster," *New York Times*, 14 April 1991, F1.

14. Cieply, "Fox Says 'Big Deal.'"

15. Charles Fleming, "Guffaws Grip Pix in Giggle Gamble," *Variety*, 17 June 1991, 1.

16. Ibid.

17. Richard Natale, "H'wood Bets Less Is More," *Variety*, 5 August 1991, 115.

18. Amanda Ann Klein, *American Film Cycles: Reframing Genres, Screening Social Problems, and Defining Subcultures* (Austin: University of Texas Press, 2011), 19–20.

19. Stephen Prince, *A New Pot of Gold: Hollywood under the Electronic Rainbow, 1980–1989* (Berkeley: University of California Press, 2002), 41.

20. Paul Grainge, *Brand Hollywood: Selling Entertainment in a Global Media Age* (London: Routledge, 2008), 49.

21. Jim McCullaugh, "Vid Retailers Value Hollywood Emphasis on Family Films," *Billboard*, 29 May 1993, 104.

22. Stuart Miller, "Vid Ad to Head *Home*," *Variety*, 25 March 1991, 100.

23. Paul Sweeting, "*Home Alone* Is August Swell-Thru," *Billboard*, 18 May 1991, 85.

24. Ibid., 1.

25. Ibid.

26. Pepsi-Cola, "Pepsi Summer Chill Out," PR Newswire, 7 May 1991; Kevin Maney, "Pepsi Fires Up Summer Ad Blitz," *USA Today*, 10 May 1991, 1B.

27. "Home Video," *Communications Daily*, 15 May 1991, LexisNexis Academic; Ty Burr, "*Alone* Again, Promotionally," *Entertainment Weekly*, 23 August 1991.

28. "Home Video," *Communications Daily*, 15 May 1991; Sweeting, "*Home Alone* Is August Swell-Thru," 1.

29. Sweeting, "*Home Alone* Is August Swell-Thru," 1, 85.

30. Ibid., 1.

31. Gerry Yandel, "Video Rental Chain Rates Films to Help Parents," *Fredericksburg (VA) Free Lance-Star*, 2 May 1988, TV-3.

32. David J. Fox, "Blockbuster Video Rates NC-17 Films Unsuitable for All," *Los Angeles Times*, 14 January 1991, http://articles.latimes.com/1991-01-14/entertainment/ca-198_1_blockbuster-video.

33. Barney Warf and Thomas Chapman, "Cathedrals of Consumption: A Political Phenomenology of Wal-Mart," in Stanley D. Brunn, ed., *Wal-Mart World: The World's Biggest Corporation in the Global Economy* (London: Routledge, 2006), 176.

34. McCullaugh, "Vid Retailers Value Hollywood," 104.

35. Sweeting, "*Home Alone* Is August Swell-Thru," 85.

36. Jim McCullaugh and Paul Verna, "FoxVideo's *Home* Delivery Just in Time, Say Retailers," *Billboard*, 7 September 1991, 70.

37. Ibid.
38. Ibid.
39. Ibid.
40. "FoxVideo Lines Up 4 *Home Alone* 2 Tie-Ins," *Video Week*, 19 April 1993, 2.
41. Janet Wasko, *Hollywood in the Information Age: Beyond the Silver Screen* (Cambridge: Polity, 1994), 208.
42. Geoffrey Deitz, "Studios Play Along with Video Games," *Variety*, 18 November 1991, 1.
43. "More Expensive, Commercial Movies for 1992," Associated Press, 23 January 1992, LexisNexis Academic.
44. William Grimes, "*Home Alone* 2: Sequel Success? Or Pow! Splat!," *New York Times*, November 15, 1992, H15.
45. Ibid., H20.
46. David J. Fox, "Marketing Mania: Movies from *Aladdin* to *X* Try to Cash In on Tie-Ins," *Los Angeles Times*, October 21, 1992, http://articles.latimes.com/1992-10-21/entertainment/ca-522_1_profit-center; Matthew Grimm, "Fox Finds Friends to Go Alone," *Brandweek*, November 2, 1992, 3; Jennifer Pendleton, "Studios Rolling Out Big Guns to Market Yule Pix," *Daily Variety*, November 11, 1992, 2.
47. Tim Halloran, *Romancing the Brand: How Brands Create Strong Intimate Relationships with Consumers* (San Francisco: Jossey-Bass, 2014), 199.
48. Donna Rosato, "Culkin Pitches Sprite," *USA Today*, 12 March 1992, 1B.
49. "*The New York Times*, Twentieth Century Fox and Bloomingdale's Plan Joint Promotion Keyed to New *Home Alone* Motion Picture," PR Newswire, 9 November 1992, LexisNexis Academic.
50. Ibid.
51. Dave McNary, "*Home Alone* 2 Sets Box Office Record," United Press International, 23 November 1992.
52. "*Home Alone* 2: Box Office Summary," Box Office Mojo, http://www.boxofficemojo.com/movies/?id=homealone2.htm.
53. "*Home Alone* 2: Foreign Box Office," Box Office Mojo, https://www.boxofficemojo.com/movies/?page=intl&id=homealone2.htm.
54. Eileen Fitzpatrick, "No Express For Grocery Videos: Confab Examines Complexity of Tie-Ins," *Billboard*, 5 August 1995, 78.
55. Paula Parisi, "*Home* 2 gets $16 Mil Push from FoxVideo," *Hollywood Reporter*, April 16, 1993, LexisNexis Academic.
56. Ibid.
57. "FoxVideo Lines Up 4 *Home Alone* 2 Tie-Ins," 2.
58. "*Home Alone* 2 Ships 7.5 million," *Video Week*, 12 July 1993, 3.
59. Peter M. Nichols, "Home Video," *New York Times*, 6 August 1993, D15.
60. Jim McCullaugh, Earl Paige, and Seth Goldstein, "*Bodyguard* in Rush to Sell-Thru," *Billboard*, 18 September 1993, 4.
61. Thomas R. King, "Coming For Christmas: *Home Alone* 2 Goodies," *Wall Street Journal*, B1; Fox, "Marketing Mania."
62. Gerard Evans, "In the Court of King Culkin," *Daily Mail*, 4 December 1992, 50.

63. Bruce Horovitz, "New Twist in Tie-Ins: *Home Alone 2* May Redefine Merchandising,' *Los Angeles Times*, 12 November 1992, http://articles.latimes.com/1992-11-12/business/fi-433_1_merchandising-empire.

64. Carolyn Jess-Cook, *Film Sequels: Theory and Practice from Hollywood to Bollywood* (Edinburgh: Edinburgh University Press, 2009), 1.

65. "Home Alone 2 Lost in New York" (flyer), Tiger Toys (Vernon Hills, Ill., 1992).

66. Horovitz, "New Twist in Tie-Ins."

67. Ibid.

68. Ibid.

69. Parisi, "*Home 2* gets $16 Mil Push."

70. "FoxVideo Lines Up Tie-Ins," 2.

71. Babette Morgan, "The Talk of Toyland: A Shortage of Talkboys Has Santas Scrambling," *St. Louis Post-Dispatch*, 19 December 1993, 1F.

72. Ibid.

73. Michelle Healy, "Shelves Are Bare of These Hot Toys," *USA Today*, 9 December 1994, 1D; "Tiger's Got '94's Hottest Toys Galore," PR Newswire, 16 November 1994, LexisNexis Academic; Carolyn Susman, "Relax Mom: You Can Find That Hot Toy," *Palm Beach Post*, 29 November 1995, 1D.

74. Claudia Eller, "Johnson to Direct *Day* for Hughes," *Daily Variety*, 16 March 1993, 1.

75. Leonard Klady, "Summer Pix: Snaps, Crackles & Flops," *Variety*, 29 August 1994, 1.

76. 20th Century Fox, "Production Information: *Baby's Day Out*," 1994, 4; this booklet was part of the film's press kit.

77. Ibid.

78. Judy Brennan and John Evan Frook, "Bright Lights May Clear Fog at Fox," *Variety*, 17 October 1993, 1.

79. "*Baby's Day Out*: Weekly Box Office," Box Office Mojo, http://www.boxofficemojo.com/movies/?page=weekly&id=babysdayout.htm.

80. Leonard Klady, "Distribs Need Some Late Summer Sizzle," *Variety*, 11 July 1994, 1.

81. "*Baby's Day Out*: Box Office Summary," Box Office Mojo, http://www.boxofficemojo.com/movies/?id=babysdayout.htm.

82. Klady, "Summer Pix."

83. Tim Apello, "Varied Hughes," *Entertainment Weekly*, 2 December 1994.

84. Peter M. Nichols, "Home Video," *New York Times*, 9 December 1994, D17.

85. "1995 Top Video Rentals," *Billboard*, 6 January 1996, 57.

86. Eileen Fitzpatrick, "Shelf Talk," *Billboard*, 25 February 1995, 130.

87. "Top Video Sales," *Billboard*, 13 May 1995, 97; "Top Video Sales," *Billboard*, 27 May 1995, 70.

88. "Hi Tech Expressions to Change Name," Business Wire, 6 June 1994, LexisNexis Academic.

89. "Video Notes," *Video Week*, 11 July 1994, 6; "Video Notes," *Video Week*, 3 October 1994, LexisNexis Academic.

90. Jonathan Carter and Chip Carter, "Kids Extra Video Games Reviews,"

Entertainment Weekly, 21 October 1994, ew.com / ew / article / 0,,304115,00 html.

91. Susan Spillman, "John Hughes Revives a Christmas *Miracle*," *USA Today*, 25 October 1993, 4D; Beth Laski, "*Miracle* Refund Promo Produces Few Takers," *Daily Variety*, 7 December 1994, 6.

92. "Boys and Girls 6–8: Open Casting Call," *New York Times*, February 4, 1994, C14.

93. Howell J. Maljham Jr., "To Her, It's Kids' Stuff," *Los Angeles Times*, 26 July 1994, http: // articles.latimes.com / 1994-07-26 / entertainment / ca-19883_1_mara-wilson.

94. Jane Galbraith, "Reluctant Macy's Rains on New *Miracle on 34th Street*'s Parade," *Los Angeles Times*, 17 April 1994, http: // articles.latimes com / 1994-04-17 / entertainment / ca-47060_1_34th-street.

95. Stuart Elliott, "'New Miracle on 34th Street,' This Time without Macy's," *New York Times*, 18 November 1994, D21.

96. Galbraith, "Reluctant Macy's Rains on Parade"; Elliott, "New Miracle on 34th Street," D1.

97. Howell J. Maljham Jr., "Sami and Santa: *Miracle*'s Mutual Appreciation Society," *Los Angeles Times*, 20 November 1994, http: // articles.latimes. com / 1994-11-20 / entertainment / ca-65012_1_deaf-girl.

98. Jean Oppenheimer, "2nd *34th*: The Remaking of a Christmas Classic," *Boxoffice*, 1 November 1994, 22.

99. "Short Takes," *Daily Variety*, 18 October 1994, 19.

100. "A *Miracle* About to Happen at Radio City!," Business Wire, 17 October 1994, LexisNexis Academic.

101. Army Archerd, "Just for Variety," *Daily Variety*, 10 November 1994, LexisNexis Academic.

102. See, for example, Oppenheimer, "2nd *34th*."

103. "*Miracle on 34th Street*: Weekly Box Office," Box Office Mojo, http: // boxofficemojo.com / movies / ?page=weekly&id=miracleon34thstreet.htm.

104. Beth Laski, "*Miracle* or Money Back," *Daily Variety*, 23 November 1994, 1.

105. "Fox Offers *Miracle* Guarantee," United Press International, 22 November 1994, LexisNexis Academic.

106. Laski, "*Miracle* or Money Back," 1.

107. See, for example, Arlene Vigoda, "Rush's Turkey Day," *USA Today*, 23 November 1994, 1D; Lois Romano, "The Reliable Source," *Washington Post*, 23 November 1994, D3.

108. Laski, "*Miracle* Refund Promo," 6; "Holiday *Miracle*," Business Wire, 6 December 1994, LexisNexis Academic.

109. "*Miracle on 34th Street*: Box Office Summary," Box Office Mojo, http: // boxofficemojo.com / movies / ?id=miracleon34thstreet.htm.

110. Ibid.

111. "*Variety* International Box Office," *Variety*, 2 January 1995, 14.

112. Eileen Fitzpatrick, "Batman Faces Holiday Battle with Santa," *Billboard*, 2 September 1995, 118.

113. Ibid.

114. John Brodie and Timothy M. Gray, "H'Wood Needs Yule Fuel," *Variety*, 27 November 1995, 1.

115. Seth Goldstein, "Managing Ever-Changing Sell-Through," *Billboard*, 6 January 1996, 43; Goldstein, "Wal-Mart, Blockbuster Top Vid Sales," *Billboard*, 30 March 1996, 9.

116. S. Goldstein, "Managing Ever-Changing Sell-Through," 43.

117. Peter Dean, "Rentals Slow but Sales Brisk in '95 U.K. Vid Business," *Billboard*, 23 December 1995, 79.

118. "20th Century Fox Announces Open Casting Call for Eight-Year-Old Boy for *Home Alone 3*," *Business Wire*, 30 September 1996, LexisNexis Academic.

119. "*Home Alone 3*: Weekly Box Office," Box Office Mojo, https://www.boxofficemojo.com/movies/?page=weekly&id=homealone3.htm.

120. "Video Notes," *Video Week*, 24 November 1997, LexisNexis Academic.

121. "*Mouse Hunt*: Weekly Box Office," Box Office Mojo, https://www.boxofficemojo.com/movies/?page=weekly&id=mousehunt.htm.

122. "*Mr. Magoo*: Weekly Box Office," Box Office Mojo, https://www.boxofficemojo.com/movies/?page=weekly&id=mrmagoo.htm.

123. "*Home Alone 3*: Weekly Box Office."

124. "Video Notes," *Video Week*, 13 April 1998, LexisNexis Academic.

125. Ibid.

126. "Video Notes," *Video Week*, 20 April 1998, LexisNexis Academic.

127. Steve Traiman, "Studios Retool Websites for Video Sales," *Billboard*, 27 June 1998, 73.

128. "Top Video Sales," *Billboard*, 15 August 1998, 74; "Top Video Rentals," *Billboard*, 22 August 1998, 75.

129. "Fox Enters DVD with Eight Titles," *Video Store*, 16 August 1998, 1.

130. Noel Brown, *The Hollywood Family Film: A History, from Shirley Temple to Harry Potter* (London: Tauris, 2012), 227.

131. Richard Natale, "Hollywood's 'New Math': Does It Still Add Up?," *Variety*, 23 September 1991, 95.

132. "50 to Watch," *Variety*, 28 August 1995, 62.

Chapter 8: Slapstick, Sentimentality, and the American Family

1. Amanda Ann Klein and R. Barton Palmer, eds., introduction to *Cycles, Sequels, Spin-offs, Remakes, and Reboots: Multiplicities in Film and Television* (Austin: University of Texas Press, 2016), 19.

2. Holly Chard, "'Give People What They Expect': John Hughes' Family Films and Seriality in 1990s Hollywood," *Film Studies* 17 (Autumn 2017): 113.

3. Ibid., 117.

4. Noel Brown, "The 'Family' Film and the Tensions between Popular and Academic Interpretations of Genre," *Trespassing* 2 (Winter 2013): 29.

5. Robert R. Shandley, *Hogan's Heroes* (Detroit: Wayne State University Press, 2011), 43.

6. Peter Krämer, "Clean, Dependable Slapstick: Comic Violence and the Emergence of Classical Hollywood Cinema," in *Violence and American Cinema*, ed. J. David Slocum (New York: Routledge, 2001), 107.

7. Steven Shaviro, *The Cinematic Body* (Minneapolis: University of Minnesota Press, 1994), 109.

8. Louise Peacock, *Slapstick and Comic Performance: Comedy and Pain* (Basingstoke, UK: Palgrave Macmillan, 2014), 143–144.

9. Richard Maxwell Brown, *No Duty to Retreat: Violence and Values in American History and Society* (Norman: University of Oklahoma Press, 1991), 155, 158.

10. Marsha Kinder, *Playing with Power in Movies, Television, and Video Games* (Berkeley: University of California Press, 1991), 218.

11. Peacock, *Slapstick and Comic Performance*, 143.

12. Ibid., 139.

13. James R. Kincaid, *Erotic Innocence: The Culture of Child Molesting* (Durham, NC: Duke University Press, 1998), 116.

14. Filipa Antunes, "Attachment Anxiety: Parenting Culture, Adolescence and the Family Film in the US," *Journal of Children and Media* 11, no. 2 (2017): 217.

15. Sandra Chang-Kredly, "Cinematic Representations of Childhood: Privileging the Adult Viewer," in *Childhoods: A Handbook*, ed. Gaile S. Cannella and Lourdes Diaz Soto (New York: Lang, 2010), 209.

16. Robert C. Allen, "Home Alone Together: Hollywood and the 'Family Film,'" in *Identifying Hollywood's Audiences*, ed. Richard Maltby and Melvyn Stokes (London: BFI, 1999), 127.

17. Henry Giroux, "Public Pedagogy and the Responsibility of Intellectuals: Youth, Littleton, and the Loss of Innocence," *JAC* 20, no. 1 (Winter 2000): 12.

18. Peacock, *Slapstick and Comic Performance*, 35.

19. Fredric Jameson, "Postmodernism and Consumer Society," in *The Cultural Turn: Selected Writings on Postmodernism, 1983–1998* (London: Verso, 1998), 9.

20. Molly Haskell, *From Reverence to Rape: The Treatment of Women in the Movies* (Baltimore: Penguin, 1974), 163–170.

21. Joe Leydon, "*Home Alone 3*," *Variety*, 8 December 1993, 112.

22. Jack Boozer, *Career Movies: American Business and the Success Mystique* (Austin: University of Texas Press, 2002), 56.

23. Giroux, "Public Pedagogy and Intellectuals," 17.

24. Anne Higonnet, *Pictures of Innocence* (New York: Thames and Hudson, 1998), 194.

25. Susan Spillman, "Hughes at *Home*: Suburban Life Is Movie Material," *USA Today*, 19 November 1992, 1D.

26. Dolores Barclay, "Video View: Home Video News and Reviews," Associated Press, 12 December 1994.

27. Bill Carter, "Him Alone," *New York Times*, 4 August 1991, SM44.

28. Alan Siegel, "*Home Alone* Hit Theaters 25 Years Ago. Here's How They Filmed Its Bonkers Finale," *Brow Beat* (blog), *Slate*, 16 November 2015, http://www.slate.com/blogs/browbeat/2015/11/16/home_alone_hit_theaters_25_years_ago_here_s_how_they_filmed_its_bonkers.html.

29. Joe Kincheloe, "Home Alone and Bad to the Bone: The Advent of a

Postmodern Childhood," in *Kinderculture*, ed. Shirley R. Steinberg and Joe L. Kincheloe (Boulder, CO: Westview, 1997), 45.

30. Francie Ostrower, *Why the Wealthy Give: The Culture of Elite Philanthropy* (Princeton, NJ: Princeton University Press, 1995), 36.

31. "New York from the 1940s to Now," Center for Urban Research, City University of New York, c. 2012, https://www.gc.cuny.edu/Page-Elements/Academics-Research-Centers-Initiatives/Centers-and-Institutes/Center-for-Urban-Research/CUNY-Mapping-Service/Projects/New-York-from-the-1940s-to-now.

32. Jameson, "Postmodernism and Consumer Society," 10.

33. Mark Connelly, "Santa Claus: The Movie," in *Christmas at the Movies*, ed. Mark Connelly (London: Tauris, 2000), 122.

34. "Move Over, Macaulay," *Hamilton (ON) Spectator*, 19 November 1996, B8.

35. Ibid.

36. Allen, "Home Alone Together," 125.

37. Chard, "Give People What They Expect," 120.

Conclusion

The chapter epigraph comes from Ty Burr, "Video Review: *Curly Sue*," *Entertainment Weekly*, 3 April 1992, ew.com/ew/article/0,,310101,00.html.

1. Bill Carter, "Him Alone," *New York Times*, 4 August 1991, SM32.

2. Mark Gallagher, *Another Steven Soderbergh Experience* (Austin: University of Texas Press, 2013), 26.

3. Amanda Ann Klein and R. Barton Palmer, introduction to *Cycles, Sequels, Spin-offs, Remakes, and Reboots*, ed. Amanda Ann Klein and R. Barton Palmer (Austin: University of Texas Press, 2016), 12.

4. Janet Maslin, "*Some Kind of Wonderful*," *New York Times*, 27 February 1987, C17; Richard Schickel, "Teen Turmoil: *Some Kind of Wonderful*," *Time*, 9 March 1987, 86; Jill Rachlin, "Video Review: *Only the Lonely*," *Entertainment Weekly*, 29 November 1991, https://ew.com/article/1991/11/29/only-lonely.

5. Amanda Ann Klein, *American Film Cycles: Reframing Genres, Screening Social Problems, and Defining Subcultures* (Austin: University of Texas Press, 2011), 6.

6. Delores Hayden, *Building Suburbia: Green Fields and Urban Growth, 1820–2000* (New York: Pantheon, 2003), 3.

7. Christina Lee, *Screening Generation X: The Politics and Popular Memory of Youth in Contemporary Cinema* (Farnham, UK: Ashgate, 2010), 1.

8. Anita M. Busch, "Hughes and Mestres Team in Disney-Based Great Oaks Ent.," *Variety*, 20 February 1995, 22.

9. Ibid.

10. Ibid.

11. "John Hughes and Ricardo Mestres Create New Media Partnership Great Oaks Entertainment," Los Angeles, Business Wire, 15 February 1995, LexisNexis Academic.

12. "Frank Wells, Disney's President, Is Killed in a Copter Crash at 62," *New York Times*, 5 April 1994, B8.

13. Robert W. Welkos, "Disney Plans to Bring New *101 Dalmatians* to Life," *Los Angeles Times*, 22 March 1995, http://articles.latimes.com/1995-03-22/entertainment/ca-45538_1_john-hughes.

14. Douglas Feiden, "A Big-Bucks Bye-Bye: Disney Ax Worth $125 Mil to Ovitz," *New York Daily News*, 14 December 1996, 4.

15. Buena Vista TV, "*101 Dalmatians: A Canine's Tale*," PR Newswire, 25 November 1996, LexisNexis Academic.

16. Melanie Wells, "Sponsors Make Pilgrimage to T-Day Parade," *USA Today*, 25 November 1996, 11B.

17. "*101 Dalmatians* (1996): Box Office Summary," Box Office Mojo, https://www.boxofficemojo.com/movies/?id=101dalmatiansliveaction.htm.

18. Janet Maslin, "Run, Spot, Run. Act, Spot, Act," *New York Times*, 27 November 1996, C9.

19. Claudia Puig, "What's Up, Doc? Disney, Warner Launch Frenzy of Movie Tie-In Merchandising," *Calgary Herald*, 22 October 1996, D11.

20. Joe Leydon, "*Flubber*," *Variety*, 24 November 1997, 63.

21. "*Flubber*: Box Office Summary," Box Office Mojo, https://www.boxofficemojo.com/movies/?id=flubber.htm.

22. Stephen Galloway, "Mestres Splits with Hughes, Starts Own Firm," *Hollywood Reporter*, 5 November 1997, LexisNexis Academic.

23. "Hughes and Mestres Create New Media Partnership."

24. Busch, "Hughes and Mestres Team"; "News in Brief," *Screen International*, 23 June 1995, 2; Richard Natale, "Too-True Tales," *Los Angeles Times*, 9 August 1995, http://articles.latimes.com/1995-08-09/entertainment/ca-33111_1_fairy-tale.

25. "Film 93—John Hughes Interview," 5 April 1993, posted to YouTube by VHS Video Vault, 3 April 2018, https://youtu.be/SDHNbHJOFf4; Busch, "Hughes and Mestres Team."

26. Angela Dawson, "Reno Revisits Time Travel Hit," BPI Entertainment News Wire, 4 April 2001, LexisNexis Academic.

27. Adam Dawtrey and Alison James, "*Visiting* Team Steps Up to Bat," *Variety*, 2 April 2001, 4.

28. "*Just Visiting*: Box Office Summary," Box Office Mojo, http://boxofficemojo.com/movies/?id=justvisiting.htm; Dawtrey and James, "*Visiting* Team Steps Up." *Variety*'s reporters noted that the budget may have been in the region of $70–$100 million.

29. "*Reach The Rock*: Box Office Summary," Box Office Mojo, http://boxofficemojo.com/movies/?page=main&id=reachtherock.htm.

30. Lael Loewnstein, "*Reach the Rock*," *Variety*, 19 October 1998, 75; Anita Gates, "Problems Only a Night in Jail Will Cure," *New York Times*, 16 October 1998, E22.

31. Susan Wloszczyna, "Teen Film Genre Is a Hughes Family Vocation," *USA Today*, 21 February 2000, Life, 4D.

32. Ibid.

33. "*New Port South* (film)," D23: The Official Disney Fan Club, n.d., https://d23.com/a-to-z/new-port-south-film/.

34. Angie Errigo, "What on Earth Ever Happened to John Hughes?," *Empire*, September 2008, 137.

35. David Kamp, "Sweet Bard of Youth," *Vanity Fair*, March 2010, 209–210.

36. Ibid., 160.

37. Kevin Smith, *Tough Sh*t: Life Advice from a Fat, Lazy Slob Who Did Good* (New York: Gotham, 2012), 239–244.

38. Dave McNary, "'The Heat' Helmer Paul Feig Gets Honest Laughs," *Variety*, 13 June 2013, https://variety.com/2013/film/people-news/the-heat-helmer-paul-feig-gets-honest-laughs-1200496384/

39. Patrick Goldstein, "John Hughes's Imprint Remains," *Los Angeles Times*, 25 March 2008, http://articles.latimes.com/2008/mar/25/entertainment/et-goldstein25.

40. Ibid.

41. Roz Kaveney, *Teen Dreams: Reading Teen Film from "Heathers" to "Veronica Mars"* (London: Tauris, 2006), 3.

42. Kirsten Smith, "YAC Hit List: Teen Girl Movies," *Los Angeles Review of Books*, 12 April 2013, https://lareviewofbooks.org/article/yac-hit-list-teen-girl-movies/.

43. Steve Rose, "The Legacy of Heathers 30 Years On," *Guardian*, 4 August 2018, https://www.theguardian.com/film/2018/aug/04/michael-lehmann-on-the-legacy-of-heathers-cult-teen-film.

44. Rick Altman, *Film/Genre* (London: BFI, 1999), 80.

45. Noel Brown, *The Hollywood Family Film: A History, from Shirley Temple to Harry Potter* (London: Tauris, 2012), 188–189.

46. Stephen Prince, *A New Pot of Gold: Hollywood under the Electronic Rainbow, 1980–1989* (Berkeley: University of California Press, 2002), 213.

47. Catherine Driscoll, *Teen Film: A Critical Introduction* (Oxford: Berg, 2011), 48.

48. Glenn Kenny, "The Y.A. Surge at Neflix Is On," *New York Times*, 30 August 2018, https://www.nytimes.com/2018/08/30/movies/netflix-to-all-the-boys-ive-loved-before-sierra-burgess-is-a-loser.html.

49. Janet Staiger, "Authorship Approaches," in *Authorship and Film*, ed. David Gerstner and Janet Staiger (New York: Routledge, 2003), 4.

50. Timothy Shary, *Teen Movies: American Youth on Screen* (London: Wallflower, 2005), 76.

51. Nell Minow, "Greta Gerwig on 'Lady Bird,'" *Huffington Post*, 11 January 2017, https://www.huffingtonpost.com/entry/greta-gerwig-on-lady-bird_us_59f9a6fee4b0b7f0915f6307.

52. Helen Barlow, "*The Grand Budapest Hotel*: Wes Anderson Interview," SBS, 10 April 2014, https://www.sbs.com.au/movies/article/2014/04/10/grand-budapest-hotel-wes-anderson-interview.

53. Kaleem Aftab, "Director Rick Famuyiwa Flips Black Stereotypes with His John Hughes–Influenced 'Dope,'" Vice, 4 June 2015, https://www.vice.com/en_us/article/qbx8zd/director-rick-famuyiwa-flips-black-urban-stereotypes-with-his-john-hughes-influenced-dope-456.

INDEX

Printed in the USA
CPSIA information can be obtained
at www.ICGtesting.com
LVHW040011120824
787865LV00003B/103